MIMESIS
INTERNATIONAL

C000066025

HASEKURA LEAGUE INTERCULTUR
n. 4

Editorial Board

FURUSATO

'Home' at the Nexus of History, Art, Society, and Self

Edited by
Christopher Craig, Enrico Fongaro, Aldo Tollini

This book has been subjected to a peer review process.

© 2020 – MIMESIS INTERNATIONAL – MILAN
www.mimesisinternational.com
e-mail: info@mimesisinternational.com

Isbn: 9788869772771
Book series: *Hasekura League Intercultural Studies Editions,* n. 4

© MIM Edizioni Srl
P.I. C.F. 02419370305

TABLE OF CONTENTS

EDITORS' PREFACE

This volume is a collection of essays based on papers presented at the Hasekura League International Symposium held on 15-16 November 2018 at Ca' Foscari University of Venice. The title of the conference was "Furusato: 'Home' at the Nexus of Politics, History, Art, Society, and Self", and a group of European, Japanese, and North American scholars assembled to consider the theme from a diverse array of academic approaches. Setting out from the multifaceted Japanese concept of '*furusato*' (written variously as 故郷, ふるさと, or 古里 and translatable as home, hometown, or place of origin), participants identified and ruminated upon both its forms in Japan and related ideas in the outside world.

The papers included in the current book are divided into 4 major sections. After an introductory essay by Aldo Tollini that explores the place of *furusato* in Buddhism and Buddhist enlightenment, the first section is concerned with *Furusato* in Image and Imagination. Tijana Žakula presents an account of the transportation of Dutch art theory from Europe to Asia and the processes by which it found a home in Japan (Chapter 1), Ozaki Akihiro's essay focuses on the imagination and understanding of *furusato* as an essential element of disaster recovery (Chapter 2), and Myōki Shinobu offers a look at one community's mobilization of its unique folklore to promote local revitalization (Chapter 3). Section 2 is entitled Being at Home and includes an essay examining poetry and philosophy in the search for a more inclusive form of *furusato* by Marcello Ghilardi (Chapter 4), another considering vastly different genres of writing to find a philosophical basis to escape feelings of alienation by Gerard van der Ree (Chapter 5), and a third exploring ideas of homelessness in the works of Martin Heidegger and Friedrich Nietzsche by Lukas Daniel Peter (Chapter 6). The third section, devoted to ideas of *Furusato* across Space, includes an anthropological study by Kawaguchi Yukihiro of collective identity among populations of Chinese and Japanese emigrants resident overseas (Chapter 7), an analysis by Sonia Favi of efforts to escape *furusato* among domestic travelers in early modern Japan (Chapter 8), and a discussion by Davide Bitti of the migration of the mythical earthquake catfish from its original hometown to the city of Edo after the 1855 Ansei Earthquake (Chapter 9). The four chapters of the final section are comprised of Kuroiwa Taku's investigation into the revealing nature of the use of the term "*furusato*" in the first Japanese translation of the Song of Roland (Chapter 10), Mária Ildikó Farkas' survey of the romanticization of home in the development of national consciousness in Japan and Central Europe (Chapter 11), Zakota Yutaka's exploration of *furusato* as a means of connecting past and present in literature from Europe and Japan (Chapter 12), and Yoshida Shigeru's examination of the character and importance of homeland in indigenous Mayan literature (Chapter 13).

What emerges in this diverse array of studies is a questing for and testing of ideas of home whose aggregate supplements the insights offered by the works it contains. Several subthemes weave through and between the individual chapters and across the four sections, giving a shape to the concept of *furusato* and highlighting both expected and surprising aspects of the concept. The original call for papers issued in connection with the Venice symposium identified the subthemes of collective pasts, identity, nationalism, and nostalgia, and the chapters in the present volume take these up and develop them. The shared past as a form of *furusato* is discussed in connection with local folklore in contemporary Japan (Chapter 3), among populations of Chinese and Japanese ex-pats (Chapter 7), and in the preservation of indigenous identity in Mexico (Chapter 13).

The derivation of personal and collective identity from *furusato* links considerations of post-disaster recovery (Chapter 2) with satiric imagery in early mass media (Chapter 9). Nationalism and national membership connect early modern Japanese travel (Chapter 8) with poetic expressions of patriotism (Chapter 11). And nostalgia represents a thread running through the whole of the book.

Less anticipated were themes that often seem at first sight contrary to the idea of *furusato*. Examinations of homelessness and alienation expose the reverse side of *furusato* and raise questions about the limitations of standard ideas of home (Introduction and Chapters 5 and 6), the impermanence and mobility of *furusato* challenge key assumptions connected to it (Chapters 1, 8, and 9), and considerations about the essentializing, ahistorical, and contingent nature of home (Chapters 7, 10, and 12) reveal some of its negative aspects.

Taken as a whole, the works collected in this volume present an ambitious and enlightening first foray into an interdisciplinary and multi-regional exploration of the concept of *furusato*. Readers are encouraged to take the chapters on their own terms and to read across them in pursuit of shared concerns and themes. It is the hope of the editors that the book will inspire further research into and treatment of *furusato* as a means of exploring ideas of home, origin, and belonging.

ALDO TOLLINI[1]

FURUSATO IN JAPANESE BUDDHISM AS A SPIRITUAL PLACE

I will deal with *furusato* in medieval Japan using poetry, since the concept of *furusato* is mostly emotional and therefore I think that it is better expressed by poems, all of which are my translations.

I would like to open this chapter with a poem by Murō Saisei 室生犀星 (1889-1962) entitled *My hometown is far*（「ふるさとは遠きにありて」）:

ふるさとは遠きにありて思ふもの
My hometown is far, but I keep it in my heart
そして悲しくうたふもの
and with nostalgia I compose poems for it.
よしや
However,
うらぶれて異土の乞食となるとても
if I should be reduced to misery and become
somewhere a beggar
帰るところにあるまじや
shouldn't I have a place to return to?
ひとり都のゆふぐれに
Alone, in the dusk of my capital
ふるさとおもひ涙ぐむ
remembering my hometown I would weep.
そのこころもて
With these feelings
遠きみやこにかへらばや
I want to go back to my faraway hometown!

遠きみやこにかへらばや
I want to go back to my faraway hometown!
（『小景異情ーその二』より）[2]
(From *Shōkei Ijō*, n. 2)

Hometown becomes *furusato* only when we are separated from it, that is when it is transformed into the beloved place of one's childhood or youth, from which, however, we are now far and where we will probably never return. It is an idealized image in contrast with the present situation, an antithesis to the present that lives in minds and memories.

This sentiment is well expressed by Zen monk Ryōkan 良寛 (1758-1831) in his *Kashū* [Collection of Poems] 『歌集』, poem n. 644[3] entitled *Thinking of the furusato* （「故郷をおもひて」）:

草枕	*During the journey,*
夜毎にかはる	*every night*
やどりにも	*sleeping in a different place,*
結ぶはおなじ	*but dreams always*
古里のゆめ	*are of my furusato*

Here we can see the fundamental disposition of the Japanese toward the *furusato*. The following points are the most relevant (apart from the omnipresent sentiments of nostalgia)

1. The *furusato* is a distant place that has been left for the needs of life;

2. It is a coveted place that inspires security; it is our own refuge;

3. There is a strong desire to return (called *bōkyō* 望郷, "desire to return to hometown").

---

2   From https://www.aozora.gr.jp/cards/001579/files/53241_49665.html

3   Yoshino Hideo 吉野秀雄, *Ryōkan kashū* [The Poems of Ryōkan] 『良寛歌集』 (Tokyo: Heibonsha 平凡社 , Tōyō bunko 東洋文庫 n. 556, 1992). See also: Ōshima Kasoku 大島花束, *Ryōkan kashū* [The Poems of Ryōkan] 『良寛歌集』 (Tokyo: Iwanami shoten 岩波書店, 1933; see University of Virginia Electronic Text Center http://jti.lib.virginia.edu/japanese/ryokan/kashu/RyoKash.html)

Homesickness is the feeling of 'I do not belong here'. It happens when someone feels a disconnection between his or her physical and emotional parts. Hometown is a sort of safe haven, where we can rediscover peace and security. It is like a family in whose bosom we can really be ourselves.

The conception of *furusato* also plays an important role in Japanese Buddhism, where the secular formulation is taken and transferred in the spiritual sphere. The native country here is understood differently. It is the original being, the true and authentic self cleansed of all the superstructures that, over the course of life and through various vicissitudes and experiences, have accumulated and created a false self. It is the pristine and pure self, which corresponds to our original Buddha-nature. The search, that is the rediscovery and return to the original self, is the task in pursuit of which Buddhist practitioners put themselves through their trying practice. The path consists in dropping all the superstructures and returning to original purity. This fundamental nature of ours (the *furusato*) is called in Zen "our original face" (*honrai no menmoku,* 本来の面目).

Buddhism follows the same conception of the mundane dimension but translates it into a Buddhist discourse:

1. We are far from our *furusato* (=our true self);
2. *Furusato* (=our true self) is the place of peace and wisdom;
3. *Furusato* (=our true self) is the object of research (desire to return to it).

While the *furusato* in general understanding is a real and physical place, in Buddhism, it is a "spiritual place", that is, it is located within ourselves, and there we must find it. Therefore, it is the object of a "spiritual search", because returning to the *furusato* is a search at a spiritual level, a quest for enlightenment. Our true *furusato*, our true abode, from the beginning is the state of our original perfection, free from attachments and illusions. In other words, returning to our "true self" means to see ourselves as a manifestation of the Buddha-nature.

Probably, the first to consider *furusato* as a spiritual place

dates back to China of the 7th century. This was master Zendō 善
導 (613-681) of Pure Land Buddhism, who in the poem *Kikyorai*
[Return to the hometown] 「帰去来」 in *Kanmuryōjukyō* [Sutra
of Visualization of Measureless Life] 『観無量寿経』 writes:

歸去來。	*Let's return back.*
魔郷不可停。	*We should not stay in this perverse hometown*
曠劫來流轉	*For a very long time on life-and-death have continued to repeat*
六道盡皆經	*in the realm of the Six Existences* (六道)
到處無餘樂	*where there is no pleasure*
唯聞愁歎聲。	*but only the voice of suffering can be heard.*
畢此生平後	*After ending a good life (based on Budddhist practice)*
入彼涅槃城。	*we will enter the dimension of nirvāṇa* [4]

Here Zendō uses the word *makyō* 魔郷, "perverse hometown"
to refer to our worldly *furusato*, that is, our present condition of
illusion. We should abandon it and strive to enter *nirvāṇa*, which
is our true *furusato*.

We can find another important reference in Kamo no Chōmei
鴨長明 (1155 ca.-1216), a devoted practitioner of Pure Land
Buddhism, in his collection of poems *Kamo no Chōmeishū*
[Works of Kamo no Chōmei] 『鴨長明集』 (poem n. 103, *The
fall of flowers while I described the image of Pure Land*):[5]

たえずちる	*There are also flowers*
花もありけり	*that fall endlessly,*
ふる里の	*but blooming of plums and cherries*
梅もさくらも	*in my hometown*

4   THE SAT *Daizōkyō* Database 大蔵経 DB, No. 1753, in vol. 37
     (http://21dzk.l.u-tokyo.ac.jp/SAT/satdb2015.php).

5   Ōsone Shōsuke, Kubota Jun 大曾根章介、久保田淳 (ed. by), *Kamo no
     Chōmei zenshū* [The Complete Works of Kamo no Chōmei] 『鴨長明全集』
     (Tokyo: Kichōhon kankōkai 貴重本刊行会, 2000, pp. 335-346). See also:
     Kamo no Chōmeishū [The Works of Kamo no Chōmei] 『鴨長明集』 (http://
     lapis.nichibun.ac.jp/waka/waka_i144.html#i144-001)

うしや一とき   *alas! Lasts only a short instant*

In the Western Paradise of Pure Land, flowers fall endlessly and beauty lasts forever, but in my poor real life (*furusato*) they last only for an instant.

Furusato in Buddhism has a double meaning: 1. Our conventional self, a construction of our ego, and 2. Our true self, the self of enlightenment. The purpose of the Buddhist Way is to let us understand that the first *furusato* is illusion and is devoid of meaning, and therefore it must be abandoned (*shukke* 出家, "leaving home") in order to devote ourselves to the quest for the true *furusato*, i.e. our true self, which is a no-self (*anattā* 無 我). This quest has two steps: 1. Leaving the *furusato*, and 2. Returning to the *furusato*. Both aspects are important and both are widely dealt with in Buddhist scriptures.

A. Leaving the *furusato*

In Buddhism the famous example of the Buddha Shakyamuni, who left home and family to devote himself to practice and search for the Way that leads to extinguishing suffering, has always been the model to be imitated. Leaving one's own home, family, and village means taking the decision to move away from what is believed to be proper to us, from the root of one's conventional (and source of suffering) self, to follow the path that leads to detachment from the ego and its appeasement.

The native village represents in Japan, in a sense, one's origin, one's most genuine self, one's roots, in a word, one's authenticity; to depart from it, is to leave behind an important part of one's self. It is something like what the French call *dépaysement*, the feeling of not being at home, in a foreign or different place, not usual and not familiar and where we lose the known coordinates.

At the same time, in Buddhism, it is a renunciation of the roots of our ego: we can say that it is a sort of "eradication of ourselves". It is necessary to put ourselves in a position to

undertake a journey in search of the true self without the bonds
that condition us to a conventional ego.

While in general understanding the self is intended as solid,
true, and genuine and is an object of search, in Buddhism the
fundamental doctrine says that our self, on the contrary, is illusion,
a fabrication of our ego, and therefore must be abandoned. The
spiritual *furusato* of Buddhism is then, an object of search, but
at the same time one of rejection. Finding the true self means to
recognize its illusionary existence and its inconsistence. What
we consider to be our true self is, on the contrary, illusion.

In Dōgen's 道元 texts, and other Buddhist scriptures, we
often find expressed the necessity of leaving home (*shukke*),
and he devotes an entire chapter to this subject (*Shukke*). The
following sentences are taken from *Shōbōgenzō* and *Shōbōgenzō
Zuimonki*:[6]

1.
はやく出家受戒して、諸仏諸祖の道を修習すべし。曠大劫
の仏因ならん。

*...soon leave home, receive the precepts, and practice the
truth of the buddhas and the patriarchs, and this will be a cause
of buddhahood for vast eons.*

(*Shōbōgenzō, Sanjūshichi bon bodai bunpō* 「三十七品菩提
分法」)

2.
しかのみにあらず、知家非家、捨家出家、入山修道、信行
法行するなり。造仏造塔するなり、読経念仏するなり。

*It is not only that: it is "to know that a home is not one's home,
to forsake one's home and to leave home, to go into the mountains*

6   As to *Zuimonki*, the Chōenjibon 長円寺本 version is used here. The
      source for *Shōbōgenzō Zuimonki* is: Nishio Minoru 西尾実 (et al. ed. by),
      Shōbōgenzō, Shōbōgenzō Zuimonki『正法眼蔵、正法眼蔵随聞記』, in *Nihon
      koten bungaku taikei* [Series of Classical Japanese Literature]『日本古典文学
      大系』, vol. 81, 1965, pp. 317-438 ("Shōbōgenzō Zuimonki"), while that for
      Shōbōgenzō is: Etō Sokuō 衛藤即応 (ed. by), *Shōbōgenzō*『正法眼蔵』, 3 vols.
      (Tokyo: Meicho fukyūkai 名著普及会, 1986).

and practice the truth, and to do devotional practice and Dharma practice"; it is to build buddhas and to build stupas; it is to read sutras and to be mindful of the Buddha.
(*Shōbōgenzō, Hotsu-Bodaishin* 「發菩提心」)

3.
遁世隱居山林、不絕我重代家、
Separate yourself from the world and go to live hidden in the deep mountains, break the deep bonds you have with your family.
(*Shōbōgenzō Zuimonki*, 2-18)

It goes without saying that, the term "leaving home" (*shukke*) has a broad meaning and refers to the concept of leaving one's position in life and embarking on the path of asceticism and research, taking the vows of the monk and practicing under a master.

To find oneself, our, true self, we must first abandon our conventional self, and this is realized with the renunciation of what we think is "ours". We should "undress" and become naked, so to speak, in order to become something completely new. This journey must be accomplished with a lightened *kokoro*, as far as possible emptied of everything that binds us to the idea of our social self. Everything that concerns us should be dropped, left behind or forgotten. The native village is symbolically the sum of all aspects of our ego. From the secular point of view, then the *furusato* is "being ourselves" in a positive sense, but from the point of view of Buddhist doctrine this is the idea of a self, that is, a strong impediment: it is attachment.

Furusato (the true one) is our original enlightened nature. In the long journey of our life, we often lose sight of our origin and of our authentic self and the realization of having lost something important stimulates the nostalgia for our original state and fosters the desire to start a search, that is a journey back.

The search is a long journey within ourselves. However, as well explained in the *Ten Oxherding Pictures* (『十牛図』), the *furusato*, or our true self, which coincides with enlightenment, is reached returning to the origin:

Step n. 9: 返本還源已費功[7]

"Returned to the origin, come back to the source, after having spent so many efforts."

So many efforts spent to search so far, while it was under our eyes all the time!

In sum, as Dōgen says:
衲子（のつす）ハ雲ノ如ク定（さだま）レル住処モナク、水ノ如クニ流レユキテヨル所モナキヲ、僧トハ云（いふ）ナリ。
A monk should be without a fixed abode, like the clouds, and like water flow without a resting place. This should be the monk.
(*Shōbōgenzō Zuimonki*, 6-22)

This is because not dwelling anywhere means not having attachment for oneself and letting oneself flow freely and accept one's transience. In Dōgen's words,
夫れ出家は、我と我所と無きが故に
In general, those who leave family life are without me and mine.
(*Shōbōgenzō, Shukke*).

Dōgen's fundamental teaching, *shinjin datsuraku* 身心脱落, or "dropping off our own body and mind" is nothing else than leaving our self, and the illusion of it, becoming "naked," and from that position starting a search for the "real self" which is nowhere and everywhere. *Shinjin datsuraku* correspond to *shukke*: a monk is one who has renounced his "me and mine". This "me and mine" is an expression which means all the attachments which allow us to suppose the existence of a solid self. *Furusato* is indeed one of the strongest bonds that leads to the construction of a self-identity. Leaving home, leaving the family (*shukke*), means leaving the idealized construction of our identity. *Furusato* is in large part an idealized place, "ideal"

---

7   From the site of Manpukuji 萬福寺 on Hōju mountain 寶樹山: http://www. tees.ne.jp/~houjuzan/jugyuzu.html.

though real, a construction of our imagery. For Buddhism, longing for an idealized place may be a stimulus to start a search, but only if well directed. This search for the "real" place must start from letting go of everything – the new birth begins from having nothing within.

A monk must be free of all attachments, his hometown, family, country must be forgotten, he is alone in the search for the Way.

B. Returning to the *furusato*.

In *Genji monogatari*'s *Suma* 「須磨」, when Hikaru Genji 光源氏 is exiled to a distant place from the capital, which is his *furusato*, he writes the following poem:[8]

ふるざとを	*In which spring*
いずれのはるか	*will I be able to see again*
ゆきてみん	*my hometown (furusato)?*
うらやましきは	*I look enviously at the wild geese*
かえるかりがね	*which fly back home*

This poem expresses the yearning desire of Genji to return to his native place. However, in Buddhism the return to hometown has a deeper, spiritual meaning.

When Dōgen returned from his sojourn in China in 1227 (or 1228), he did not bring with him Buddhist *sūtras* as was usual. He "came back to his hometown (Japan) empty-handed" (*kūshu genkyō* 空手還郷), as he said. What he wanted to mean was that instead of bringing back intellectual knowledge, he brought his true self, or "original face" 「本来の面目」, which he found under his master Nyojō 如浄. His "back to hometown" is coming back to Japan bringing with him enlightenment or his "true self".

---

8   Yamagishi Tokuhei 山岸徳平 (ed. by), *Nihon koten bungaku taikei*, cit., vol. 15, *Genji monogatari* 『源氏物語』 (Tokyo: Iwanami shoten, 1959), vol. 2, pp. 11-54.

However, *genkyō* 還郷 may be interpreted both as coming back to Japan or coming back to his "true self".

From that time on, for Dōgen the *furusato* was the "true self", or "original face". In his *waka* collection *Sanshō dōei* [Compositions of the Way of Sanshō] 『傘松道詠』 we find a poem entitled 「涅槃妙心」 *The mysterious mind of nirvāṇa:*[9]

いつもたた	*The flowers*
我ふる里の	*of my hometown*
花なれは	*never change their colour*
色もかはらす	*even when*
過し春かな	*spring has passed.*

Here Dōgen means that the dimension of enlightenment or *nirvāṇa*, that is, the original state without contamination, once reached, never changes. His "hometown" is his true self found once and for all. From that spiritual place he will never separate. He is back there to stay.

The monk Jien 慈円 (1155-1225) of the Tendai school 天台宗, who was also a great scholar, the author of the *Gukanshō* [Treatise for low-level administrators] 『愚管抄』, and a fine poet, expresses Buddhist sentiments regarding enlightenment with a poem included in *Shin Kokinwakashū* (n. 985):[10]

さとり行く	*Entering the path*
まことの道に	*leading to enlightenment,*
いりぬれば	*treading the way of sincerity*
恋しかるべき	*I have no more a hometown*
古郷もなし	*to yearn for*

Here Jien tells us that, during the journey towards

---

9   Dōgen's poems in *Sanshō dōei* are taken from: *Sanshō dōei*, in *Sōtōshū zensho* 曹洞宗全書 [The complete texts of the Sōtō school], DVD/ROM version published by Sōtōshū zensho kankōkai 曹洞宗全書刊行会, (Kyōto: Hōjōdō shuppan 方丈堂出版, 2014).

10   Hisamatsu Shin'ichi 久松真一 (et al. ed. by), *Nihon koten bungaku taikei*, op. cit., vol. 28, *Shin Kokinwakashū* 『新古今和歌集』 (Tokyo: Iwanami, 1958).

enlightenment, the *furusato* for which to long has vanished and with it also the desire to return.

It is interesting to speculate whether the *furusato* here is understood as a physical or spiritual place: in the first case, it means that those who are on the Way lose their attachment to their native country because they are detached from the worldly bonds. If, on the other hand, we understand *furusato* as the spiritual hometown, as is most likely, then Jien intends to say that treading the path of the Buddhist Way he has dropped his conventional ego. This means that he has let his illusory self go, so that he no longer has a spiritual *furusato* to be attached to.

Imaginarily, Dōgen answers him with the following poem in *Sanshō dōei* entitled 「父母所生身即證大覺位」 *This body born from a father and a mother is the great enlightenment itself*:

尋ね入	*Far away among the mountains,*
深山の奥の	*the village*
さとそもと	*where at last I arrived*
我住馴し	*is nothing else than my capital city (furusato)*
都なりける	*where I have always dwelled*

Dōgen, in retiring to the mountains of Echizen 越前 (today Fukuiken 福井県) where Eiheiji is located, practicing the Way away from the turmoil of society, but also far from his physical *furusato*, has finally reached his spiritual *furusato*, his true self. To his surprise, he notes that this true and authentic self (the *furusato*) is nothing but the place where he has always dwelled, where he has always been, from the beginning. The spiritual *furusato* is not far away, or in another dimension, but it is none other than that which is present every day, has always been present and will always be there. However, it is a *furusato*, or an I, which is now seen with different eyes, and a different consciousness.

Among the poems in Chinese of Dōgen there is one that takes up the theme of the return to the house (i.e. the *furusato*). It is in

Gen oshō geju [Buddhist poems of the reverend Kigen (Dōgen)]
『玄和尚偈頌』, (poem n.22):[11]

行世夢然休覓跡	*Treading the way of this world as in a dream, I cease searching the tracks.*
杜鵑啼處動頭輕	*I listen to the cuckoo singing and exhorting me to go back to my home, and I turn my head towards it*
誰教退步歸家路	*to see who urges me to turn back on the way of my home.*
盡大地人莫問程	*O you all, people of this world! Do not ask me which is this way back home [it is every step of the Buddhist Way].*

Here Dōgen tells us that the way back to our home is that of the Buddhist Way. It brings us back to our true origin, to our original nature.

The cuckoo in literature and myth is associated with the longing of the spirits of the dead to return to their loved ones. Here it means, a voice that urges the poet to go back to his home, that is to his spiritual *furusato*. However, this "way back" is nothing else than every step of the Buddhist Way. Everywhere is the Path, everywhere is the *furusato*.

In the same mood is another great Zen master, Musō Soseki 夢窓疎石, (1275-1351) who lived about one century after Dōgen. Musō combines the two points of view quoted above (have a *furusato* no longer, and everywhere is *furusato*). In the anthology *Fūgawakashū* [Collection of Elegant poetry] 『風雅和歌集』 (poem n. 2063)[12] we find the following poem by Musō:

ふるさとと	*When you have*
さたむるかたの	*no furusato anywhere*
なきときは	*to return to,*
いつくにゆくも	*everywhere you go*

---

11   Ōtani Tetsuo 大谷哲夫, *Dōgen Eihei kōroku, shinsan, jisan, geju*『道元、広録、真賛、自賛、偈頌 』(Tokyo: Kōdansha 講談社, 2014), *Geju*, pp. 95-190.

12   *Fūgawakashū* (http://lapis.nichibun.ac.jp/waka/waka_i019.html)

いへちなりけり　　　　*that is the way back home.*

We should realize, practicing the Buddhist Way, that our *furusato* (our self) is an illusory construction, a mirage or a dream from which we should awake: it is not something solid, reliable and real. Dropping the illusion is to awake to true reality, and to understand that our self is diluted and liquid, just like water that constantly changes its form and never rests anywhere. It is everywhere and nowhere.

However... though being deeply conscious of what has been said above, and having taught the necessity of dropping our self (and our *furusato*), Dōgen writes in *Sanshō dōei* the following poem,

都には　　　　　　*In the capital now*
紅葉しぬらん　　　*the leaves of the maples are coloured.*
おく山は　　　　　*Here in the deep mountains*
夕へも今朝も　　　*yesterday evening and also today*
あられ降けり　　　*a hailstorm.*

The capital, Kyoto, is Dōgen's *furusato*. Now living among the mountains in the northern part of the country where the climate is harsh, he turns his thoughts to his *furusato*, famous for the coloured leaves of autumn...His words are filled with unexpressed nostalgia.

The great Buddhist master sometimes returns to humanity, with his worldly sentiments and fragility.

The other great Zen master Eisai 栄西 (1141-1215) too, founder of the Rinzai school 臨済宗, during his sojourn in China wrote a poem included in *Shoku Kokinwakashū* [Collection of poems ancient and new: Continuation] (poem n. 906),[13] remembering his *furusato* with nostalgia:

13　*Shoku Kokinwakashū* 『続古今和歌集』 (http://lapis.nichibun.ac.jp/waka/waka_i013.html#i013-002).

もろこしの	*It is so sad to see*
こすゑもさひし	*the leaves that fall*
ひのもとの	*here in China.*
ははそのもみち	*Perhaps also in Japan*
ちりやしぬらむ	*the leaves of the maples are now*
	falling...

Concluding remarks

In Japanese culture, the *furusato* is a longing for a lost dimension: our own dimension, that is our self. However, longing (for *furusato*) is in the Buddhist view a strong attachment and is not being free: it means dissatisfaction, frustration and uneasiness. The *kokoro* is disturbed and does not find rest. It is a projection of our anxiety: a calmed *kokoro* has no longing. Besides, according to Buddhist doctrine, our own self is considered illusion and therefore, its quest must lead to the final abandonment of the idea of a self.

In medieval Japan, Buddhism became the spiritual reference of many forms of culture and arts. The arts drew inspiration from the concept of self abandonment, and the sedated *kokoro* became the spiritual state in which the perfection of art could grow.

Zeami, in *Fūshi kaden* [The Transmission of the Flower of Elegance] 『風姿花伝』, 5th chapter *The deep meaning*, says:

In pursuing a Way, in devoting oneself to an art, one obtains one's virtues by means of abandoning oneself.

In the Way of Tea, *sadō* 茶道, also the aesthetic conception of *wabi* 侘 [taste for the simple] is based on *kanjaku kotan* 閑寂枯淡: *kanjaku* stands for "tranquility and solitude", and *kotan* for "dried up and extinguished", referred to one's self.

Therefore, the quest for *furusato* in Buddhism becomes a spiritual quest which should lead to enlightenment. However, this quest, is a special one because consists in dropping attachment and in the last analysis also in dropping the quest itself.

PART I
FURUSATO IN IMAGE AND IMAGINATION

TIJANA ŽAKULA[1]

DUTCH ART THEORY AT HOME IN JAPAN

An Abridged History of Gerard de Lairesse's *Groot Schilderboek*'s Presence in Japan and Its Influence on Japanese Art

On January 1, 1795, Dr. Ōtsuki Gentaku 大槻玄沢 (1757-1827) of Edo threw the first annual celebration of the Dutch New Year (fig. 1).[2] This extraordinary event was organized on the premises of the first private school for Dutch studies in Japan, which this preeminent *rangakusha* (蘭学者 Dutch studies scholar) had founded in 1787. For this festive occasion Dr. Gentaku was sporting a Dutch captain's hat and coat, and, as a master of ceremonies, he entertained a company of the most prominent scholars of Dutch learning. Among these thirty distinguished men was his former student Morishima Chūryō 森島中良 (1756-1810), who, together with Gentaku, had authored the *Kōmō Zatsuwa* [Red-hair Miscellany] 『紅毛雑話』 in 1787. This book included a section on European art, which was lavishly illustrated with the images copied from Gerard de Lairesse's *Groot Schilderboek*.[3]

De Lairesse's massive volume was first published in 1707 — 17 years after he had gone blind.[4] This encyclopedic treatise elucidated a program that was meant to help future painters of all

1   Utrecht University
2   Calvin L. French, *Through Closed Doors: Western Influence on Japanese Art, 1639-1853* (Rochester: Meadow Art Gallery & Kobe City Museum, 1978), p. 121.
3   Grant Kohn Goodman, *The Dutch Impact in Japan (1640-1853)* (Leiden: Brill, 1967), pp. 10-11; Yoriko Kobayashi-Sato, 'Japan's Encounters with the West through the VOC', in Thomas DaCosta Kaufmann and Michael North (ed. by), *Mediating Netherlandish Art and Material Culture in Asia* (Amsterdam: Amsterdam University Press, 2014), p. 283.
4   Gerard de Lairesse, *Het Groot schilderboek*, (Amsterdam: by de Erfgenaamen van Willem de Coup, op 'tRokkin, 1707).

Figure 1

stripes create images of unparalleled beauty and perfection. This perfection was in De Lairesse's vocabulary defined by the term *antique*. Even though through the adoption and endorsement of the *antique*, which was "followed by the most polite nations," De Lairesse, his patrons and followers aspired to reach out beyond the borders of the Northern Netherlands, not in their wildest dreams did they expect that the *Groot Schilderboek*'s would land in Japan. This article is going to trace its critical fortune in Japan as is described and assessed in existing sources, the possible influence of the *Groot Schilderboek* on Japanese art, and propose a hitherto neglected lead that deserves further scholarly attention.

Interpreters, Readers and Admirers

It is not known when exactly De Lairesse's treatise reached Japan. A copy of its 1740 edition is still to be found in the Municipal museum of Kyoto.[5] As testified by a number of images and writings on art of few Japanese artists active around this time – most notably

---

5   Keiichi H. Okano, *Die Malkunsttheorien von Satake Shozan und Shiba Kôkan: europäische Einflüsse auf die Malkunst des 18. Jahrhunderts in Japan* (Cologne: University of Cologne Dissertation, 1971), p. 87.

Odano Naotake 小田野直武 (1749-1780), Satake Shozan 佐竹曙山 (1748-1785), and Shiba Kōkan 司馬江漢 (1747-1818), Gerard de Lairesse's treatise seems to have made an indelible impression on them and changed their artistic idiom forever.

This would perhaps not have been such a remarkable feat, if the book was not procured to Japan during the most draconian period of self-isolation recorded in the history of the civilized world.[6] In this fashion the whereabouts and influence of Gerard de Lairesse's *Groot Schilderboek* – to the extent they can be retraced – relate an extraordinary account about political, social, and artistic affairs in eighteenth-century Japan.

In all likelihood the *Groot Schildeboek* was first owned by a Nagasaki interpreter and physician, Yoshio Kōsaku 吉雄幸作 (1724–1800), who facilitated communication between the Dutch and the Japanese.[7] The Dutch, or the 'red-hair people', were as of July 24, 1641 confined to the man-made island of Deshima, and remained hidden from the inquisitive glimpses of the locals behind an imposing wall. The name 'red-hair people' had to do with a long-held belief that Europeans, much like demons, were identifiable through their blue eyes and ginger hair.[8] Any Japanese who would venture to the island, with the exception of interpreters, would be closely monitored.[9]

In these circumstances, it is little wonder that Kōsaku's title of interpreter was not infrequently a euphemism for a spy. And in this particular case, a spy, who, under the threat of death penalty, would not communicate with the other party beyond the absolute minimum. But a well-placed bribe, as one encounters many a time in history, seems to have opened many doors. This means that images, illustrated manuals, as well as books on art would end up in an interpreter's private collection. Be it in the capacity

6   Matthi Forrer and Yoriko Kobayashi-Sato, 'The VOC on Deshima and Its Impact on Japanese Culture', in Thomas DaCosta Kaufmann and Michael North (ed. by), cit., pp. 239-244.

7   Keiichi H. Okano, *Die Malkunsttheorien von Satake Shozan und Shiba Kôkan*, cit., pp. 87-89; Grant Kohn Goodman, *The Dutch Impact in Japan*, cit., pp. 10-11.

8   Calvin L. French, *Through Closed Doors*, cit., p. 3.

9   Matthi Forrer and Yoriko Kobayashi-Sato, 'The VOC on Deshima', p. 240.

of a bribe, or as a gift to a young man who in his writings praised the Dutch beyond any conceivable measure, a copy of the 1740 edition of the *Groot Schilderboek* is likely to have found its new home in the collection of Yoshio Kōsaku.[10]

In the course of the year 1770 Kōsaku received an extraordinary guest, who had had a compelling task on his hands. This guest was Hiraga Gennai 平賀源内 (1729-1779), who as of 1765 started collecting Dutch books and was in need of a competent translator. A *rōnin* 浪人 by choice and out of disgruntlement with the limitations of the Japanese feudal system, Gennai was a brilliant botanist and an engineer interested in everything from matchlock guns to ceramics, from dinosaur bones to theatre plays.[11] Little wonder that he was interested in painting as well. This fascination spurred Gennai to purchase the *Groot Schilderboek* from Yoshio Kōsaku.[12]

Figure 2

10   Calvin L. French, *Through Closed Doors,* cit., pp. 59-60.
11   Grant Kohn Goodman, *The Dutch Impact in Japan,* cit., p. 71 and p. 143; Cal French, *Through Closed Doors,* cit., p. 4-5.
12   Hiroko Johnson, *Western Influences on Japanese Art: the Akita Ranga Art School and foreign books* (Amsterdam: Hotei, 2005), p. 71.

Gennai's role in the dissemination of Western pictorial devices was more that of a promotor than a practitioner. There is only one extant painting loosely attributed to him (fig. 2), and not of particularly laudable quality. This makes it safe to say that his contribution to the endorsement and promulgation of Western artistic formulae largely relied on several important Western books he owned and is likely to have made available to his students.[13]

Art-loving Akita Samurai: Satake Shozan and Odano Naotake

In 1773 Gennai was invited to the remote Akita domain in the capacity of the undisputed authority on mining technology. According to a popular anecdote, at the house of a local sake brewer, where Gennai had taken up lodgings, he took notice of a screen painting. This discovery led him to Odano Naotake. Rumor has it that upon meeting Naotake, Gennai asked him to draw *kagami mochi* 鏡餅 — two round rice cakes prepared for a Shinto altar — placed one on top of another as seen from above. The result of this exercise was disappointing, as Gennai could not tell what the drawing represented: a tray, or a ring. This allegedly prompted him to introduce Naotake to the technique of chiaroscuro, for in Asian painting no shading was added to create depth.[14]

Be it as it may, towards the end of 1773 we find Naotake in Edo, where he stayed for three years under the ambiguous and unprecedented title of Agent for Mining and Goods. It has been assumed that Gennai saw Naotake fit to illustrate Sugita Genpaku's 杉田玄白 (1733-1817) *Kaitai shinsho* 『解体新書』, the first translation of an anatomy book, and had him move to Edo.[15]

This was Naotake's first encounter with Gerard de Lairesse, for

---

13   Calvin L. French, *Through Closed Doors,* cit., p. 124.
14   Calvin L. French, *Shiba Kōkan: Artist, Innovator and Pioneer in the Westernization of Japan* (New York: Weatherhill, 1974), p. 79; Calvin L. French, *Through Closed Doors,* cit., pp. 126-127; Hiroko Johnson, *Western Influences on Japanese Art,* cit., p. 31.
15   Robert Parthesius and Kris Schiermeier, *Japanse verwondering: Shiba Kōkan, 1747-1818: kunstenaar in de ban van het westen* (Amsterdam: Amsterdam Historisch Museum, 2000), p. 18. Hiroko Johnson, *Western Influences on*

the last four illustrations of the anatomical instruction were based on De Lairesse's images for Govert Bidloo's *Anatomia Humani Corporis*. The way Naotake went about copying these, points out to the discrepancies in artistic idioms, and to nearly insurmountable difficulties Naotake must have been facing while trying to change the scale of De Lairesse's illustrations. While Bidloo's book measured 50cm by 36cm, the Japanese counterpart was reduced to nearly half the size (figs. 3 and 4).[16] The differences in the representations of the *Tendons of the Dorsal of the Hand* show why the tri-dimensionality of the original was lost in Naotake's translation. Not only did he remove the cutting board providing the perspective lines, but Naotake's inexperience in shading made the surgical instruments, which De Lairesse so masterfully employed not only to demonstrate the course of the procedure but also to indicate spatial relations, look as though they were hovering in the air.

Figure 3

Japanese Art, cit., p. 32. Yoriko Kobayashi-Sato, 'Japan's Encounters with the West through the VOC', cit., pp. 275-278.

16   Hiroko Johnson, *Western Influences on Japanese Art,* cit., p. 58.

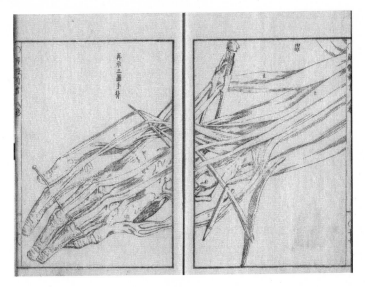

Figure 4

Naotake got better, though. Only a glance at his superb *Shinobazu ike zu* 不忍池図 (fig. 5), provides us with a glimpse into the three compositional elements Naotake had adopted from Western art: the low horizon line with a distant landscape, the water element in the middle ground serving as a reflective surface, and close-up objects in the foreground that introduce the eye of the beholder into the linear perspective set-up of the image. Several illustrations of De Lairesse's instruction, particularly those showing landscapes, would have been of indispensable help in translating the Japanese *en-kin* (遠近, far and near) technique into what looks like a full-blown Western one-point linear perspective. Especially useful would have been the engraving that illustrates the division of landscape into five grounds (fig. 6). The motifs that differ in size and that are placed on different grounds create a sense of distance and lead the eye of the beholder towards the vanishing point.[17]

---

17   Yoriko Kobayashi-Sato and Mia M. Mochizuki, 'Perspective and Its Discontents or St. Lucy Eyes', in Dana Leibsohn and Jeanette Favrot Peterson (ed. by), *Seeing Across Cultures in the Early Modern World* (Farnham and Burlington: Routledge, 2012), p. 39; Yoriko Kobayashi-Sato, 'Japan's Encounters with the West through the VOC', cit., p. 283.

Figure 5

Figure 6

Regardless of his evident success, Naotake intimated that the Dutch drawings were so great, that an untalented person like himself should not have been included in such a project. He went on to say that if it were not for his good friend, he would have never embarked on such a demanding enterprise.[18]

---

18   Hiroko Johnson, *Western Influences on Japanese Art*, cit., p. 32.

The friend in question was lord Satake Shozan of the Akita domain. Shozan was a samurai and autodidact who profoundly enjoyed discussing and making art. He was the founder of the *Akita ranga* 秋田蘭画, or the *Akita school of painting,* and the first to author a treatise on Western art and theory.[19]

We cannot be sure of Shozan's ability to read Dutch. It is certain, though, that through the use of visual language, Shozan tried to compile a comprehensive overview of Western painting techniques and pictorial devices. While doing so he heavily relied on the *Groot Schilderboek,* as is evidenced by his illustration of the nude female figure, which was originally meant to show the correct proportions of the female body. Shozan did not trace its contours, but copied from the original. His method of going about this is best visible in the decidedly different expression of the face, and slight muddling around the fingers, both due to the use of a brush.[20]

The influence of the *Groot Schilderboek* is also evident in Shozan's musings on reflections and the use of chiaroscuro. Shozan wrote that "Any object close to the surface of the water has reflections on the water. They should be depicted (see: Lairesse (1712), pp. 228-29 and p. 258). At night or in the dark, the reflections of the objects cannot be seen. But when the moon shines or the light illuminates the object, their reflections and shadows can be seen (see: Lairesse (1712), p. 309). In such cases, the reflections on water should not be forgotten. Therefore, when painting, the rule for indicating light and shade is that artists differentiate the lighted and shaded areas by using light or dark ink in front of or behind the object. In this way, differences in distance and the height of the object are indicated (see: Lairesse (1712), p. 258 and p. 287). Therefore, the views of the sphere, semi-circle and circle, or of the treacherousness of the mountains, the currents of the river, the frontal view of the nose, and the interior view of the room all can be indicated by using the shading principles."[21]

---

19   Hiroko Johnson, *Western Influences on Japanese Art*, cit., p. 10.
20   Hiroko Johnson, *Western Influences on Japanese Art*, cit., p. 114 and p. 121. Yoriko Kobayashi-Sato, 'Japan's Encounters with the West through the VOC', cit., pp. 282-284.
21   Translated and cited in Hiroko Johnson, *Western Influences on Japanese Art*, cit., p. 147 and p. 160.

Shiba Kōkan: a true connoisseur or a gifted storyteller?

The *European Man and Lady,* now in the Manna Art Museum
in Osaka, was a collaborative effort of Satake Shozan and Shiba
Kōkan, the best known Japanese Western-style artist, who also
had trained with Hiraga Gennai. While Kōkan was responsible
for the figures, Shozan painted the trees in the backdrop.[22]

In order to master the Western idiom in the best possible way,
Kōkan ventured to Nagasaki in search of someone who would
be willing and able to train him. However, instead of meeting a
Western artist, he obtained a Dutch book from Isaac Titsing, the
then-*operhoofd* on Deshima. In Kōkan's own words, this book
on art, which was entitled *Konst Schilderboek,* "carried [him]
into an intoxicating world. After a careful study of it, [he] finally
attained a perfect command of its principles, and [could then]
draw whatever [he] wished with complete ease – landscapes,
birds, flowers, men, or beasts."[23]

Kōkan's claim that this book was the *Groot Schilderboek* needs to
be re-examined, though, for it may well have been an embellishment
of his travel account. Although there is no question that Kōkan
knew Titsingh, it is impossible that they met at the time that Kōkan
indicated. When Kōkan visited Nagasaki in 1788, Titsingh was not
in Japan. Similarly, during Titsingh's stay in Edo in 1780 or 1782,
it is highly unlikely that he would have been in a position to give
the book to Kōkan. Moreover, the *Groot Schilderboek* had been
circulating at least several years before Titsingh arrived in Japan.
Shozan's sketchbook, which was in any case completed before
1780, contained illustrations directly taken from De Lairesse's
treatise. This means that in all likelihood Kōkan got acquainted with
the *Groot Schilderboek* through the preeminent and indefatigable
champion of western art, Hiraga Gennai.

Much like Shozan, Kōkan probably did not understood

---

22   Calvin L. French, *Shiba Kōkan,* cit., p. 80, p. 79; Calvin L. French, *Through
      Closed Doors,* cit., p. 127; Hiroko Johnson, *Western Influences on Japanese
      Art,* cit., p. 143.
23   Shiba Kōkan, *Seiyōga Dan,* NZT, 6:809, cited and translated in Calvin L.
      French, *Shiba Kōkan,* cit., p. 80.

a word of Dutch, but drew his knowledge from the copious illustrations of De Lairesse's treatise. In his *Seiyōga Dan* 『西洋画談』, a discussion treating Western painting, Kōkan said that "By employing shading, Western artists can represent convex and concave surfaces, sun and shade, distance, depth, and shallowness. The pictures are models of reality and thus can serve the same function as the written word, often more effectively. The syllables used in writing can only describe, but one realistically drawn picture is worth ten thousand words. For this reason, Western books frequently use pictures to supplement descriptive texts, a striking contrast to the inutility of the Japanese and Chinese pictures, which serve no better function that that of a hobby to be performed at drinking parties."[24]

Figure 7

Be it as it may, Kōkan is said to also have used the *Groot Schilderboek* as a source of inspiration for his own works. However, and despite the fact that it is undeniable that Kōkan had the access

---

24   Shiba Kōkan, *Seiyōga Dan*, cited and translated in Calvin L. French, *Shiba Kōkan*, cit., pp. 171-174.

Figure 8

to the copy owned by Gennai, which was later passed down to Gennai's pupil Morishima Chūryō,[25] he is unlikely to have modelled his paintings on the illustrations from De Lairesse's treatise.

Kōkan's representation of the *Dutch Woman beneath the Tree* (fig. 7) was thought to be inspired by De Lairesse's tableau of *Vanitas* (fig. 8), while its pendant, showing the *Hollander on a pier,* was allegedly modeled after the image of a Sailor from Abraham a Sancta Clara's 1759 *Iets voor Allen.* Even though these assumptions seemed perfectly plausible at first glance, Isozaki Yasuhiko 磯崎康彦 has aptly demonstrated that both Kōkan's works were modelled after the illustrations from Jan and Caspar Luyken's 1694 *Menselyk Bedryf* (fig. 9 and fig. 10).[26]

Kōkan's exhaustive knowledge of the *Groot Schilderboek* thus remains tenuous. In spite of his claim to have learned everything from De Lairesse's treatise, Kōkan's images fall short of showing evidence to support this. Kōkan may have perused the *Groot Schilderboek* during his collaboration with Hiraga Gennai and used its illustrations as a source of inspiration for his theoretical musings,

---

25   Masanobu Hosono, *Nagasaki prints and early copperplates* (Tokyo: Kodansha Internat., Shibundo, 1978), p. 68 and p. 99.

26   Yasuhiko Isozaki, 'De invloed van Jan en Caspar Luyken op de Japanse schilderkunst', in *Antiek* (1979-80), pp. 197-210, esp. pp. 203-204.

Figure 9   Figure 10

while his painted oeuvre is much more likely indebted to the printed sources he had at hand – the *Menselyk Bedryf* being one of them.

Legend has it that after having announced his own death to the world in 1813, Shiba Kōkan retreated to Kamakura, where he became the follower of the Zen priest Seisetsu 誠拙 (1745-1820). In his letter to Yamane Kazuma of 1815 Kōkan wrote that his "only desire [was] to leave behind paintings that can be seen by posterity, so that [his] fame will live on."[27] And indeed, he left a laudable oeuvre of hybrid images that mixed the elements of Japanese artistic idiom with decidedly European traits. Upon seeing them, however, a Japanese person would certainly be excused for not acknowledging them as his own, while a Westerner is likely to not be able to instantaneously recognize them as modelled on European artistic traditions.[28]

---

27   Calvin L. French, *Shiba Kōkan,* cit., p. 162.

28   Sherman E. Lee and Michael R. Cunningham, *Reflections of Reality in*

Figure 11

The Aftermath

Some ten years after Kōkan's retreat from society, the first of Hokusai's 北斎 (1760-1849) series of *36 Views of Mt. Fuji* 『富嶽三十六景』 appeared in 1823 and introduced a new standard of excellence. The existing visual evidence, especially the illustrations from the third volume of Hokusai's celebrated fifteen-part *Hokusai Manga*『北斎漫画』 (fig. 11), indicate that he may well have derived his knowledge of the linear perspective from the *Groot Schilderboek.*[29] What has escaped scholarly attention so far, though, is that Hokusai's representations of different acts of daily life might, too, be indebted to De Lairesse's *magnum opus* (fig. 12). In the first volume of the *Hokusai Manga,* Hokusai drew a number of figures striking different poses while being engaged in an array of activities.[30] One sees men and women crouching, sleeping, reading, walking, holding forth, etc.— all of them irresistibly calling to

---

    Japanese Art (Cleveland: The Cleveland Museum of Art, 1983), p. 191.

29   Matthi Forrer, 'Hokusai, the old man mad about painting', in *Simiolus 40,* p. 195.
      Masanobu Hosono, *Nagasaki prints and early copperplates,* cit., pp. 126-127.

30   Edmond de Goncourt, *Hokusai,* (Parkstone International, 2012), pp. 138-139.

mind De Lairesse's representations of four sorts of movements (fig. 13). Hokusai was no stranger to the Dutch, and their artistic tradition. After Opperhoofd Jan Cock Blomhoff and his assistant Johan van Overmeer Fisscher had acquired books illustrated by Hokusai during their stay in Edo in 1822, Hokusai and his studio were commissioned a vast number of paintings by the Dutch at Deshima.[31] Works of art and literature that Hokusai had consulted before showing off his knowledge of Western pictorial devices to the Dutch commissioners still need to be identified.

Be that as it may, Hokusai's landscape prints of the 1820s, 30s, and 40s, as well as those of Hiroshige 広重 (1797-1858), Kuniyoshi 国芳 (1797-1858), and Kunisada 国貞 (1786-1865), assimilated Western pictorial devices of perspective, foreshortening, and chiaroscuro into a decidedly Japanese artistic idiom. The tables were about to turn, and announce their conquest of progressive Western European artistic scene, which was soon to be seduced by the beguiling charm of Japanese art.[32]

Figure 12

31   Matthi Forrer, 'Hokusai', cit., p. 207.
32   Calvin L. French, *Through Closed Doors*, cit., p. 24.

Figure 13

List of Illustrations

Fig. 1 Ichikawa Yo, 1795. Tokyo, Waseda University Library.

Fig. 2 Hiraga Gennai (attributed), *European Lady*, 1734 -1779. Kobe, City Museum.

Fig. 3 Gerard de Lairesse, *Muscles and tendons of the forearm and hand*, from Govert Bidloo, *Anatomia corporis humani*, Amsterdam 1685, plate no. 70.

Fig. 4 Odano Naotake, *Tendon of the dorsal of the hand*, in Sugita Genpaku, *Kaitai shinsho*, Tokyo 1774.

Fig. 5 Odano Naotake, *Shinobazu Pond*, after 1774. Yokote, Akita Museum of Modern Art.

Fig. 6 Illustration showing objects marking five-ground landscape, from Gerard de Lairesse, Groot schilderboek, 2 vols., Amsterdam 1712, vol. 1, p.350.

Fig. 7 Shiba Kōkan, *Hollander on a pier and Dutch woman beneath a tree*, ca. 1784. Kobe Museum, Kobe.

Fig. 8 Philip Tideman, *Vanitas*, Illustration from Gerard de Lairesse, *Groot Schilderboek*, 2 vols., Amsterdam 1712, vol. 1, facing p. 189.

Fig. 9 Jan Luyken, *The Sailor*, ca. 1690. *Het Menselyk Bedryf,* Amsterdam 1694, plate no. 94.

Fig. 10 Jan Luyken, *Het Menselyk Bedryf,* Amsterdam 1694, frontispiece.

Fig. 11 Katsushika Hokusai, *Hokusai Manga,* 1814-1879. Tokyo, National Museum.

Fig. 12 Katsushika Hokusai, *Hokusai Manga,* 1814-1879. Tokyo, National Museum.

Fig. 13 Illustration of the motions, from Gerard de Lairesse, *Groot Schilderboek,* 2 vols., Amsterdam 1712, vol. 1, following p. 30.

Ozaki Akihiro 尾崎彰宏[1]

THE GREAT EAST JAPAN EARTHQUAKE AND FURUSATO/HOME

Towards *furusato* as a Sacred Space

Introduction: What 3/11 Made Visible

The sound of the term *furusato*/home (hometown, birthplace, homeland, native place, or *Heimat* in German) evokes an unconscious sense of nostalgia for the Japanese. Such feelings might even increase, as one gets older. While we are not normally conscious of *furusato*, it may well represent a key to opening the door to human sentiments. This article will use the concept of *furusato* to consider the Great East Japan Earthquake of March 11, 2011, which wreaked horrific destruction across the Tōhoku and Kantō regions, and how the area has recovered and revived since the disaster.

The Disappearance of furusato *and the Wealth of Things*

Furusato has been heralded in Japanese poetry as a term and concept from antiquity to the present. The *Man'yōshū* 『万葉集』 anthology, compiled from the latter half of the 7th century through the latter half of the 8th century, and the *Kokinwakashū* 『古今和歌集』 anthology, dating to 901, both include frequent mentions of the term *furusato*. Its appearances in these two anthologies express two different meanings. First, poem 992 in the *Man'yōshū* refers to Asuka as the poet's *furusato*, and then creates a pun on different characters for the term Asuka referring to Nara. Here the term refers to an old, dilapidated village. In the past *furusato* meant old lands that were previously cities or capitals. The second usage, found in *Kokinwakashū* poem 42, states that the scent of past flowers reminds the poet of his *furusato*. Thus, the term here means a land long loved and familiar to the poet. From antiquity the definition of *furusato* included something similar to what we might today call nostalgia. Beginning in the Meiji period (1868-1912), the term came to refer to thoughts of somewhere far off, of traveling to a city where one succeeds and then returns home, covered with honors. Thus, *furusato* refers both to the place of one's birth, for which one is nostalgic, and at the same time to its exact opposite, the advanced place or country where one lives in the present, busy with work and the accumulation of wealth.

This is not to suggest that the term had universally positive associations. Dazai Osamu's 太宰治 (1909-1948) novel *Tsugaru* 『津軽』 (1944) includes a scene where the protagonist takes pains not to speak the Tsugaru dialect, his native form of the language. This is a typical example of a situation in which identification with rural roots becomes as source of embarrassment. *Furusato* equaled the countryside, a place seen as providing raw resources in the forms of labor and foodstuffs but offering little else. Conversely, this means that, while the countryside produces resources and labor, rural areas are not themselves understood as sites of consumption or places to work. Thus, these areas are supporting actors, and people there come to internalize the idea that they inhabit places that progress left behind.

Let us take the situation of power companies in Japan to highlight an example of the ways ambiguous feelings toward *furusato* shape rural realities. Electric power companies in Japan, which are public utilities, often face criticisms that they take advantage of feelings of inadequacy in the countryside by promoting themselves as standing at "the cutting edge of civilization" and by promising rural areas that host them financial grants and local job creation as part of Japan's nuclear power policies. The major power companies have been divided in accordance with the eight major regions of Japan, and each of them is tasked with providing its region with electrical power. Based on that regional division, the Tohoku Electric Company should be responsible for the running of the Fukushima nuclear plants where the nuclear crisis occurred in 2011 and where even now the difficult work of stabilizing the reactors continues. However, despite the fact that the Fukushima nuclear plant is located 250 km from Tokyo, it is managed by the Tokyo Electric Company and functions as a power generation base for the capital region. It is an example of the situation discussed above, in which a local government allowed a power company to establish nuclear facilities dedicated to other regions in order to create employment opportunities and to enrich the local area through supplemental grants. *Furusato* as the countryside became emblematic of places that were simply less developed than their urban analogues. For areas with historical associations and those known for agricultural success, tourism offers some hope for local prosperity, but this promise often turns out to be false. Most areas fail to generate enough interest to maintain viable populations, leading to the loss of local cultural heritage, for example when local arts or festivals fail to be passed on to succeeding generations. This can cause already struggling communities to be further marginalized. There appears a vicious cycle in which a dearth of economic opportunities leads to the abandonment of villages and towns by their residents, contributing to a further darkening of local economic prospects.

This is not a new story. Situations like that described above have been standard in the course of government-directed modernization from the Meiji period onward. The plans of officials focused on the belief that wealth building was possible and that its pursuit justified significant sacrifices. Natsume Sōseki 夏目漱石 (1867-1916) understood the dangers of this path and what would result. His novel *Sanshirō* 『三四郎』 (1908) recounts its title character's journey to Tokyo from Kumamoto in Kyūshū in order to study at Tokyo Imperial University. Sitting in the railway carriage, his eyes widened as he saw how ever-progressing Japan was changing and spoke of his excitement. The middle-aged man sitting next to him poured cold water on the young man's enthusiasm, suggesting that the current version of progress could only end in destruction. Japan today, a century after *Sanshirō*, is no different. People continue to press forward with single-mindedness, eyes constantly on what is ahead in order to live. The shadow of the Meiji era darkens the present, still defining modern Japan.

The Great Hanshin-Awaji Earthquake of January 17, 1995, 16 years before the Great East Japan Earthquake, was a clear warning. And yet, we continued to stand by and disregard the impatience and despair that modern Japan evoked prior to that. Contrary to that indifference, the Great East Japan Earthquake and the nuclear plant accident it caused has led to radical reconsideration of the dominant ways of life and value systems in Japan. The scale of the destruction was immense, spreading more than 300 km from Fukushima to Iwate and Kantō. It was a disaster of a nearly unparalleled magnitude in Japan, but previous centuries faced their own repeated disasters, though smaller in scale. The Great Kantō Earthquake of 1923 and Sanriku earthquakes and tsunami in 1896 and 1933 are ready examples of these. The accident at the Fukushima nuclear facility, however, was a disaster that defied, and continues to defy, imagination.

Nine years have now passed since the disaster. When I hear how recovery is proceeding in the different areas, it only strengthens my sense of how difficult it is to do the cleanup after a nuclear accident. Progress is being made in the decontamination of the radiation-contaminated region, and restrictions have been lifted on parts of the evacuation zone. Still, progress remains slow on the return of displaced people to their evacuated homes. There is a lack of detailed information on the health of the citizens affected by the radiation, making it difficult to obtain accurate information and doing little to reassure former residents.

Recovery and regeneration after the March 11th disasters involve discussions about the building of seawalls that are higher than previously thought necessary, the creation of safety measures to protect coast lines that could be overwhelmed by tsunami, and the movement of residential areas to higher ground. And yet, that process has been less welcomed by the residents than expected. Why is it not linked to their desire to live active lives?

Undoubtedly the ability to live in safety is important to them, but their reluctance to take what have been deemed appropriate measures betrays a deep sense of dissatisfaction. Much of this feeling surely derives from thoughts of being separated from the lands where they and their families have lived for so long. This is a clear demonstration that human life is not something simply built on safety and convenience.

So, what can be done? The answer isn't easy. Let us change our perspective and ask again. Instead of asking what can be done, we must consider what links people so determinedly to the places where they have lived for long times, for the lands where their ancestors lie buried. Why are these locations so essential? Solutions to the current problems will surely come from such questions.

From Scenic Spot to Landscape

Many of the disaster zones were background zones, the regional or countryside areas I mentioned previously that support the prosperity of the cities, or industrial areas, places that contribute both labor and materials. These areas served important roles in the course of Japan's development. As a result, the group structures of traditional religion, the organizations and collective practices connected with ancestors, have been neglected. If we talk about the blood links that connect people, the landscapes of a community that has grown over time, the cold mornings of winter when one is enveloped in a soft warm overcoat, these are the impressions that undergird human lives. This is why the residents feel such nostalgia for their *furusato*. This nostalgia evokes in human hearts images of such scenes, such landscapes.

Since antiquity, poets in Japan have written prose regarding scenic spots and landscapes. Those scenes were then implanted in the hearts of their readers. Not simply sad, or happy, or lonely, they contained internal realities that could not be conveyed to others. Ariwara no Narihira's 在原業平 (825-880) poem about the evanescence of a cherry tree, "Were there no cherry blossoms/in all the world,/how tranquil in the spring/would the hearts/of people be (*Yononaka ni taete sakura no nakari seba, hito no kokoro wa nodokekaramashi*, 世の中にたえて桜のなかりせば春の心はのどけからまし) ", is well known from the *Kokinwakashū* anthology. Cherry blossoms, first noticed when they begin to bloom, reach full bloom very quickly and have fallen and scattered in a matter of days. Because the flower's existence is so short, it evokes a sense of pity in the hearts of those who view it. It stands as a symbol of the transience of life. The scene described by Narihira spreads in an instant to the hearts of all those who read the verse.

Then we can consider another example of evoking a scene or landscape. That is Bashō's 松尾芭蕉 (1644-1694) famous verse, "The summer grasses/for many brave warriors/the aftermath of dreams (*Natsukusa ya tsuwamono-domo ga yume no ato*, 夏草や 兵どもが 夢の跡)", presents another example of the affecting depiction of the human and natural landscapes. This poem evokes human fate, its rise and fall, composed on the site of an old battlefield in Hiraizumi in Tōhoku. It refers to the tragic end of Yoshitsune no Minamoto, chased by the forces of his older brother, the first shogun Yoritomo no Minamoto, to the far north, where he took his own life at age 30 after being betrayed by the second son of his erstwhile host, Hidehara Fujiwara. The stage for the decisive battle is today a plain of waving grass with only shadows of the great families' existences remaining. This poem speaks with deep emotion of the fleetingness of human endeavors. Here too, rather than a long rambling text, the succinct 17-morae verse form conveys a limitless sentiment seemingly in opposition to its textual brevity. The reader senses that expanse, and indeed the power of the imagery overshadows that of its specific content. And yet, the evoked image is not the bare description of a scene. It is suffused with narrative elements that inject movement and human life into an actual landscape, a real place. The text imposes the transience of the human experience to the still and unchanging backdrop. The verse presents a tableau, yes, but strictly speaking it is not only a tableau.

From a Land of the Gods to a Real-World Land – Furusato *in Europe*

The ancient Greeks and Romans were aware of the *furusato* concept, and this awareness persisted in the Europe of later centuries. The Renaissance - a term that speaks specifically of a rebirth of ancient classical culture – can also be seen as a "*furusato* and rebirth movement." At the same time, the view that one's individuality was based on one's birthplace, those who live there, and particularly the language spoken there can be traced back at least as far as 14th century Italy. In parallel there began to be an awareness of each region as landscape or scenic view.

The 16th century saw various dramatically opposing movements emerge. In northern Europe painters rediscovered the ruins of ancient Rome and, beginning with Jan Gossaert, individuals and groups traveled from the Netherlands to Italy, where they were moved by the works of the Italian Renaissance and antiquity. The Romanists recognized the previously unvalued ancient works as their own source and began to include similar imagery in their paintings. In the process, the classics and antiquity became part of their own identity. And yet, their devotion did not represent simple and unadulterated praise for antiquity. The antiquity that they celebrated expressed different qualities than that idealized in Italy. In other words, the Renaissance based on antiquity did not exist solely in Italy, it took on other forms in northern Europe. While northern artists took Italy as their source, their creativity was all the more strengthened by the pains they took to distinguish themselves from Italy. This movement, this search for individual identity, repeated over and over again until the 18th century German Romantics. As they assigned increasing importance to their places of birth, their *furusato* came to be expressed in ways that went beyond the purely spiritual. Indeed, where they were from was also a political matter, their own selves standing at the center of the world. This reflected another type of *furusato* that already existed separately from *furusato* as source or origin. In the early 13th century in Europe, the place where one was raised and lived one's everyday life came also to be recognized as *furusato*. The concept that one's duty to defend one's ancestral land was loftier than the feudal duty of a vassal to one's lord was expressed by legal scholars. The idea gradually spread that what was important was not a far-off heavenly realm, a land of the gods as described by Augustine, but rather a land of the gods here on earth. This thinking, which emerged from one aspect of Christianity, saw in the midst of the Reformation a heightening of the meaning of pride in one's own land. While previously such land was depicted in painting as background without much importance, the land where people lived, rather than the royal family, came to be used as the central subject of painting. This worked in tandem with the recognition of landscape paintings as a genre. These places were sanctified by their depiction in painting, enshrining within them the voices of the nameless multitudes. The landscape was their identity and its symbol.

Let us consider the *Baptism of Christ* in the *Turin-Milan Hours* by Jan van Eyck, the painter credited with bringing realistic depiction to Northern European art. The viewer's gaze immediately shifts from the scene of Christ's baptism in the foreground to the landscape behind. The depiction of nature is arresting. The castle reflected on the river's surface and the landscape that spreads out from both banks of the river show that the person who conceived the composition did not want to focus attention on the heavens, but rather on the earthly realm. God's realm is thus shown to exist on Earth, and at the same time the scenery depicted is not the town of Bethlehem on the outskirts of Jerusalem, but rather evokes a sense of the Netherlandish countryside. Heaven is realized on Earth, and the painting entrusted to the hearts and emotions of the people who live there the answering of the question of whether their faith was strong enough to accept this.

Eventually the Netherlandish landscape shifted from the 16th century painters Joachim Patinir, Pieter Bruegel and others to 17th century Holland, where it became the medium for expressing the identity and pride of the citizenry. In other words, there came to be the understanding that landscape paintings were a way to create visible forms of a person's own identity. The birth of landscape painting can be seen as a sign that God's realm had shifted from the heavens to the Earth. The pursuit of that realm represented a movement in accord with the Protestant Reformation and, in turn, became linked with various forms of community based on *furusato*. The landscape functioned as a medium linking people into social groups, and people who viewed landscapes as such recognized the world around them as landscapes.

What factors shaped people's awareness of the landscape as visualizations of *furusato*? The answer to that question can be found in Blaise Pascal's famous words about painting: "How useless is painting, which attracts admiration by the resemblance of things, the originals of which we do not admire." (*Pensées,* 134). If painted in a picture, even an uninteresting person can appear remarkable. Pascal emphasized the falseness of paintings, describing it as something that imitates the actual form in an effort approximating vanity. What he holds up for derision, however, is precisely where others find the principle value of painting. This same situation also arises for landscapes. Encountering their own *furusato* in a landscape, the people who see it (as well as the artist who rendered it) rediscover that place as a special location. The *furusato* as seen in a picture was an element that paved the path for the consciousness of modern citizenry. We can see Johannes Vermeer's famous *View of Delft* (1660-1661) as a typical example of this concept. Vermeer's painting reveals his *furusato* as a shining holy place, replete with a sense of quiet solemnity.

In 17th century Europe, there was a shift from the teleological view of the world to the mechanistic view of the world, and religious spaces became human spaces that could be measured. This transformation in European history, in which the main actors shifted from a set ruling class to the citizenry, was also seen in Japan. The Warring States period ended in the century-long Ōnin War of the late 16th century in an extended political transformation that concluded with the unification of the country under Oda Nobunaga and Toyotomi Hideyoshi. At the beginning of the 17th century, Tokugawa Ieyasu destroyed both these rivals and forged the polity that would become known as the Edo shogunate. Peace was established and the foundations laid for what would become a 250-year long period of relative peace and stability. By the 18th century, the merchants who helped develop the economy made great strides in cultural terms, and though, art, and aesthetics began to focus more on such emotive qualities as beauty and pleasure, rather than on religious concepts. The flourishing culture of the townspeople displayed in *ukiyoe* 浮世絵 arts – the "floating world (*ukiyo* 浮世)" – took root in cities and cultural products alike.

Discovery of the Landscape and the Rebirth of furusato

And yet, this movement, too, was to pass. As previously noted, Japanese society was plunged into turmoil when its leaders chose to open the country after pressure from the West in the latter half of the 19th century. This brought about a fundamental change in the dominant social systems. The movement from the Tokugawa-led government to the self-consciously modern Meiji government centered on four clans, those of Satsuma, Chōshū, Tosa and Hizen, who together assumed important roles in the events leading to the Meiji Restoration. The previous social caste system, which centered on samurai, farmers, craftsmen and merchants, was abolished and the four classes were made nominally equal. The moral basis for society began to undergo a broad shift from Confucianism to the rationalism and the economic theories presented in Adam Smith's *Wealth of Nations*. New technologies and Western individualistic viewpoints were introduced. From the previous human relationships based on master-servant basis, Western ideas of the worth of the individual began to spread.

The thought that civil society was made up of a gathering of individuals was backed up in landscapes. The discovery of the landscape is thoroughly discussed in the well-known "Fūkei no hatsugen 風景の発言" chapter of the long essay *Origins of Modern Japanese Literature* by Karatani Kōjin 柄谷行人 (1941-). The key point of this chapter was that the landscape was discovered in Japan in 1887, and Kunikida Doppo's 国木田

独歩 (1871-1908) *Musashino* 『武蔵野』 (1898) and *Wasureenu hitobito* 『忘れえぬ人々』 (1898) were important milestones in the process of its spread and acceptance. In particular, *Wasureenu hitobito* clearly shows a shift in values in which the painter turns towards the inner man before sketching the landscape.

Karatani's book describes the narrative paradigm in which the protagonist struggles with the eternal questions of human life, nostalgically thinking of different people as he suffers a sense of loneliness and isolation. During this process, we are told, it is landscape scenes, not images of people, that come to his mind. The unforgettable people of his life have been absorbed into the landscape. Though completely uninterested in the person in front of him, Doppo feels a sense of identification with the chance-encountered person who is absorbed in the landscape he is looking at as "none other than me." Karatani says that the person who views the landscape is the person who does not see "the external". It is essential to notice one's own existence in order to discover the landscape on a personal basis. In the shift from the Edo to the Meiji periods, there was a rethinking of morals and social structures and systems. During that process people lost track of their support systems but were able to discover themselves through the landscapes. In other words, rather than being absorbed in their relationships with the gods or the Buddhas, it was necessary for them to find a place where they could have an emotional transference as the other who is aware of the self.

In this manner scenery was transfigured into landscape. This entailed a de-familiarization with the visually known landscape elements, and through that process an imbuing of the landscape with the emotions of unease, sadness and nostalgia. While a landscape is an ordinary scene that might be anywhere, for the viewer it is an inimitable scene; this is what makes it a landscape. It could also be thought of as a shining, sacred place. Luminescence is transformed into personal autonomy, and is reborn as a will to live.

In Conclusion – The Restoration of Furusato *is a Milestone on the Path towards a Worthy Nation*

Since the birth of modern Japan, and especially from the 1960s onwards, *furusato* has been a site in which country is placed at odds with city in a manufactured conflict that has contributed greatly to the expansion of high-level capitalism. This order was shaken by the Great East Japan Earthquake and subsequent nuclear plant accident. The damage the disasters caused, both economic and material, was almost irreparable. Devastated landscapes cause deep despair, yet if we can discern a holy light in the destroyed *furusato*, we will remember the forgotten narrative in the wind that flows from lost places. These are the lands where generations of ancestors sleep, sacred and connected to the hearts of people. Thus, *furusato* as a site of prayer is a place filled with a multitude of spirits, it is a land of affection, a place in which life has ended and will revive itself.

The restoration of *furusato* done to support people's spirits is not a case of a subordinate relationship between country and city; it is the rebuilding of a country with *furusato* as an organic body that closely binds the two. As 19th century French historian Jules Michelet has stated in his *The History of France*, such a nation resonates with the people's character, and as a laudable nation that honors individuality, it can project an exemplary social nature internationally.[2]

Main References

Jirō Abe 阿部次郎, *Tokugawa jidai no geijutsu to shakai* [Art and society in Tokugawa period] 『徳川時代の芸術と社会』 (Tokyo: Kadokawa Shoten 角川書店, 1971 [1931]).

Hiroki Azuma 東浩紀, *Genron* 『ゲンロン』 (Tokyo: Genron ゲンロン, 2017).

2   Jules Michelet, *Histoire de France*, Japanese version published by Fujiwara Shoten, 2010, pp. 165-166.

Augustin Berque, *Nippon no fūkei, seiō no seikan* 『日本の風景・西欧の景観』(Tokyo: Kōdansha gendai shinsho 講談社現代新書, 1990).

Piero Camporesi, *Le belle contrade* (Milano: Il saggiatore, 1992).

Kenneth Clark, *Landscape into Art* (New York: Harper and Row, 1976).

Osamu Dazai 太宰治, *Tsugaru* 『津軽』(Tokyo: Shinchōsha 新潮社, 2004).

Shunsuke Hirose 廣瀬俊介, *Fūkei shihonron* [Capitalistic theory of landscape] 『風景資本論』(Tokyo: Rōbundō 朗文堂, 2011).

Norihiro Katō 加藤典洋, *Nippon no fūkeiron* [Theory of Japanese landscape] 『日本の風景論』(Tokyo: Kōdansha gakujutsu bunko 講談社学術文庫, 2000).

Hiroshi Kainuma 開沼博, *"Fukushima"ron: genshiryokumura ha naze umaretanoka* ["Fukushima" theory: Why did atomic power villages appear?] 『「フクシマ」論：原子力ムラはなぜうまれたのか』(Tokyo: Seidosha 青土社, 2011).

Hiroshi Kainuma, *Hajimete no fukushimagaku* [Introduction to fukushimology] 『はじめての福島学』(Tokyo: East Press イーストプレス, 2015).

Kojin Karatani, *Origins of Modern Japanese Literature (Post-Contemporary Interventions)* (Durham: Duke Univesity Press, 1993).

Riken Komatsu 小松理虔, *Shinfukkōron* [New theory of reconstruction] 『新復興論』(Tokyo: Genron, 2018).

Doppo Kunikida, *Musashino* (including Wasureenu hitobito) (Tokyo: Shinchō-bunko 新潮文庫, 1949).

Koichirō Kuniwake 国分功一郎, *Genshiryoku jidai ni okeru tetsugaku* [Philosophy in the age of nuclear power] 『原子力時代における哲学』(Tokyo: Shōbunsha 晶文社, 2019).

Jules Michelet, *Furansushi* [The History of France] 『フランス史』(Tokyo: Fujiwara shoten 藤原書店, vol. 1, 2010).

Raffaele Milani, *L'arte del paesaggio* (Bologna: Il mulino, 2001).

Masaki Ōsawa 大澤真幸, *Sekaishi no tetsugaku-Kinsei hen*

[Philosophy of world history – The modern age] 『〈世界史〉の哲学 近世篇』(Tokyo: Kōdansha, 2017).

Susumu Nakanishi 中西進, *Man'yōshū* 『万葉集』 (Tokyo: Kōdansha, 1978).

Akihiro Ozaki 尾崎彰宏, 'The Beginning of the Never-ending Struggle', in: Christopher Craig, Enrico Fongaro, Akihiro Ozaki (ed. by), *Knowledge and Arts on the Move: Transformation of the Self-Aware Image through East-West Encounters* (Milan: Mimesis, 2018).

Akihiro Ozaki 尾崎彰宏, 'AFTER 3.11: Toward a Rehabilitation of the Mind', in: Christopher Craig, Enrico Fongaro, Andreas Niehaus (ed. by), *3.11: Disaster and Trauma in Experience, Understanding, and Imagination* (Milan: Mimesis, 2019).

Shigetaka Shiga 志賀重昂, *Nihon fūkeiron* [Theory of Japanese landscape] 『日本風景論』 (Tokyo: Iwanami shoten 岩波書店, 1995 [1894]).

Natsume Sōseki, *Sanshirō* (London: Penguin Classic, 2017).

Hideo Takahashi 高橋英夫, *Mikurokosumosu: matsuo bashō ni mukatte* [Microcosmos: toward Matsuo Bashō] 『ミクロコスモス―松尾芭蕉に向かって』(Tokyo: Kōdansha, 1992).

Yutaka Tanaka 田中裕, Shingo Akase 赤瀬信吾 (ed. by), *Kokinwakashū* (Tokyo: Iwanami shoten, 1981); Shin'ichi Yamamuro 山室信一, *Kimera: Manshūkoku no shōzō* [Chimera: a portrait of Manchuria] 『キメラ―満洲国の肖像』(Tokyo: Chūōkōron shinsha 中央公論新社, 2004).

Akira Yoshimura 吉村昭, *Sanriku kaigan ōtsunami* [The big tsunami of Sanriku shore] 『三陸大津波』(Tokyo: Bungeishunjūsha 文藝春秋社, 2004).

Yutaka Zakota 座小田豊 (ed. by), *Shizenkan no hensen to ningen no unmei* [Changement of nature's vision and destiny of human beings] 『自然観の変遷と人間の運命』(Sendai: Tohoku University Press 東北大学出版会, 2015).

Myōki Shinobu 妙木忍[1]

THE REDISCOVERY OF FURUSATO AND THE INHERITANCE OF FOLKLORE

A Case Study of Yamashiro, Tokushima Prefecture

1 *Introduction*

As of November 2019, there are three designated *kai isan* (怪遺産, *Kai* heritage, namely heritage relating to mystery) areas in Japan.[2] Sakaiminato in Tottori Prefecture was designated in 2007, Yamashiro in Tokushima Prefecture in 2008, and Tōno in Iwate Prefecture in 2010. These have the common characteristics of giving rise to stories of *yōkai* (妖怪), mysterious creatures in Japanese folklore.

Sakaiminato is the hometown of Mizuki Shigeru (水木しげる, 1922-2015), creator of the *yōkai* manga *GeGeGe no Kitarō*. Tōno, meanwhile, is the setting of Tōno monogatari (The legends of Tōno) written by Yanagita Kunio 柳田國男 (1875-1962) in 1910, and the book's 100th anniversary was in 2010. Finally, Yamashiro is known as the birthplace of the *Konaki-jijii* (こなきじじい, 児啼爺, a *yōkai* with the face of an old man and the voice of a crying baby) legend.

Taking the perspective of Contents Tourism Studies, I conducted my fieldwork in these areas, focusing on the relationship between folklore and tourism.[3] In the process,

---

1   Tohoku University
2   *Kai* heritage areas are designated by the *Sekai yōkai kyōkai* (世界妖怪協会, World Yōkai Association, whose first and honorary posthumous president is Mizuki Shigeru).
3   I conducted my fieldwork in Tōno (25-26 November 2016, 11-12 and 24 February 2017, 22-23 July 2018, and 20 October 2018), Sakaiminato (12-15 October 2017 and 8 July 2018), and Yamashiro (10-11 October 2017, 10-12 November 2017, 4-7 August 2018, 24-25 November 2018, and 16-17 November 2019).

I found that Yamashiro bears a unique history and process in the inheritance of folklore.[4] The town has many legends related to *yōkai*, but the stories were rediscovered and highlighted by the efforts of a Yamashiro native resident outside the town, resulting in the local residents' efforts to pass down that folklore. Accordingly, this paper takes Yamashiro as a case study. Here, the concept of *furusato* (ふるさと, 故郷) refers to the place where someone was born and brought up, and this term plays an important role in this paper.

This paper is structured as follows. First, I describe the characteristics of Yamashiro as a place where the transmission of *yōkai* folklore was able to take place, clarifying the questions of how and why its appeal as a *furusato* was rediscovered from outside. Second, I outline how and why *Konaki-jijii*'s birthplace was identified. Third, I analyze the local residents' activities which were spurred by the above two rediscoveries. Fourth, I examine how *yōkai* legends have functioned in the community. Finally, this study will reveal a particular way in which the inheritance of folklore takes place in contemporary Japan.

2 *The Rediscovery of the Furusato's folklore*

Yamashiro is located in central Shikoku. It is famous for its beautiful natural landscape, including the Ōboke and Koboke gorges (see Figure 1). The town is surrounded by sheer mountains, and this rugged landscape is of relevance to the existence of *yōkai* folklore. That is, these stories were needed to protect people, especially children, from natural dangers.

In 1995, Shimooka Shōichi (下岡昭一, 1936-) was invited to a meeting held by *Kinki Yamashiro Ōboke kai* (近畿山城大歩危会, an organization consisting of Yamashiro natives resident in the Kansai region), where he was asked for suggestions regarding

---

4   As regards the similarities and differences between these three sites and analysis, see Myōki Shinobu, 'Yōkai Tourism in Japan and Taiwan', in Yamamura Takayoshi, Philip Seaton (ed. by), *Contents Tourism and Pop Culture Fandom* (Bristol: Channel View Publications, 2020), pp. 98-115.

Figure 1: The Ōboke gorge. (Source: Author, 10 November 2017)

the revitalization of their hometown.[5] Shimooka is also from Yamashiro, but he was living in Shizuoka Prefecture at the time. According to him, he suggested planting Japanese maple trees because there were beautiful surroundings in the Fujikawadani Valley.[6]

After that meeting, Shimooka began trying to discover the state of the *furusato* as it had once been, which he believed could then be put to use for its future. He read official town histories, also consulting references on geography, history, topography, geology, and other aspects of the town. Subsequently, he began conducting interviews. He originally focused on the samurai who patrolled the province's borders (now the borders of the prefecture) in premodern times. In doing so, he realized that he encountered stories of *yōkai* wherever he went. Since the turn of the century, he has been collecting folklore in earnest. Village residents asked Shimooka "are my stories worth telling or

---

5   This paragraph and the next are based on an interview with Shimooka conducted by the author at the Yōkai House (*Yōkai-yashiki*) and Stone Museum in Yamashiro (5 August 2018), as well as an additional telephone interview conducted by the author by telephone (6 June 2019). The *Kinki Yamashiro Ōboke kai*, meanwhile, was established in 1991 and has 355 members and 49 associate members as of 9 June 2019. The members live in Osaka, Hyōgo, Kyoto, Nara, Shiga, Wakayama, and Mie Prefectures, while the associate members are resident in the Shikoku, Tōkai, Kantō, and Chūgoku regions. This information is based on an interview with Kubohara Kazuhiro 窪原和弘, the head of Office at *Kinki Yamashiro Ōboke kai*, conducted by the author via e-mail (24 June 2019).

6   Later, the *Fujikawadani no kai* [Fujikawadani Association] 藤川谷の会 was established in 1996.

important?", and Shimooka affirmed that they were. They then began to tell Shimooka about additional stories and willingly guided him to related places. Shimooka considered this process to be a movement that involved the mutual discovery of value.[7]

Shimooka himself had previously heard these kinds of *yōkai* stories in his youth, so he was already familiar with them. However, when he observed his *furusato* from outside of Yamashiro, he rediscovered the significance that such stories hold. He later returned to Tokushima (Awa Ikeda) in 2006. In 2009, 2012, and 2017, Shimooka edited three volumes of *yōkai* stories that, as shown later, he gathered in Yamashiro.

3. *The Rediscovery of the* Konaki-jiji*'s birthplace*

Konaki-jijii is a famous *yōkai* in *GeGeGe no Kitarō*. In manga and anime, *Konaki-jijii* is given a likeness, but originally it appeared only in texts based on folklore. In Yanagita Kunio's *Yōkai-meii* (「妖怪名彙」), a glossary that includes 80 kinds of famous Japanese *yōkai* written in 1938-1939, *Konaki-jiji* (written in *katakana* and rendered phonetically as コナキヂヂ) was described as a *yōkai* found in villages in the mountainous regions of Awa province (present-day Tokushima Prefecture).[8] Takeda Akira 武田明 identified the name *Konaki-jiji* (コナキジジ), provided an explanation for it, and attributed it to "Sanmyōson [village] Aza Taira (三名村字平, present-day Taira in Kamimyō (上名), Yamashiro Town, Tokushima)".[9]

A local historian named Takita Masahiro 多喜田昌裕 from

---

7   In the process of his interviews, he realized that there were many people there who remained cheerful and hardy, even though Yamashiro was (and remains) a depopulated area. He felt a new appreciation for the value of every individual.

8   Yanagita Kunio 柳田國男, *Yōkai-meii* [The glossary of Japanese yōkai] 「妖怪名彙」, *Minkan denshō* 3, no.10 (Tokyo: Minkan denshō no Kai, 民間伝承の会, 1938), p.12.

9   Takeda Akira, 武田明, *Sanson-goi* [The vocabulary of mountain villages] 「山村語彙」, *Minkan denshō* 4, no.2 (Tokyo: Minkan denshō no Kai, 1938), p.12.

Anan City in Tokushima began his research on *Konaki-jiji*'s precise birthplace, and he found three people who had heard of the *Konaki-jiji* legend. In 1999, he confirmed that its origin was the Kamimyō area of Yamashiro.[10] After Takita's confirmation, a stone stature of *Konaki-jijii* was created in 2001 in Yamashiro, and its unveiling ceremony became the first festival held by *Fujikawadani no kai*. At an earlier stage, the association also held the Yōkai Momiji Maple Festival, which later became the Yōkai *matsuri* (祭り, festival).

Ichikawa Hiroya 市川寛也 explored the processes through which *yōkai* are formed: from legends, to conversion into text, visualization, the propagation of images through manga, the excavation of *yōkai* folklore, and how all of these become resources for regional regeneration.[11] The reconfirmation of the *Konaki-jiji*'s birthplace contributed to this revitalization, resulting in further revelations concerning *Konaki-jiji*'s *furusato*, as shown below.

4. The Inheritance of Folklore and Two Rediscoveries

What did these two rediscoveries bring to Yamashiro? In short, they led to resonance.

In 2008, Shikoku-no-hikyō Yamashiro Ōboke yōkai mura (四国の秘境 山城・大歩危妖怪村, Yamashiro Ōboke Yōkai Village in Shikoku's Secluded Areas, hereafter 'Yamashiro Ōboke Yōkai Village') was established and was certified as a *kai* heritage site

10   Takita Masahiro 多喜田昌裕, 'GeGeGe no Kitarō no manga-ka Mizuki Shigeru shi wo tazunete' [Visiting *GeGeGe no Kitarō* manga creator Shigeru Mizuki] 「「ゲゲゲの鬼太郎」の漫画家水木しげる氏を訪ねて」, Tokushima shinbun 徳島新聞, 4 July 2002, p.12.

11   Ichikawa Hiroya 市川寛也, 'Chiiki shakai ni okeru yōkai kan no keisei to keishō - Tokushima ken Miyoshi shi Yamashiro chō no jirei kara' [Formation and Tradition in the Representation of Japanese Monstrous Beings in Local Communities: A Case Study on Yamashiro Town, Miyoshi City, Tokushima Prefecture] 「地域社会における妖怪観の形成と継承—徳島県三好市山城町の事例から」, *Bunkashigengaku* 文化資源学 11 (Tokyo: Bunka shigen gakkai 文化資源学会, 2013), pp.127-138.

in the same year. Then, in December 2008, the village unveiled a development plan declaring that they would make use of regional resources such as history, legends, local residents (storytellers, guides), and the natural landscape.

Shimooka Shōichi edited a book titled *Yōkai mura densetsu* (『妖怪村伝説』, Yōkai Village folklore)[12] in 2009, *Otoroshiya* (『おとろしや』, 'Frightening' in the local dialect)[13] in 2012, and *Omoshiro Yamashiro tanukibanashi* (『おもしろ やましろ たぬき話』, Interesting Yamashiro Tanuki Tales)[14] in 2017, all of which were published by Yamashiro Ōboke Yōkai Village (see Figure 2).

In 2010, Yōkai-yashiki to ishi no hakubutsukan (Yōkai House and Stone Museum, hereafter Yōkai-yashiki) opened. Its exhibits are made up of visualized images of *yōkai*: handmade *yōkai* dolls produced by local residents (see Figure 3). Shimooka is also known as *Yōkai hakase* (Dr. Yōkai) or *Yōkai jiisan* (Grandpa Yōkai) and he sometimes visits the museum to receive questions from children and explain *yōkai* culture to visitors. In 2013, Yamashiro Ōboke Yōkai Village was awarded the Suntory Prize for Community Cultural activities. Yamashiro residents themselves took the initiative in order to transmit their *furusato*'s legends to future generations.

Along Fujikawadani road, which runs between the town and mountains, wooden *yōkai* statues welcome tourists (see Figure 4). On this road is the former Kamimyō Elementary School, the grounds of which are now used as a venue for the Yōkai Festival (held by *Fujikawadani no kai*). I participated in the 17th, 18th, and 19th Yōkai Festivals between 2017 and 2019 (see Figure 5). As an example of the activities done in connection with the festival, on 12 November 2017 Shimomyō (下名) Elementary School

---

12 Shimooka Shōichi (ed. by), *Yōkai mura densetsu* [Yōkai village folklore] 『妖怪村伝説』(Miyoshi: Shikoku-no-hikyō Yamashiro Ōboke yōkai mura 四国の秘境 山城・大歩危妖怪村, 2009).

13 Shimooka Shōichi (ed. by), *Otoroshiya* ['Frightening' in the local dialect] 『おとろしや』(Miyoshi: Shikoku-no-hikyō Yamashiro Ōboke yōkai mura, 2012).

14 Shimooka Shōichi (ed. by), *Omoshiro Yamashiro tanuki-banashi* [Interesting Yamashiro *tanuki* stories] 『おもしろやましろたぬき話』(Miyoshi: Shikoku-no-hikyō Yamashiro Ōboke yōkai mura, 2017).

Figure 2: Shimooka Shōichi at the 6th Kai Forum, held in Yamashiro. Pictured on right is a part of an enlarged version of *Otoroshiya*'s cover, drawn by Shimooka. (Source: Author, 12 November 2017)

Figure 3: Handmade *yōkai* dolls at Yōkai-yashiki (Source: Author, 10 October 2017)

Figure 4: A wooden *yōkai* statue. This *yōkai* is called '*Mado*'. (Source: Author, 10 October 2017)

Figure 5: A local Yamashiro *yōkai* named 'Yamajichi' at the 18th Yōkai Festival. (Source: Author, 25 November 2018)

students thought of ideas for *yōkai* sweets and sold them with cards featuring explanations of the concept of the foods, sketches of *yōkai*, and messages reading "they're delicious, try one!" (see Figure 6) This demonstrates that not only adults, but also children participate in the maintenance and transmission of folklore.

At the 3rd Yamashiro Tanuki Festival in 2017, a new *tanuki*-themed station building was unveiled (see Figure 7), and, at the same festival the following year, there was an exhibition of drawings depicting *tanuki* legends in Yamashiro (see Figure 8). At that year's festival, meanwhile, I also saw *kamishibai* (紙芝居, picture-story show) about local *yōkai* stories performed at a local kimono store. Through pictures, local residents and tourists can travel through the past and imagine life in the vanished past.

5. *The Function of* Yōkai *Folklore and its Significance in the Community*

According to Shimooka,[15] *yōkai* stories fulfil a number of functions in everyday life. These include the protection of children, an avenue to forgiveness for people (by, for example, attributing their behavior to *yōkai*), a way to stop dwelling on unfortunate events, and warnings of danger. In other words, they are inherited knowledge that serves to maintain the community or a mechanism for sustaining it. This wisdom comes from the danger of the mountains and fear in the darkness. *Yōkai*, therefore, are a frightening presence, yet one that people are eager to see and meet.

In the preface of one of the books that he edited (*Yōkai mura densetsu*),[16] Shimooka writes: "*Yōkai* in Yamashiro are necessities for coexisting with a harsh natural environment, a

---

15   Interview conducted by the author at the *Yōkai-yashiki* in Yamashiro (5 August 2018). This paragraph is based on this interview.

16   Shimooka Shōichi (ed. by) *Yōkai mura densetsu* 『妖怪村伝説』 (Miyoshi: Shikoku-no-hikyō Yamashiro Ōboke Yōkai Mura (四国の秘境　山城・大歩危妖怪村, 2009). Quoted sentences are from the preface written by Shimooka. The quotation is the author's translation from Japanese.

Figure 6: *Yōkai* sweets shop at the 17th Yōkai Festival. The *Yōkai* sweets sold out immediately. (Source: Author, 12 November 2017)

Figure 7: The 4th Yamashiro Tanuki Festival with the *tanuki*-themed station building unveiled in 2017 in the background on the right. (Source: Author, 24 November 2018)

Figure 8: At 4th Yamashiro Tanuki Matsuri festival, *tanuki* legends were drawn as pictures by Shimooka and a group of four women group known as '*osone-chan.*' (*Osome-danuki*, おそめ狸, is one *tanuki* legend in Yamashiro.) (Source: Author, 24 November 2018)

product of parental love wishing to ensure children's safety (…) *Yōkai* are important treasures that we should pass on to future generations."

Yōkai legends in Yamashiro have served a necessary purpose in daily life and may be unremarkable if seen from the inside. However, when seen from the outside, the reasons why and the process of how human beings make use of *yōkai* legends is of relevance to their wisdom. This, then, reveals the insight of the people who live wisely as they give birth to these *yōkai* legends. This human activity merits examination because *yōkai* legends have provided them with assistance and solutions for living in a severe natural environment. *Yōkai* are an invisible presence, but one that is definitely present in the lives of residents. *Yōkai* not only enter their lives this way, they also give them vitality to survive. This function of *yōkai* has been reevaluated and highlighted again from outside of the *furusato*, then protected and reinforced inside it.

Yōkai legends disappear when those who tell them pass away. In this sense, the work of residents connected with *yōkai* are efforts to leave behind memories. Oral legends that were not written down in the past are recorded in books and visualized as *yōkai* dolls. From visible characters and dolls, future generations can learn memories of the past. *Yōkai* legends are also used in children's education. Children can learn how people in the past thought and explore the reasons why they needed to create these legends. Children's activities such as food and woodcraft enable them to develop their imaginations about the past.

Another example is the *Ōboke Yōkai Saishū* (大歩危妖怪採集, Ōboke Yōkai Collection), which relates to *yōkai* creation. Participants walk around Yamashiro Town and use their imaginations to create *yōkai*. This activity is based on participants' efforts to get to know the region and create products of the imagination. The event is held by Yamashiro Shinkō Co. Ltd., which operates Yōkai-yashiki.[17] Currently, it is held once

---

17   This information, as well as that in the following three sentences, is based on an interview with Nagamoto Kazuaki 永本和明, the Representative Director of Yamashiro Shinkō Co. Ltd., conducted by the author via e-mail

a year, most recently during the summer vacation. About half of the participants are from Miyoshi City or neighboring towns and villages, while the rest are from outside of Tokushima Prefecture. Most of them are families with children. I think this event (and others like it) shows that *yōkai* can serve as a communication tool that transcends generations.

These phenomena do not arise only within Yamashiro itself. Today, natives of town in the *Kinki Yamashiro Ōboke kai* and current residents exchange information on their shared *furusato*. In the past, the *Kinki Yamashiro Ōboke kai* organized "*furusato tanbō*" (ふるさと探訪, exploring *furusato*) in 1992 in order to enable its members to get know the *furusato* better. To 2008, they held twelve *furusato tanbō* as official events of the organization.[18] These events involved travelling to the Yamashiro by private-hire bus and visiting attractions and historic sites. As well as strengthening the friendships between member-participants, these events also resulted in deepening members' individual feelings towards and emotional ties with the *furusato*. Even today, they come together and meet (such as by participating in the Yōkai Festival and the Yamashiro Tanuki Festival).[19] There is ongoing communication between Yamashiro residents and Yamashiro natives resident elsewhere rooted in the term *furusato*. Here, not just the *yōkai*, but also general aspects of the *furusato* seem to play important roles, but it appears that

---

(1 February, 2020). According to Nagamoto, a "Yokai Saishū notebook" is sold at the reception desk of Yōkai-yashiki, both at the event and on a regular basis.

18 This sentence and the next are based on an interview to Kubohara conducted by the author via e-mail (24 June 2019).

19 The *Kinki Yamashiro Ōboke kai* cooperates with Yamashiro inhabitants to publish '*Furusato dayori*' (a thrice-yearly published Furusato newsletter named '*Yamashirokko*' (やましろっ子, a native or inhabitant of Yamashiro), edited by the Yamashirokko editorial committee). For example, *Yamashirokko* (no. 65, 2018) includes the selection of the Ōboke gorge as a must-visit tourism destination by an American travel magazine, the rapid increase of foreign tourists, an introduction of newly opened tourism accommodation in a traditional Japanese-style house, reports on local festivals, announcements from the Yamashiro library, an serialized essay by a member of *Kinki Yamashiro Ōboke kai*, a report from a new year's party in Osaka, and child birth information.

the *yōkai* elements have gradually grown in importance. In this way, both groups conduct exchange both inside and outside of Yamashiro, and *yōkai* legends seem to be one of their common points of interest.

Although Yamashiro also has beautiful landscapes and its own history, *yōkai* have become another important component of the town's image, a process boosted by the popularity of *yōkai* in mass media.

Conclusion

This paper first describes the characteristics of Yamashiro, and the reasons why *yōkai* folklore is needed there. Then, it relates the process of the rediscovery of the *furusato*'s appeal from outside of the town. On one hand, two folklorists made references to the *Konaki-jiji* and a local historian later confirmed the location of the *yōkai*'s birthplace. Before that, however, there was the visualization of the *Konaki-jiji* and the propagation of its image thorough manga.

These two separate events, the confirmation of *Konaki-jiji*'s origin and Shimooka's interviews, accelerated the revitalization of the area through local Yamashiro *yōkai*. Shimooka's efforts to re-recognize and reevaluate local Yamashiro *yōkai* stories revealed that *yōkai* in Yamashiro played an important role in maintaining community. Not only adults, but also children cooperate to pass down *yōkai* folklore to future generations.

Today, both inside and outside of Yamashiro, the *furusato* is considered to be an important place, worthy of protection. Through this case study of Yamashiro, this paper approaches the dynamism of folklore's inheritance. Yamashiro has been through its own process of community formation. *Yōkai* as an element of popular culture served as an impetus for Yamashiro's development as a *yōkai* town, but at the same time, residents value *yōkai* in a folkloristic sense. *Yōkai* culture has a connection with their own daily lives. Yamashiro exhibits a rare case of the development of a *yōkai* town in connection with a challenging natural environment and *yōkai* legends. That is to say, the town conveys its significance as it is.

Acknowledgment

This study was supported by a JSPS (Japan Society for the Promotion of Science) grant titled 'International Comparative Research on the Spreading and Reception of Culture through Contents Tourism' (Kiban A, grant number 26243007, grant period 2014-2019).

PART II
BEING AT HOME

MARCELLO GHILARDI[1]

THE PLACE AND THE WAY

Heidegger, Matsuo Bashō, and Art as Being-at-Home

> *"Philosophy is properly homesickness,*
> *an urge to feel at home everywhere"*.
>
> Novalis

> *"The places we have known do not belong solely to the*
> *world of space in which we situate them for our greater*
> *convenience.*
> *They were only a thin slice among contiguous*
> *impressions which formed our life at that time; the memory*
> *of a certain image is but regret for a certain moment; and*
> *houses, roads, avenues are as fleeting, alas, as the years"*.
>
> M. Proust, *In Search of Lost Time*, vol. 1, *Swann's Way*

1. No doubt, Novalis' statement about philosophy exhibits properly the Romantic mood and an overall idea about the exercise of thought as a form of (or as an answer to) what in those years was called by German thinkers *Sehnsucht*, a melancholic or dramatic grieving, an anxiety or tension toward infinity. But his incisive description tells us something more, and connects to the theme of *furusato* 故郷 in a wider sense, that is not limited to early 19th century European thought. In fact, it displays in a few words a dialectical relationship between the need to come back to our original place, the home we are longing for, and the awareness that this place is nowhere, that we cannot grasp it. The origin is at the same time nowhere and everywhere. We could mention the Japanese idiomatic expression *tada ima* ただ

いま: "just now" (but also "I'm back home"), in order to express
the idea of "being right there", in the right place we should be.
This feeling can be compared to a sort of peak experience, or to
the happening that springs up during a calm contemplation. In
zazen 坐禅, for instance, the sitting meditation fostered by the
Zen tradition, the concentration on breathing and the letting go
of every thought and attachment convey, a deep understanding:
saṃsāra (the ceaseless "pilgrimage" of the individual, full of
desire and sorrows) is at the same time *nirvāṇa* (the "extinction"
of sorrow, the true awakening to reality itself). "Home" is thus the
realization of this understanding; no one is really separated from
enlightenment, or Buddhahood (*Busshō* 仏性, or the "Buddha-
nature").[2]

Nonetheless, a ticklish question arises, if we only keep in
mind the risk of turning the philosophical mentions of terms
such as "home", "homeland", "country", "ground", or "place"
into a sort of despotic, totalitarian, and exclusive ontology. That
was the case for a significant part of modern thought, in the
East as well as in the West, when nationalism and imperialism
arose and affected philosophy.[3] How can we avoid the risk that
the notion and value of "home" becomes something that finally
absorbs and annihilates the singular event of existence? Or how
can we move away from exclusion (when we consider only our
homeland and its qualities as something good and desirable) to
inclusion (thinking, for instance, that the notion of homeland or
homecountry is an ideal one, and it can be shared by humans in
their different experiences)? As it is well known, philosophers
have not always hesitated at plunging headlong in bad mistakes

---

2   See C. Bielefeldt, 'Shōbōgenzō busshō正法眼藏佛性: Buddha Nature (Part
     1)', *Dharma Eye* (*Hōgen* 法眼) 25 (Spring, 2010), pp. 23-49.
3   See for instance R. Kipling, 'The White Man's Burden', *McClure's Magazine*
     12 (Feb. 1899), as a famous example of ethnocentrism and Western
     imperialism; or H. Ott, *Martin Heidegger: A Political Life* (New York: Basic,
     1993). About the entanglements with a strong nationalism in prewar Japan,
     see J.W. Heisig, J.C. Maraldo (ed. by), *Rude Awakenings: Zen, the Kyoto
     School, and the Question of Nationalism* (Nagoya: Nanzan Library of Asian
     Religion and Culture, 1995); B. Victoria, *Zen at War* (Lanham: Roman &
     Littlefield, 1997).

of perspective or patently nationalistic views. Last, but not least, we have to face the problem of avoiding an outcome in which the very notion of *furusato* turns itself into a bundle of ruins or mere historical and ideological remains.

If we only consider some terms springing out of two languages, English and Japanese, we have to acknowledge a constellation of different notions that sometimes overlap and sometimes distinguish themselves from each other in a definite way: home, country, culture, identity, us..., and *bunka* 文化, *machi* 町, *kuni* 国, *mura* 村... This constellation produces a complex net of emotions, desires, ambitions, fears, hopes, and often, in political discourse or in the public arena, feelings and ideological frames that are very influential and take their toll.

2. The question is, then, what can help us to live in a balanced relation with our "native village", whether it is a physical *furusato* or a spiritual homeland? Is there any human device or activity we can exploit to avoid the risk of fostering a new outbreak of nationalism or ethnocentrism? My reflections here concern some hints or glimpses we can get through a short reading of Martin Heidegger's ideas about the notion of *Feldweg*, on the one hand, and of Matsuo Bashō's experience of poetry, on the other hand. My intent is not fulfil a complete scrutiny of their work, of course, but rather I would like to show through some of their writings that art can be a form or an opportunity to feel at home, even when we are still wandering or still looking for our inner *furusato*.

I think indeed that a possible path can be shown through *artistic experience* – if we consider it as an endeavour and desire to recompose the original break, fracture, the separation from the primary wholeness, without forcing that wholeness in a precise, singular identity. Art can be indeed a sort of intensification of our senses and experience, in order to *give a form* to our yearning: put in Japanese, this becomes *dōkei* 憧憬, in which both characters show the Chinese radical for heart (心 → 忄), and the second character adds the phonetic element of "scenery, landscape" (*kei* 景), perhaps pointing to a hypothetical "place of the heart".

The Japanese term we usually translate as "art", *geidō* 芸
道, displays a *kanji* in which the radical alludes to a natural
growing of plants rooted in the earth (*gei* 芸), coupled with
the well-known character *michi* 道, "way, path, itinerary" (but
also "method" or "process"), that gives birth to an interesting
complexity. We could dare to interpret the artistic move as a
process or dynamic transformation that allows something to
grow while staying rooted in its soil, in its matrix or womb. If this
metaphorical interpretation of artistic practice is acceptable, we
could conclude that art may be connected to a remembrance of
the place from which we came, with a nostalgia for the absolute
that we cannot possess.[4] Through art, we can try to *build a place
to rest while moving forward*. Let us take as a possible example
this passage, written by a contemporary Japanese calligrapher,
Morita Shiryū 森田子龍 (1912-1998):

> Because there is no self by itself and no brush by itself, no relationship
> comes about between some prior "me" and some prior "brush". Rather, we
> must say that what exists is a whole we may call "me and my brush". The
> one, inseparable whole lives here and now, and that is the very substance
> of my being a calligrapher here and now. Let us call this single totality
> *place*. [...] In the sense that I and my brush are born in a place and that a
> place gives birth to us. [...] In the unity of the place, I and the brush are
> one.[5]

Here, we do not find any hint or mention of the notion of
furusato. But we can clearly see how the notion of "place"
(*basho* 場所) plays an important role in the mutual definition
of the calligrapher and the brush, the artist and the work of art.
The unity of subject and object – if we want to use a Western
terminology – is granted by that particular place that opens
between the "I" and the "brush" and gives space to the artistic
process. To be "at home", in this occasion, does not mean only
to find oneself in the right spot, at the right time, but also to be

---

4   See G. Steiner, *Nostalgia for the Absolute* (Toronto: House of Anansi Press,
     1997).

5   S. Morita, 'Sho to chūshō kaiga' [Calligraphy and Abstract Painting] 「書
     と抽象絵画」, in J. Heisig, T. Kasulis, J. Maraldo, *Japanese Philosophy. A
     Sourcebook* (Nagoya: Nanzan University Press, 2011), pp. 1200-1202.

centered, at ease, and above all to lo(o)se the attachment to the idea of a substantial and autonomous self.

The true, authentic place is the "way", the way of artistry, the way a single artist tries every day to follow in order to realize a work of art, and to realize him or herself, too. Vice versa, *the way of artistry can be regarded as the "place"*, the invisible environment in which human nature can nurture itself and find new meanings and new resources while avoiding the feeling of *Unheimlichkeit*, or weirdness, eeriness (but also, etymologically, "lack of feeling at home", disorientation).

We cannot find in Martin Heidegger's writings a high praise to the virtue of wandering; on the contrary we are presented with his fear for the rootless character of modernity. Moreover, his stubbornness on the themes of soil, roots, and the mythology rooted around his hut in Todtnauberg, near the Black Forest in Germany, brought him close to the Nazi ideology of *Blut und Boden* ("Blood and Soil").[6] Clearly what is central in Heidegger's thought is our finding ourselves already "there", situated in the world, in a "place". Nonetheless, in a later work titled *Feldweg-Gespräche* (*Country Path conversations*), we can find some hints that open a new direction – even if this direction may not have been premeditated by the philosopher himself. A sentence that Heidegger himself wrote in italics in the imaginary dialogue between "the Teacher" and "the Tower Warden" says: *"From everywhere we must continually turn back to where we truly already are"*.[7] Indeed, the Teacher replies to the Tower Warden (who thus spoke) that what he says "sounds even more obscure" than what he said before. But we can understand the statement as the belief that a turning back can be also a form of turning outward, looking not only at a lost origin, but scrutinizing what is coming out, moving close. Let us give a brief glance at the composition of the word in this peculiar title, *Feldweg*. Imagine

---

6   See J. Malpas, *Heidegger's Topology: Being, Place, World* (Cambridge: MIT Press, Bradford book, 2008); A. Sharr, *Heidegger's Hut* (Cambridge: MIT Press, 2017).

7   M. Heidegger, *Country Path conversations* (Bloomington: Indiana University Press, 2010), p. 115.

that we are walking on an ever-reliable country path. This path leads through a "field" (*Feld*) wherein we become aware of things as they truly are by walking on the "way" (*Weg*). So, even here we get close to the idea that the true field or (home) country in which we can find a rest – our place – is indeed a *path*, a way upon which we must walk. Being-at-home (an expression we could compare to that of being-in-the-world) means, thus, to keep moving, to be in search of something, or again to be wandering endlessly, when we can trust in a reliable direction.

3. Rendering this concept into a short and incisive phrase, I would try to translate it into a four-*kanji* Japanese expression: *basho soku dō* 場所即道, or "The place *qua* the way". By the term *soku*, a logic of "implication-and-opposition" takes shape. It is a logic we can detect at the core of the notion of *soku*: "separate", and "not separate"; "facing", and "not facing". When I say A=A, the equality of unity is already a duplication of the unity. The repetition of the identity generates a split in the identity itself, so the "one" (A) is "one" but also "two", it is involved in a movement. To express the identity with itself, *within* itself, (A) displays a repetition, it brings out a difference in the core of unity. The notion of *soku* shows, by means of language, that at the root of the self there is the other; the "self" is at once the "self" and the "other". *Soku* can be regarded as a sort of "contraction" of the Hegelian speculative proposition, in which the rigidities of the judgement melt down and link to the different terms of the relation. The terms reveal themselves as processes, converging into each other. More than a theoretic solution, the logical operator *soku* fosters a problematic reconfiguration.

In this perspective, we could affirm that *furusato*, in a wider dimension, *is* – or at least it could be regarded as – the way (*dō*), i.e. the ongoing dimension of human beings; and, as we saw before, art (*geidō*) can represent at the same time an example of the endeavour, the effort on the way to recompose the original fracture or separation from our originary "home" and the capacity to feel at home while we walk on the path. This apparent contradiction works in a similar way in Eihei Dōgen's

永平道元 (1200-1253) thought, when in his *Bendōwa* 「弁道話」 (*A Talk on the Endeavor of the Path*, 1231) he states the unity of practice and awakening (*shushō ichinyo* 修証一如). Awakening is not separate from the path we follow in order to attain it – in fact, it is not something to be "grasped" or grabbed nor something that is detached from the process to which we are committed. Final goal and itinerary to pursue it are one single unity; analogously, the supposed origin, or the initial place from which we stepped out, makes a unity with the path or the way we are called to walk upon, in order to rejoin it. What prevents a place or a homeland, a metaphorical *furusato*, from being totalitarian, i.e. something that excludes "otherness"? Arguably, it is the *possibility to withdraw*, i.e. its non-imposing character, or the space of freedom that is left. Only if one's own homeland, as a spiritual origin, does not impose itself, then it can open space for something new to happen or for someone new to come. In the Western religious traditions, God lets his Holy Spirit flow, only withdrawing Himself. And Paradise carries out its meaning as long as it is lost: in that way, mankind can begin its history. We find more examples in different traditions of thought. According to Plotinus, "Before we had our becoming here, we existed There, men other than now; we were pure souls. Intelligence inbound with the entire of reality, not fenced off, integral to that All" (*Enneads*, 4, 14). From the dimension of "being *qua* being" (ὂν ᾗ ὄν) we are invited to aim to the "One" (ἕν), knowing that its quality is unconceivable and unutterable; it is our real homeland, our deepest and highest true *furusato*. In Middle-Age Christian mysticism, particularly in Meister Eckhart's thought, the notion of *Grund* ("ground", foundation, ontological basis) is replaced by the elusive, metaphorical notion of *Abgrund*. The prefix *Ab-* suggests the movement of dismissal, removing, and withdrawal; this is the sole quality that makes it possible to think through it in order to point at the encompassing dimension of the divine. Furthermore, Buddhist thought underlines the necessity of overcoming the attachment to substance and to a solid subject (*svabhāva*: "own-being", "own-becoming") towards the relieving experience of *śunyatā*, the awareness that all things are empty of intrinsic existence and nature. Nishida Kitarō, in his turn, stresses a turning point in philosophy moving out of the "place of being" (*u no basho* 有の場所), heading towards the "place of absolute nothingness" (*zettai mu no basho* 絶対無の場所). The common denominator of those philosophical strategies, even in their distance and differences, is arguing that if a notion or an experience wants to resist and to stay as the real absolute, that very notion is still something particular or relative. True absoluteness is, literally, no-*thing*: "it" cannot be defined, confined, or limited. Thus, the origin or the pivotal place at the basis of every single thought, every "native village", can be alluded only as some "thing" that is unceasingly withdrawing, changing, moving – this is the central insight also in the *Daodejing* 道德經: *Dao ke dao, feichang dao* 道可道, 非常道 ("The Dao/Way that can be trodden is not the enduring/authentic Dao/Way"). So, a true "homeland" (*Heimat*, or *furusato*) should be understood and lived as a way (*Weg*, or *dō*). The Buddhist monk Daitō Kokushi 大燈国師 (1282-1338) expressed this insight using poetic imagery:

> Having once penetrated the cloud barrier, the living road opens out north, east, south, and west. In the evening resting, in the morning roaming, neither host nor guest. At every step the pure wind rises. *Having penetrated the cloud barrier, there is no old road, the azure heaven and the bright sun, these are my native place.* The wheel of free activity constantly changing is difficult to reach. Even the golden-hued monk [Kasyapa] bows respectfully and returns.[8]

The "native place" is the all-encompassing nature: the clouds, the azure heaven, and the bright sun. It is what we could express in one word as *shizen* 自然 – not only "nature" in the modern Western meaning, but more generally as "what arises from itself", true spontaneity.[9]

---

8   See H. Dumoulin, *Zen Buddhim: A History. Japan* (New York: MacMillan, 1990), p. 186 (italics are mine).

9   On this topic, see E. Fongaro, M. Ghilardi, 'L'idea di natura tra Cina e Giappone', *Oltrecorrente* 11 (2005), pp. 143-152. In this perspective, *shizen* (also read *jinen* when its Buddhist meaning is stressed) can be compared to Dōgen's *Busshō.*

Therefore, we stumbled upon a dialectical relationship between two ostensible contradictory statements or insights. On one side, the need to come back to the original place is advocated widely by many different thinkers; on the other side, this supposed original, native place is empty, it dwells nowhere. In other words, there either is no origin or the origin is everywhere. It could seem a difficult *impasse*, and it might be that the two perspectives cannot be sublated or integrated. But we can also look at those different visions as the different, yet necessary, perspectives at work in human lives and feelings.[10] The longing for something we consider lost is the spark that helps to light the fire, the trace that helps to begin the path, Once we venture onto that trail, we recognize that the goal of our route is mere walking in its free spontaneity.

4. With his art, the Japanese poet Matsuo Bashō 松尾芭蕉 (1644-1694) built up a spiritual dimension that stood for a physical place during his endless wandering. In the opening paragraphs of his famous *Oku no hosomichi*『奥の細道』(*The Narrow Road to the Deep North*), Bashō confronts himself with nature ("the sight of a solitary cloud drifting with the wind to ceaseless thoughts..."), witnessing his everlasting compulsion to travel all over the country ("I seemed to be possessed by the spirits of wanderlust"), while at the same time his longing for one of his cherished places ("I could think of nothing but the moon at Matsushima"):

　　月日は百代の過客にして、行かふ年も又旅人也。舟の上に生涯をうかべ馬の口とらえて老をむかふる物は、日々旅にして、旅を栖とす。古人も多く旅に死せるあり。予もいづれの年よりか、片雲の風にさそはれて、漂泊の思ひやまず、海浜にさすらへ、去年の秋江上の破屋に蜘の古巣をはらひて、やゝ年も暮、春立る霞の空に、白河の関こえんと、そゞろ神の物につきて心をくるはせ、道祖神のまねきにあひて取もの手につかず、もゝ引の破をつゞ

---

10   The relationship between the two is not so far from the idea of the twofold aspect of truth taught in Buddhist tradition. About this "doctrine", see J.L. Garfield, G. Priest, 'Nāgārjuna and the Limits of Thought', *Philosophy East and West* 53 (2003-1), pp. 1-21.

り、笠の緒付かえて、三里に灸すゆるより、松島の月先心にかゝ
りて、住る方は人に譲り、杉風が別墅に移るに、

草の戸も
住替る代ぞ
ひなの家

面八句を庵の柱に懸置。

The months and days are the travellers of eternity. The years that come
and go are also voyagers. Those who float away their lives on ships or
who grow old leading horses are forever journeying, and their homes are
wherever their travels take them. Many of the men of old died on the road,
and I too for years past have been stirred by the sight of a solitary cloud
drifting with the wind to ceaseless thoughts of roaming.

Last year I spent wandering along the seacoast. In autumn I returned to
my cottage on the river and swept away the cobwebs. Gradually the year
drew to its close. When spring came and there was mist in the air, I thought
of crossing the Barrier of Shirakawa into Oku. I seemed to be possessed by
the spirits of wanderlust, and they all but deprived me of my senses. The
guardian spirits of the road beckoned, and I could not settle down to work.

I patched my torn trousers and changed the cord on my bamboo hat.
To strengthen my legs for the journey I had moxa burned on my shins. By
then I could think of nothing but the moon at Matsushima. When I sold my
cottage and moved to Sampū's villa, to stay until I started on my journey,
I hung this poem on a post in my hut:

kusa no to mo	Even a thatched hut
sumikawaru yo zo	May change with a new owner
hina no ie	Into a doll's house.

This became the first of an eight-verse sequence[11].

In the end, Bashō's melancholic meditation is expressed in a
haiku. The poem shows the possibility to turn a "thatched hut"
(*kusa no to*), made of straw and grass, into a small jewel, a decent
little "doll's house" (*hina no ie*). While a contemporary Zen
master, Sawaki Kōdō 沢木興道 (1880-1965), became famous
with the nickname *yadonashi* 宿無し ("homeless"), proving to
be at ease without taking any physical domicile, Bashō wandered

11   Matsuo Bashō, *The Narrow Road to Oku*, (Tokyo: Kodansha International,
      1996), p. 19.

for all his lifetime constantly being struck by the need to get back to his *furusato*. So we read in another *haiku*, his work *Oi no kobumi* 『笈の小文』 (*Knapsack Notebook*):[12]

旧里や	*Furusato ya*	My native home –
臍の緒に泣く	*heso no o ni naku*	weeping over my umbilical cord
年の暮	*toshi no kure*	at year's end

If a master like Sawaki wanted to stress the fact that there is no strong opposition between "home" and "homelessness", it seems that Bashō's poetic experience arose from the tension, or the de-coincidence, between the awareness of the human condition's wandering character and the yearning for a place to rest. In fact, he seems to implicitly understand that what is usually familiar can become all at once unfamiliar, estranged. Every simplistic imagination of what is "home" dissolves and gives space to the consideration that even what is supposedly familiar can reveal itself as something uncanny. "Identity" and "origin" are a bundle of contradictions, a field of tensions. Nonetheless, we are not confined to this perturbing sensation. We have rather to face and make the most with a paradox: we have never left Nature, or our ancestral home, and yet we feel alienated from it; we never lost the Buddha-nature (according to Dōgen's text *Busshō*, we *are* Buddha nature: we cannot possess it, so we can neither lose it), but we must learn how to be in it. We need to learn how to come back to where we belong, where we have always been.

The odd "circularity" of the awakening process is eminently testified by the cycle of images and poems handed down with the title of *Jūgyūzu* [*Ten Ox Herding Pictures*] 『十牛図』. The best-known version of the story is that by Kuòān Shīyuǎn (Jap.: Kakuan Shien 廓庵師遠, 12th century). This reproduction shows the path to enlightenment using the metaphor of the travel a young breeder has to undertake in order to bring back home a

---

12   D.L. Barnhill (ed. by), *Bashō's Journey.The Literary Prose of Matsuo Bashō* (New York: State University of New York Press, 2005), p. 33. Note that Bashō uses here different *kanji* to write *furusato*: 旧里 instead of 故郷 (旧 indicates "old times", or "old friends", and 里 means "village", or "parent's home").

fugitive ox. In Kuòān's series the end is not absolute emptiness (eighth picture) like it was in previous series, but a return back to the world (tenth picture), passing through an integration with nature (ninth picture).

It is likely that we should look at and read the three final stances as a threefold perspective of one single insight or dimension, because there is no more chronological progress or change, but all is one and one is all – emptiness, communion with nature, and the capacity to live in the world.[13] Getting the ox back home represents only the middle stage in the whole process. In fact, the herdsman (or Zen disciple) has to go beyond the basic feeling of ownership: awakening is not something one can possess, just as the authentic "native village" of one's soul is not to be searched in a physical realm outside one's self. *Furusato* reveals itself to be at the same time absolute nothingness (*mu* 無), nature as spontaneity (*shizen*), and the ordinary life in which everyone

---

13   See Ueda Shizuteru, 'Emptiness and Fullness; Sunyata in Mahayana Buddhism', *The Eastern Buddhist* XV-1 (Spring 1982), pp. 10-22.

lives and struggles, with his or her own limits and possibilities. Ueda Shizuteru 上田閑照 (1926-2019) wrote on this topic:

> on the basis of this incarnational reality that confirms selflessness and sustains it, there appears the selfless self which, by its very selflessness, takes the hyphenated "between" of the I-Thou, as its own existential inner realm of activity. The third picture shows us an old man and a youth meeting on a road, but it is not the chance encounter of two different people that is being depicted there. "An old man and a youth" means the selfless self-unfolding of the old man. For the self in its selflessness, whatever happens to the other happens to itself. This communion of common life is the second resurrected body of the selfless self. The self, cut open and disclosed through absolute nothingness, unfolds itself as the "between." I am "I and Thou," and "I and Thou" are I.[14]

Finally, we can maintain that the authentic place in which human beings dwell and meet each other is just the invisible place that stays in-between, the "between" of the I-Thou. Mankind, or human beings, are expressed in Japanese as *ningen* 人間. Literally, what lies between a human being and another human being. Not a substance, not a definite place, but the empty gap that allows the necessary distance to open up a dialogue. In that "in-betweenness" resides humans' *furusato*: more than a physical spot, it is a live openness, related to plurality, inclusion, and compassion among human beings.

---

14 Ueda Shizuteru, "'Nothingness' in Meister Eckhart and Zen Buddhism', in D. Papenfuss, J. Söring (ed. by), *Transzendenz und Immanenz: Philosophie und Theologie in der veränderten Welt* (Stuttgart: Kohlhammer, 1977), p. 163.

GERARD VAN DER REE[1]

BUILDING A HOME IN THE WORLD

Belonging in the Wilderness

Introduction

Belonging is a question for me. Throughout most of my life, I have experienced a sense of un-belonging, a sense of not-being-at-home in the world. That experience took the form of both an absence and a presence. The belonging that was lacking was often highly present *as* a lack and gained much of its shape, form, and colour through its absence. It was because of this that the Japanese word *furusato* (lost hometown) immediately resonated with me during our conference in Venice. Its associations of home being something lost, as something to long for, directly spoke to my own experiences.

In this chapter, I want to work out the question of *furusato* as a doing. Or, put otherwise, I want to understand the word "home" as a verb, as "home-making". This home-making can be understood as a quest for belonging, of finding or making a belonging in this world. Home-making is a response to a human experience of un-belonging. Such a sense of unbelonging, or homelessness, is not merely an emotional phenomenon. As will be shown, it comes out of an existential relation to our own being. To exist, existentially speaking, is to face up to the fact that there is only one "me" and that my being-in-the-world ultimately is mine to give shape. I have to find a way of relating myself towards the world somehow. My home is going to be my home-making.

Even though home-making starts off from an individual, existential perspective, it immediately translates into a way

---

1   University College Utrecht

of connecting myself to others. The way I relate myself to my own homelessness is going to shape the way in which I relate to the people around me. If I avoid ownership of my existential homelessness, I will be owned by the group that I inhabit. If, in turn, I embrace such ownership, I can relate to others from a position of freedom and openness.

The dynamics of home-making, then, shape how we deal with others, and, more precisely, with otherness. Who my "other" is depends on how I relate myself to my homelessness. If I seek to build my home through the group of people that I live with, my "others" will become the people outside of that group. As a consequence, they will become visible to me as a threat to my home. However, if I base my home-making on my own being-in-the-world, then *all people* are my "others". This means that I will have nowhere to unproblematically "blend in", or belong. Yet at the same time, none of them pose a threat to my homeliness, since that is not in their hands. I can relate to them outside of the logic of in-group and out-group. In this way, my relations with others will depend on how I relate to my *furusato*.

How I Go About

I want to work out the notion of belonging in a way that does justice to the tensions that the word *furusato* itself brings forth. If *furusato* suggests that home is a lost home, and that belonging lies within un-belonging, I want to speak to it in a vocabulary that itself is unable to belong to it, yet in a certain way still does. A vocabulary that is not even able to properly belong to itself. I want to work out *furusato* as a doing by connecting different registers of voice, which can never completely come together, which always leave open an incompleteness, an un-belonging; and yet, in doing so, reveal something meaningful about what belonging is or can be.

The registers of voice I will work with are Heidegger's late philosophy, the postcolonial political science scholarship of Naeem Inayatullah and David Blaney, and the work on belonging by social psychologist Brené Brown. At the first glance, these three sources seem to have in common that they are Western, and, as such, already do not belong to the Japanese origins of *furusato*. But even between themselves, they also come with deep contradictions: Heidegger was deeply suspicious of the social sciences in general and psychology in particular, let alone American popular self-help literature. Postcolonialism questions the hegemony of Western philosophy as well as Americanised "common sense" as forms of political impositions. And Brené Brown purposefully eschews both philosophic and academic registers of voice (even though her work is based on social scientific research) in order to speak to the everyday lives of everyday people. Moreover, the three of them come with completely different epistemologies: Heidegger speaks to the level of ontology, of being itself; postcolonialism interrogates the political world in terms of a knowledge/power nexus; and Brené Brown recovers everyday practical wisdom in everyday terms. There is very little they have in common.

Bringing these voices together expands the notion of interdisciplinarity beyond the scope of academic disciplines. This is no longer a conversation between scientific schools of thought, this is an encounter between genres. In order to sustain them together, then, I want to be both careful and playful, both scholarly and adventurous. I am not looking for unity or a harmonious whole. But neither do I want to tell three separate stories that do not connect with one another. I will try to bring them together in movements, in action, in such a way that they respond to one another, as dancers in modern dance. My choreography does not seek to bring closure or unity between the participants in the dance, but rather, in being attentive towards their plurality, it explores the way their movements shape a space between them.[2] I hope to reveal meaning in the gaps that these sources will leave open.

In a way, then, the form of this chapter will resemble its content. If *furusato* locates belonging in un-belonging, and home in the home that we have lost, then my aim will be to explore this

---

2   Thieu Besselink, 'Learning Choreography', in: John Moravec (ed. by), *Knowmad Society* (Minneapolis: Education Futures LLC, 2013), pp. 89-128.

puzzle by carving out an unstable, unattainable, yet meaningful belonging between these voices that do not belong together. They are not at home together, so if there is something of a home possible between them, it needs to be a doing, a practice, a politics. In other words, if "home" is a "making", then this is an attempt at home-making.

There is something idiosyncratic in the way these three sources were selected. During my intellectual journey as a scholar, they became visible to me as very different, yet similar ways of dealing with the question of belonging. All three of them speak to my own questions about, and struggles with, belonging and seeking a home in the world. All three articulate something that I experience in my own life. Yet simultaneously, placing them in interaction with one another speaks to the world we commonly share. They connect the world of our being (Heidegger), our social life (Brown), and the realm of politics (Inayatullah and Blaney). In bringing these three together, something about belonging, unbelonging, and the possibility of building a home in the world will hopefully emerge. If this is a dance, then, it is an intimate one; yet at the same time, it exposes a shared, public experience. That sounds right to me. The question of *furusato* is one that speaks to humanity as a whole, yet simultaneously at each of us individually.

Movement One: Home is Home-making

Heidegger works out the relation between "being at home" and "making a home" in his 1951 essay *Building, Dwelling, Thinking*. He does so by contrasting the notions of dwelling and building. Dwelling ("*wohnen*" in the German original) denotes being-at-home, while building ("*bauen*") emphasises the aspect of home-making. In our conventional thinking, we would assume that building precedes dwelling: we build a house in order to dwell in it. To be at home, then, would mean to have finished the building; and to dwell, then, implies that we have a home to dwell in.

However, Heidegger argues, the relation between building and dwelling is not that straightforward. Building a house does not imply being at home there. Our modern houses, he argues, may be "well planned, easy to keep, attractively cheap, open to air, light, and sun, but—do the houses in themselves hold any guarantee that dwelling occurs in them?".[3] After all, the physical structure in itself is not what determines the being-at-home. Our house, even if it is the place that shelters us, is not necessarily our home. A truck driver may well be at home on the highway, but does not have his shelter there. The chief engineer is at home at the station, even though he does not dwell there. Apparently, building and dwelling are not sequential.

Heidegger explores this puzzle by examining the ways language roots our understandings of the two words. Etymologically, he notes, building (*bauen*) comes from the same root as dwelling (*wohnen*): "*buan*". This word, lost in German, signifies not just to build, but also to stay, to remain in one place. Building, then, originally meant dwelling as well. And this, he emphasises, extends further than our relation to our environment. The German for "I am" and "you are" also come from the verb *buan*: "*ich bin*" and "*du bist*". Our being itself, then, was originally captured with the word that came to denote building. Originally, dwelling, being, and building mean, somehow, the same thing.

In order to explain this, Heidegger works out the meaning of building in a twofold way. On one hand, building means raising up edifices; that is, to construct something. On the other, building means to preserve or to cultivate. In German, a farmer is a "*bauer*", a builder, because farming means to cherish, protect, and nurture the land on which he lives. Building, then, is not just constructing; it is also preserving and cultivating the world around us. Building is our way of "being on the earth".[4] Building is dwelling.

Simultaneously, the origin of the word dwelling (*wohnen*) does not merely signify inhabiting a place. Its root word in

---

3   Martin Heidegger, 'Building, Dwelling, Thinking', in Albert Hoftstadter (ed. by), *Poetry, Language, Thought* (New York: Harper and Row, 1971), pp. 143-159, p. 155.

4   Martin Heidegger, 'Building, Dwelling, Thinking', cit., p. 145.

Gothic (*wunian*) denotes "being at peace" or "remaining at peace". Peace here should not be understood as the absence of war, though. Peace ("*Friede*") means to be preserved ("*fry*", or free) from harm or danger. The meaning of dwelling, then, is letting things be, not through disinterest, but by sparing them, preserving them, setting them free in their own being.

Bringing together these lost meanings of the words dwelling and building, two things become clear. First, building and dwelling are the same thing. To build a home is to be at home. Second, the fundamental character of dwelling, of being-at-home, is to preserve, to spare, to set things free. To be at home, then, is a practice of preservation, of cultivation, of setting things free in their own being. Being-at-home is home-making: actively relating ourselves to the world around us such that we can let it be.

Movement Two: Social Life and "Belonging to Oneself"

In her 2017 book *Braving the Wilderness*, social psychologist Brené Brown explores the theme of belonging from a different angle. Basing herself on interviews, surveys, conversations and personal experiences, she addresses a paradox that is becoming increasingly pronounced in the 21st century: we group together with like-minded people more and more, yet we are lonelier than ever. This puzzle strikes at the heart of how we conventionally understand belonging. If belonging is about fitting in, about being part of a likeminded group, then why do we not experience this in our highly segregated and sorted "bubbles" of people of the same ethnicity, class, political conviction, and lifestyle? Why are we increasingly experiencing a sense of loneliness?

Brown starts off by making a distinction between loneliness and being alone. She argues that loneliness is not an expression of solitude, but of a lack of meaningful social interaction.[5] For most of us, then, to be lonely does not come from being alone,

---

5   Brené Brown, *Braving the Wilderness: The Quest for True Belonging and the*

but from the quality of being together. In our modern way of flocking together, the quality of togetherness takes the form of a double dynamic. On the one hand, we come together on the basis of fear of the "other" and the outside world. Fear, Brown argues, lies at the root of modern loneliness.[6] This means that our togetherness is not based on a meaningful engagement with one another, but as a response to a sense of external danger. We cuddle together out of fear, but all of us still have our shields up. That is not a good recipe for meaningful social engagement. On the other hand, grouping together on the basis of similarity actually undermines our ability to have meaningful social engagement. If being-similar is what makes us feel safe, we will not dare to reveal to the people around us how we are different. We will not dare to show ourselves for who we are. We will not dare to be vulnerable. Instead, we will try to "fit in". As a result, we will end up disconnecting ourselves from the group that we belong to and end up safe but lonely.

On the basis of this analysis, Brown explores how we might identify a form of belonging that goes beyond similarity and fear. Her approach includes methods from the social sciences, particularly interviews and surveys; but she is not interested in merely gathering facts or identifying causal chains. Her purpose is to bring out practical wisdom. She does not claim to have that wisdom herself, nor does she locate it in the knowledge of experts. Instead, Brown does something very similar to what Heidegger does. She assumes that wisdom is located right under our noses, hidden in plain sight. For Heidegger, such wisdom hides in our everyday language and the lost meanings that it still holds. For Brown, in contrast, wisdom is located in the stated experiences of everyday people. It merely requires asking the right questions, listening empathetically to what is being said, and interpreting the answers skilfully and generously. Wisdom, for Brown, is not to be found somewhere far away. It is present in the everyday experiences of everyday people.

Courage to Stand Alone (London: Vermillion Press, 2017), p. 52.

6   Brené Brown, *Braving the Wilderness*, cit., p. 55.

Her research reveals that people who experience a deep sense of belonging, or what she calls "true belonging", typically follow four principles of relating themselves to other people. They are:
- People are hard to hate close up. Move in.
- Speak truth to bullshit. Be civil.
- Hold hands. With strangers.
- Strong Back. Soft Front. Wild heart.[7]

I will not work out these principles here, but the general thrust is relatively self-evident. They highlight the ability to stand up to one's own peers and to get close to those who are not part of one's own group. They emphasise the capacity to hold your own values ("strong back") while being open and close to those who are different ("soft front").

This reveals a paradox of belonging. People who stand up to their own group and embrace outsiders, report a deeper sense of belonging than people who seek the safety of their peers. They experience what Brown calls "true belonging", even if it means that they stand alone. Her definition of "true belonging" is as follows:

> True belonging is the spiritual practice of believing in and belonging to yourself so deeply that you can share your most authentic self with the world and find sacredness in both being part of something and standing alone in the wilderness. True belonging does not require you to change who you are; it requires you to be who you are.[8]

There are several things to note in this definition. Firstly, that Brown's vocabulary goes straight against the conventions of the philosophical tradition. To speak of "true belonging", "authentic self", and "sacredness" without even attempting to define what could be meant by "true", "authentic", and "sacred" would raise the eyebrows of even the most eclectic academic philosophers. Such vocabulary would immediately call for clarification of terms before being admissible as a part of any philosophical text. However, this chapter is not a philosophical text. The purpose of

7   Brené Brown, *Braving the Wilderness*, cit., p. 36.
8   Brené Brown, *Braving the Wilderness*, cit., p. 40.

this chapter is to bring together, however tenuously, the work of a philosopher, a social psychologist, and two political scientists. In order to do so, I will have to resist the urge to place all of them under the analytical standards of only one of them. Brown's vocabulary will have to be understood in its own terms, rather than be dissected through the toolkit of the philosopher. She builds her vocabulary on the basis of how her interviewees report on their experiences. Words like "true belonging", "authentic", "sacred", and "wilderness" can thus be understood as ways of metaphorically capturing experience, rather than providing analytically precise definition.

Secondly, Brown locates "true belonging" in terms of independence from the social sphere. Belonging, she points out, primarily concerns belonging to yourself. It relates to authenticity and the ability "to be who you are". The image that she invokes is one of standing alone, in relation to yourself. This does not, however, suggest a hermit-like lifestyle. True belonging is the ability to "share your most authentic self with the world" and "find sacredness in *both* being part of something and standing alone in the wilderness". True belonging is therefore not located either *inside* or *outside* of social life, but in *independence* of it. To truly belong is the ability to belong to oneself, regardless of whether you are surrounded by others or not.

Finally, Brown's understanding of true belonging seems to read it as a relational process, rather than as a state. It is an act ("belonging to yourself so deeply that you can share your most authentic self with the world") that comes out of a relation to yourself ("it requires you to be who you are"). That relation to yourself, the being "who you are", is clearly not understood as a given. Being who you are is something that is positioned as a desirable state, a point on the horizon to aim for. All we can achieve is our "most authentic self", not a "fully" authentic self. Locating true belonging in the relation we have to ourselves thus highlights two aspects. On the one hand, it is an open-ended process, never finished, and a practice, rather than a state. On the other, it comes out of relating myself to myself in a certain way. This indicates a distance, a dialectic, between "me" and "myself". It implies that I take a stand on myself. In a way, then, true belonging comes out of the way I am in friction with myself: exactly because my "I" is separate from "myself" can true belonging be a possibility for me. Even in trying to be "who I am", I can never completely belong to myself.

Movement Three: Belonging in the Fourfold

Heidegger works this out in a different yet similar approach, highlighting the way in which our world and our being are inseparable. For Heidegger, belonging takes place in what he calls "the fourfold": the earth, the sky, the divinities, and mortals. That fourfold is not separate from who we are; in fact, it is located within our own being-in-the-world. Who I am, phenomenologically speaking, cannot be separated from the world that I inhabit, which I grow out of, and which is what is meaningful to me.

For Heidegger, then, who I am and what my world is are not separable from one another. It is within this context that the phrase "belonging to oneself" can be translated into his register. If I belong to myself, I belong to my world. The grounding of my belonging lies in my being-in-the-world. It is in my dwelling on the earth.

But, Heidegger argues, "on the earth" already means "under the sky". Both of these *also* mean "before the divinities" and include a "belonging to man's being with one another".[9] This is what Heidegger calls the "fourfold". It is within the fourfold of earth and sky, divinities and mortals, that my dwelling takes place and that I am making my home. If my belonging is primarily belonging to myself and I am my world, then my belonging lies within my dwelling in the fourfold.

Our dwelling *on the earth*, Heidegger says, takes the form of saving the earth. This saving, he emphasises, does not come through "snatching it away from danger" (as, for instance, the

---

9   Martin Heidegger, 'Building, Dwelling, Thinking', cit., p. 147.

sustainability movement suggests when speaking of "saving the planet"). Instead, he uses "saving" in its old meaning, similar to what being "at peace" or "free" means: to preserve, to set free in its own being. Being on the earth, then, is to be close to what grows, gives fruit, dies, and is born. Dwelling on the earth "does not master the earth and does not subjugate it".[10] But it also does not withdraw from it. Setting something free in its own being is what a gardener does to the flowers in the garden: it comes with careful tending to growth, flourishing, bearing fruit, and dying. Dwelling as belonging on the earth is attending to life.

Being *under the sky*, in turn, is to "receive the sky as the sky". It suggests a way of dwelling that lets the things that come over us, come over us. It is "to leave to the sun and the moon their journey, to the stars their course, to the seasons their blessing and their inclemency".[11] Here, too, the point of "letting be" is not to retreat, withdraw, or disconnect from the things that happen to us which are outside of our control. On the contrary, letting them come over us, allowing ourselves to be over-come by them, comes through presence and attendance. It is the opposite of panicking, running away, or trying to gain control. Dwelling as being under the sky is about receiving fate.

To be *before the divinities* is to "await the divinities as divinities".[12] This should certainly not be interpreted in religious terms. For Heidegger, the divine has nothing to do with a belief in supernatural or otherworldly entities. Instead, as Susanne Claxton puts it, for Heidegger the "divine is present in the ordinary".[13] And within that presence, we experience the divine as being subject to something that is absent, something that can never be fully made manifest. To experience joy, or music, or terror, or love, for instance, is to be subject to something that transcends our cognition, our language, our world.[14] In such experiences, we are

---

10   Martin Heidegger, 'Building, Dwelling, Thinking', cit., p. 148.
11   Martin Heidegger, 'Building, Dwelling, Thinking', cit., p. 148.
12   Martin Heidegger, 'Building, Dwelling, Thinking', cit., p. 148.
13   Susanne Claxton, *Heidegger's Gods: An Ecofeminist Perspective* (London: Rowman and Littlefield, 2017), p. 62.
14   Susanne Claxton, *Heidegger's Gods*, cit., p. 26.

present to something that is simultaneously absent, something that touches us but is at the same time withdrawn.

Awaiting the divinities, then, is the opposite of making gods or worshipping idols.[15] Those would be standing in for the absence, fill the void, and therefore end our waiting. To await the divinities as divinities is to allow for incompleteness, for longing, and for unfulfillment. It is most present in poetry, Heidegger argues, as poetry is our ability to open up language, and to point towards something that is unspeakable, a presence that is absent. "The poet", Heidegger says, "names the holy".[16] Dwelling as awaiting the divinities, then, is *poetic dwelling*: it is to inhabit a world that is silently enchanted, a world that transcends our words, a world in which "mystery is nothing special".[17]

Finally, dwelling as *man's being among each other* points towards the way we belong to our fellow humans. For Heidegger, this is not matter of living together in everyday doings. Our belonging to one another does not come from daily life, but, on the contrary, from the way human beings are mortals. "They are called mortals", Heidegger states, "because they can die. To die means to be capable of death *as* death".[18] What death means here is not death as the end of our physical lives. Instead, death should be understood as the way in which being human confronts us with the end of our own possibility of being. And it is only in looking that end of possibility into the eye that what *is* possible becomes manifest in our lives. Being-towards-death, by neither fleeing from it or resisting it, is what makes life possible.[19] Existentially speaking, death is what gives us life, because it brings forth to us what is meaningful in our lives. As Claxton puts it: "Life is Death".[20]

It is in this light that we should understand our dwelling among our fellow mortals. In dwelling together as mortals, we activate

15   Martin Heidegger, 'Building, Dwelling, Thinking', cit., p. 148.
16   Quoted in Suzanne Claxton, *Heidegger's Gods*, cit., p. 51.
17   David Cooper, *Senses of Mystery* (Abingdon: Routledge, 2018), p. 2.
18   Martin Heidegger, 'Building, Dwelling, Thinking', cit., p. 148.
19   Martin Heidegger, *Being and Time*, cit., pp. 304-311.
20   Suzanne Claxton, *Heidegger's Gods*, cit., p. 29.

being-towards-death in one another. We help one another to be more alive by "initiating" others "into the nature of death".[21] We help each other face death, not as a way of "blindly staring towards the end",[22] but as a way of unconcealing what life is. We are with them in what is, at the end of the day, real to them.

The fourfold is where our dwelling takes place; and dwelling is not just "being around", but should be understood as "building a home". Building a home, then, is done on the earth, under the sky, awaiting the divinities, and among the mortals. Or in other words: home-making is to attend to life, to let ourselves be overcome, to inhabit a silently enchanted world, and to initiate our fellow mortals into the nature of death. Building a home is to inhabit and preserve ("set free") these realms of being.

Moreover, and not unlike Brown's notion of "belonging to oneself", the fourfold is not something that is separate from our being. Our being unfolds through the fourfold. It is, in a way, our being. Belonging in the fourfold, then, is to belong to our own being.

What is absent in this picture is one thing in particular: most of our social life. Home-building connects us with other people on the basis of being mortal. But most of our human relations and communications are not like that at all. They are about collaborating in projects, leisurely chatting, comparing ourselves to others, taking part in political debates, having fun, or talking about the news or entertainment. For Heidegger, none of that contributes to our belonging. To take part in the communication about the things our social sphere cares about (the news, politics, our institutional environment) is to engage in "idle talk" ("*Gerede*" in German). For Heidegger, it is not bad or wrong to engage in idle talk – it is a necessary component of human existence. It is what produces our socialisation, the everyday averageness that human social life is built upon. All of that is fine. But it does not speak to our existential being because

---

21   Martin Heidegger, 'Building, Dwelling, Thinking', cit., p. 149.
22   Martin Heidegger, 'Building, Dwelling, Thinking', cit., p. 148.

that does not come from our socialisation, but from our own experiences with our world, our *Dasein*.

It would seem, then, that both Heidegger and Brown, each in their own repertoire, carve out a similar-yet-different picture of human connectedness. We are thrown, as humans, into our communities, into our everyday social interactions, our shared language, our habits, and our chattering. And all of that is well, but it does not provide us a ground for belonging. In fact, our social boundedness is a problem for our belonging. However, that does not mean that our belonging *excludes* other people. For both Brown and Heidegger, belonging comes with specific connection to our fellow humans. Heidegger locates that in the way that being-onto-death reveals being together with other people as being in line with the fourfold of earth, sky, divinities, and humans. Brown, in turn, suggests that in order to find belonging, we first need to take a stand on our own being. We need to belong to ourselves first, and from there we can start building our belonging with others.

All of this implies that belonging (as home-making) comes with a redefinition of human and social relationships. It means that we have to re-encounter the people around us. This is the politics of encounter.

Movement Four: The Politics of Belonging

If we cannot ground our belonging in the social relations in which we have grown up, but need to build our "belonging to ourselves" (Brown) in the fourfold (Heidegger), what does that mean for our social relations? How can we build our home such that it makes us belong with other people?

In order to start answering this question, I want to draw from a third source: Naeem Inayatullah and David Blaney's *International Relations and the Problem of Difference*.[23] Speaking from a post-colonial and post-structuralist perspective,

---

23   Naeem Inatayullah and David Blaney, *International Relations and the*

this work interprets the way in which international politics has been historically shaped around the question of difference. For Inayatullah and Blaney, both 19th century empire as well as the current post-colonial order stem from a particular historical response to cultural plurality. Modern sovereignty, they argue, is the outcome of the Western inability to deal with difference *as* difference. Rather than allowing ourselves to be confronted by others who are both similar and different, modern sovereignty carves out human communities in clear groupings of "us" and "them". This "splitting" is the cornerstone of the modern sovereign state system. It divides the world up in terms of "insides" and "outsides", associating the "inside" with similarity and the "outside" with difference. The result is that we associate otherness with threat, while similarity becomes the ground of a shared, homogenised identity.[24]

Even though the authors work this process out with a focus on International Relations, it is not difficult to see its relevance for the politics of belonging. If our home-making requires something of a re-encounter with our fellow humans, it will lead us to a confrontation with difference. We may be tempted to respond to such a confrontation through "splitting": to seek out homeliness with our own in-group. However, this can never get us towards belonging. As Brown suggests, belonging comes primarily through "belonging to oneself", the way we relate ourselves to ourselves. And for Heidegger, too, our social world is anathema to our belonging. Only in the fourfold, away from the "idle talk" of our social life, can we properly belong. If we want to encounter our fellow humans *from* belonging, we need to find an alternative response to encounter.

Splitting occurs because of the fragility of our understanding of our own being. Encounter, Inayatullah and Blaney argue, is a place of existential anxiety. It takes place in a "contact zone", where self and other meet. In this contact zone, we are confronted with difference but also with similarity. The other is

Problem of Difference (New York: Routledge, 2004).

24 Naeem Inatayullah and David Blaney, *International Relations and the Problem of Difference*, cit., pp. 18-28.

simultaneously different and similar, both alien and akin. This destabilises our understanding of ourselves. What does the "self" mean if it cannot be meaningfully delineated from the "other"? How can I be like my own "other"? Such questions interrogate the narratives that we have about ourselves. They call into question the things we take for granted, the stories of our belonging in the world, our cosmology. The contact zone, then, is a space where our understanding about ourselves destabilises and opens up to ambiguity.[25] It therefore produces anxiety.

Who we are, then, is fragile; and splitting is a protection mechanism. It guards us against the anxiety, uncertainty, and destabilisation that emerges in a contact zone. Through splitting, we can hold the other at a distance; typically we do so by mapping them out in terms of inferiority. Once that inferiority has been established and the other has been safely assigned to a "them", the anxiety of the contact zone is quenched. From there on, it becomes possible to proceed to a second movement: that of assimilation. Where in the first move, the difference between self and other is used to designate the other as inferior, in the second move, the similarities between self and other are used to assimilate them. This usually takes the form of a "developmental" strategy: the other becomes the site of our intervention and tutelage, through which we transform them to the likes of ourselves. This "double movement", Inayatullah and Blaney argue, lies at the heart of the Western modern political imaginary. It informs the way in which we organise politics (state sovereignty), trade (competition), and development (Westernisation).[26]

Splitting and the double movement are attempts at belonging. They create mutually exclusive spaces of "us" and "them", so that all of us have a place where we fit in. In this way, belonging is grounded in group membership. You either belong in the one or the other, to "us" or "them". And, through the double movement, the "other" is typically mapped out in terms of inferiority. This

---

25   Naeem Inatayullah and David Blaney, *International Relations and the Problem of Difference*, cit., pp. 10-11.
26   Naeem Inatayullah and David Blaney, *International Relations and the Problem of Difference*, cit., pp. 9-10.

keeps all of us safe from the anxiety of the contact zone, and envelops us in a narrative of superiority. The anxiety of the contact zone is kept at bay; we can feel at home.

This approach towards difference affects us profoundly in two ways. First, grounding our belonging in the split between self and other comes with a homogenisation of the self. If we locate "difference" in the outside, the inside becomes equated with "sameness". To be part of "us", then, comes at the cost of the denial of fundamental differences among ourselves. Such differences can only be tolerated insofar as they are optional add-ons, life-style-choices, or fashionable embellishments; otherwise, they will have to be policed, repressed, or marginalised.[27] To be different – to be unique, an original human being – becomes a threat to, rather than a ground for, belonging. Here, Brown's analysis of belonging comes back into view: if we seek belonging by joining the flock, we will disavow belonging to ourselves.

Second, the splitting of self and other associates difference firmly with danger. Since "their" difference cannot overlap with "our" sameness, "they" become visible in opposition to our identity, norms, and values. The safety of the inside is contrasted with the danger of the outside. Home becomes a safe place in an alien world, a herd of sheep surrounded by predators. Belonging takes the form of seeking refuge; the world becomes a threat to belonging. Attempting to belong in this way keeps fear intact, and, as Brown suggested earlier, that fear shapes our relation to ourselves and our world. Belonging to a group is the opposite of belonging to ourselves (Brown) or to the fourfold (Heidegger).

Splitting is not the only way for dealing with the problem of difference. Inayatullah and Blaney point towards an alternative that takes the form of an "ethnological moment" as a way out of splitting. In such an ethnological moment, the anxiety of the contact zone is sustained, rather than avoided. By allowing the self to be questioned by the presence of the other, however uncomfortable that may be, the other can become a source of

---

27   Naeem Inatayullah and David Blaney, *International Relations and the Problem of Difference*, cit., pp. 39.

learning for the self. And in such a dialogical process of shared learning, *both* difference and similarity will be revealed. The other, no longer radically split from the self, becomes visible within the self and vice versa. This "other within" becomes the source for self-reflection and transformative growth.[28]

In this "ethnological moment", we start seeing the outlines of an alternative politics of belonging. Rather than grounding belonging in the "self" so that the encounter with difference becomes associated with danger, the *encounter itself can become a source of belonging*. Within encounter, we are stripped from some of the "sameness" of our group and we are revealed as "misfits": unique beings who are not reducible to group properties. Encounter reveals us as singular – there is only one "me" – and therefore points to my belonging in terms of my relation to my world rather than my peer group. Even though this may come with existential anxiety, it simultaneously brings us back to our belonging in the fourfold. In order to work that out, though, we will have to return to Heidegger's philosophy one final time.

Movement Five: Belonging in Encounter

One of the staples of Heidegger's philosophy is the concept of *Ereignis*. Even though it communicates a range of meanings, all of these circle around the idea of being coming into itself. *Ereignis* is the way in which being comes into being, or as Richard Polt puts it: in *Ereignis* "the being of beings becomes our own, and at the same time, we are allowed to come into our own by entering *Dasein*".[29] It gets translated in English in multiple ways: as *event*, *bringing into view*, *appropriation*, and

---

28   Naeem Inatayullah and David Blaney, *International Relations and the Problem of Difference*, cit., pp. 13-14.

29   Richard Polt, 'The Event of Enthinking the Event', in Charles Scott, Susan Schoenbohm, Daniela Vallega-Neu, and Alejandro Vallega (ed. by), *Companion to Heidegger's Contributions to Philosophy* (Bloomington, Indiana University Press, 2001), pp. 81-104, p. 82.

en-owning. Each of these translations highlight different aspects of *Ereignis*.

Firstly, as an *event*, *Ereignis* stands for the way in which being unfolds itself. It is the structure of our being-in-the-world setting the stage for the intelligibility of an experienced world. This is not an ahistoric or unchanging state of affairs but takes place through what could be characterised as paradigmatic shifts of knowledge. *Ereignis* as an *event* is the way different eras come with different ways of being-in-the-world, each with their own language, which form the foundation for *Dasein*'s historical thinking.[30]

Secondly, coming from the German word *Eige* (*Auge*, eye), *Ereignis* "*brings into view*" the world of *Dasein*. It sets the perimeters of what is there to be seen and simultaneously determines how it is that we see things. While *Ereignis* as *event* sets the stage for the intelligibility of the world, *Ereignis* as *bringing into view* determines what we can encounter in that world. This includes the ideas that we have about our world, as our thinking is part of our encounters in the world. "The word 'idea'", Heidegger writes, "comes from the Greek εἶδος which means to see, face, meet, be face-to-face".[31] It is in this way that *Ereignis* brings our world into view.

Thirdly, *Ereignis* as *appropriation* highlights the relation between our being and what it sees in the world. It appropriates because any encounter takes place within the intelligibility that is offered to *Dasein* to begin with. We always somehow appropriate whatever it is that comes into our view by placing it within the terms of the intelligibility of the *event*. This does not mean, however, that encounter is a subjective and somehow twisted form of perception. Despite the way we appropriate what we encounter, we are also able to come near to the being of the thing that we are encountering. If we do so, "appropriation" can lead to a "proper" connection to things at the level of being. As Heidegger puts it: "Lived experiences are events of appropriation,

---

30 Daniela Vallega-Neu, *Heidegger's Contributions to Philosophy: An Introduction* (Bloomington, Indiana University Press, 2003) p. 35.

31 Martin Heidegger, *What is Called Thinking* (New York: Harper Collins, 1976), p. 41.

insofar as they live from out of what is proper [*eigen*] and live life only in this way".[32]

Finally, *Ereignis* is translated as *en-owning* because it brings us into ourselves, into our "own". As we saw in the discussion about the "contact zone", an encounter confronts us with our being, opening up the possibility for taking a stand on ourselves. It therefore invites us back to ourselves. As Polt puts it: "Only in *Ereignis* can we truly become our own selves; this does not mean returning to some fixed nature but accepting our role as the beings to whom our own being, and being in general, makes a difference. This can happen only if we enter into "owndom," that is, the there as the realm in which being is an urgent issue for a community".[33] Understood in this way, *Ereignis* is about belonging to oneself as a way of opening up the possibility of being with others.

It is through these four translations, each highlighting different aspects of the same thing, that we can start seeing the connection between encounter and belonging. *Ereignis* can be seen as the way in which being opens up a world for us and makes encounter available to us. Simultaneously, it can be the way in which encounter leads us back to our own being, and ultimately to being itself. Being makes encounter possible, and encounter brings us into being. And that being is always in the fourfold of earth, sky, divinities, and fellow mortals. Encounter is our entry point into the fourfold.

What does such an encounter look like? Heidegger uses the example of an encounter with a tree:

> we stand before a tree in bloom, for example – and the tree stands before us. The tree faces us. The tree and we meet one another, as the tree stands there and we stand face to face with it. As we are in relation of one to the other and before the other, the tree and we *are*.[34]

Encounter, then, can be understood an act of facing. Such

---

32   Quoted in Graham Harman, *Tool-being: Heidegger and the Metaphysics of Objects* (Chicago: Open Court, 2002), p. 82.

33   Richard Polt, 'Ereignis', in Hubert Dreyfus and Mark Wrathall (ed. by), *A Companion to Heidegger* (Malden: Blackwell, 2005), pp. 375-391, p. 383.

34   Martin Heidegger, *What is Called Thinking*, cit., p. 41.

facing may not be easy – encounter implies that we somehow stand "counter" to what we are facing – but in doing so, it reveals our being to ourselves and the other. Encounter, in this way, is like nakedness: it is letting ourselves be revealed through the way we reveal the other. And in this nakedness, we find our belonging; not in our social environment or our peer group, but in relation to our being.

In order to get face-to-face with things, we need to do one thing: we need to let be. Using the example of the tree again, Heidegger puts it in the following way:

> When we think through what this is, that a tree in bloom presents itself to us so that we can come and stand face-to-face with it, the thing that matters first and foremost, and finally, is not to drop the tree in bloom, but for once let it stand where it stands.[35]

To let the tree "stand where it stands" is the essence of encounter. It means: setting it free in itself. This is, as we have seen above, also the meaning of the word "dwelling". Dwelling among things ("*wohnen*") comes through setting them free in themselves. And such "letting be" is not a matter of indifference or abandonment. Quite the opposite: it comes through being face-to-face with them, by being present to them, by really "being with" them. This is where encounter and belonging become the same thing.

It is, however, not a coincidence that Heidegger uses a non-human entity, a tree, as an example of encounter. He does not articulate the encounter into human relations and it would be problematic to attempt to translate this into an ethical account of social life. He does, however, provide a groundwork for understanding encounter as "being with" in such a way that two parties come into their own being. Heidegger's *Ereignis*, then, can be seen as a way of providing a foundation for understanding encounter as an act of belonging, without translating that to our social world.

---

35   Martin Heidegger, *What is Called Thinking*, cit., p. 44.

Movement Six: Braving the Wilderness

In this chapter, I have brought together philosophy (Heidegger), social science (Inayatullah and Blaney), and condensed lived experiences (Brown). They do not add up neatly, nor do they direct us to one conclusion. They come from such disparate approaches towards the world that they almost seem to speak different languages. Yet at the same time, they seem to "rhyme" with one another: there is a meaningful resonance between them. This is why I referred to this chapter as a dance; there may not be a shared logic between them that is clearly articulable, but that does not mean that there is no coherence or meaning between them at all.

This chapter started out with understanding belonging, in a Heideggerian way, as a verb, as a form of home-building. From there, it turned to Brown's notion of "true belonging" as a form of belonging to yourself, as opposed to your social environment. Coming back to Heidegger, it then developed belonging as something that takes place in the "fourfold": on the earth, under the sky, before the divinities, and among man's being with one another. The chapter then turned to Inayatullah and Blaney in order to develop the notion of a "contact zone" as a space for encounter, providing us with different logics for belonging. On the one hand, the contact zone can lead to "splitting" between a collective self and other, on the other hand it can provide an "ethnological moment" where self and other mutually learn. And finally, it worked out an ontological link between encounter and belonging through Heidegger's notion of *Ereignis*.

In order to bring all of this to some form of incomplete completion, a final sequence that does not provide clear answers but still lands the previous movements in a meaningful way, one more idea needs to be developed: that of the wilderness.

Brown posits "braving the wilderness" as the grounds for true belonging. For her, the wilderness is where we go when we challenge, question, or disobey core values of our social peer group. It comes out of breaking the (often unwritten) rules of our tribe and typically produces violent responses of confrontation, marginalization, and exclusion. It is a place where we find ourselves alone, outside of the safety of collective protection and group cohesion. The wilderness offers "solitude, vulnerability, and an emotional, spiritual, or physical quest".[36] After having left the home of our social circles, the only home that we can find is the home that we build ourselves.

The wilderness is not merely an environment or a space that we inhabit, though; it is a way of being. Brown puts it like this: "The special courage it takes to experience true belonging is not just about braving the wilderness, it's about *becoming* the wilderness".[37] In resisting the urge to fit into our social circles, our relation to ourselves changes. In learning to belong to ourselves, we find a deeper way of connecting to ourselves and others. It is transformative. "Once we've found the courage to stand alone", Brown states, "to say what we believe and do what we feel is right despite the criticism and fear, we may leave the wilderness, but the wild has marked our hearts". And she continues: "once we've stood up for ourself and our beliefs, the bar is higher. A wild heart fights fitting in and grieves betrayal".[38]

Inayatullah and Blaney also develop a notion of wilderness. For them, wilderness contains a double meaning. On the one hand, it is handed down in Western intellectual and religious traditions with references to barbary and savage practices. It is way of delineating the "civilised" self from a "barbaric" other, both in geographic and moral terms. The wilderness then is "at once a judgment about the internal diversity of humankind, into higher and lower parts, and about the spatial borders of civilization and the monstrosities, dangers, and temptations that lie on the other side".[39] On the other hand, the wilderness comes with associations of freedom and authenticity. It echoes, in the Christian tradition, the garden of Eden as an emblem of living

---

36 Brown, *Braving the Wilderness*, cit., p. 36.
37 Brown, *Braving the Wilderness*, cit., p. 36-37.
38 Brown, *Braving the Wilderness*, cit., p. 148-149.
39 Inayatullah and Blaney, *International Relations and the Problem of Difference*, cit., p. 45.

outside of the restrictions and moral impositions of social life.[40] The wilderness, then, stands as much as a locale of danger as it presents us with the possibility of reconnecting to our "pre-social" self.

For Inayatullah and Blaney, the wilderness is the stage for encounter. Only in the wild can the "contact zone" lead to an "ethnological moment" because such a moment necessarily puts into question fundamental assumptions about ourselves. Within the confines of our established social order, such questions are typically repressed and penalised through the splitting of the self and other.[41] But in the wilderness, such collective disciplinary structures are weaker, giving way for the possibility of mutual learning. Encounter requires wilderness. If we seek to enter into a meaningful dialogue or mutual learning, we can not do so from the comfort of our established social order. We need to enter into the wild.

Heidegger's "fourfold" develops other associations with wilderness. To live "on the earth" (among what grows and dies), "under the sky" (letting events come over us), and "before the divinities" (facing incompleteness and poetic dwelling) is to inhabit being in a way that remains largely unstructured by social life. Belonging, or dwelling, thus takes place outside of the social order. This does not mean, though, that it is solitary. The fourfold also includes "man's being with one another", a way of being among one another that is based on "initiating" each other "into the nature of death".[42] In the context of the wildness of the earth, the sky, and the divinities, human connectedness takes the form of co-initiation into what life is really about.

Between these three different registers, then, wilderness becomes loosely visible as a dangerous and solitary space defined by the absence of the safety of the social sphere. Yet at the same time, it offers the possibility of dwelling, belonging,

---

40 Inayatullah and Blaney, *International Relations and the Problem of Difference*, cit., p. 46-47.

41 Inayatullah and Blaney, *International Relations and the Problem of Difference*, cit., p. 48-49.

42 Martin Heidegger, 'Building, Dwelling, Thinking', cit., p. 149.

and the freedom to belong to oneself. Belonging, as a verb, apparently requires some form of social un-belonging. And from that, a prospect of encounter emerges. Such encounter holds the potentiality of learning about oneself as well as the other. In this way, belonging could become a form of co-belonging.

I cannot draw any solid conclusions from this chapter. That was never the intention. As a piece of interdisciplinary and inter-genre exploration, the above dance is wild and takes place outside of the social standards of all the genres it includes, be they philosophy, political science, or social psychology. Seen from any of these disciplinary perspectives, this text will not make a lot of sense. Yet, by bringing Heidegger, Brown, and Inayatullah and Blaney together in that wilderness, something of a loose and playful encounter took place. Between the different movements of this dance, something became visible that otherwise would have remained difficult to see. A learning that does not seek to subsume difference under one unifying logic, but still adds to all the perspectives it includes. It will remain ephemeral and incomplete. Just like *furusato* itself.

LUKAS DANIEL PETER[1]

TRANSIENCE AND THE PROMISE OF HOME

Reconceptualising Homelessness Through Heidegger and Nietzsche

In the current age of so called "planetary urbanization"[2] homelessness has come to the fore in much of our everyday experience not only in the form of a growing population of homeless people, but as the very experience of transient modern urban life: being everywhere and nowhere. Against this background, the notion of "the home" emerges as peculiarly opposed to, and threatened by, everyday functionality. True belonging appears to be attainable only outside the confines of hectic urban life. Whether in the form of the family home, tourist destinations, or the traditional countryside, the home is positioned increasingly as a refuge *from* the very built environment of modern transience. This "promise of home" launches itself across varied channels, from advertisement and consumerism to political campaigns, capable of penetrating seemingly any domain of "modern life". Against the transience of the "built environment" of urbanisation (airports, supermarkets etc.), the home as a space of belonging, always outside-and-beyond, animates various "economies" of modern life: an incessant concern with "the home" has conquered not only urban planning and development, commerce and advertisement, but the imaginary of being-human, being-couple/family, being-nation. Thus, at multiple levels at once, the understanding of the home-under-threat sets in motion a proliferation of projects to protect, secure, and recover "the home" in the widest sense.

---

1   University of Bristol
2   N. Brenner, 'Theses on urbanization', *Public culture* 25-1 (2013), pp. 85-114. N. Brenner and C. Schmid, 'Planetary urbanization', in *The Globalizing Cities Reader* (London-New York: Routledge, 2017), pp. 479-482.

Subverting this understanding of the threatened/lost home in need of protection/recovery, I thread a vagrant line through the writings of Martin Heidegger and Friedrich Nietzsche, offering a notion of belonging that is paradoxically based on homelessness itself. Through a richly ambiguous web of etymological connections emerges an understanding of the home which allows for a critique of hostile conditions of urban living without needing to resort to an idealised outside home as a utopian place. Drawing on the original German texts of both Heidegger and Nietzsche, I hope to capture some of the etymological ambiguities often lost in translation. This playful, translational close-reading reveals the "promise of home" in a curious existential light that holds the potential to precipitate a breakdown of the oppositional pairings modernity/home and transience/belonging. This variant conceptual grounding of belonging and home(lessness) has the capacity to incite provocations for the political, social, and economic challenge of making home in an age of transience.

1. *Being-modern and "the home"*

Modernity is a tricky concept. Is it an epoch? A style? A way of life? A certain political economy? In an attempt to steer clear of the academic Bermuda triangle of defining modernity, the point of departure for this inquiry is a peculiar concern with "the home" which, in a somewhat vague sense, could be considered an expression of being-modern. Within a variety of themes and domains, it appears that a notion of the home as threatened by and potentially lost in modern life has come to constitute a key dynamism of the economies of our day-to-day lives: the home is in danger and thus in need of protection or, where already (partially) lost, recovery. Some of the themes, which have marked the popular imaginary and academic thought alike over the past century, will indicate this notion of the "home under threat" in some of its ubiquitous formations.

The threat of nuclear warfare or fallout loom over much of the second half of the 20th century, invoking a threat to the home on a national and even planetary scale. Far beyond their acute instances, first Hiroshima and Nagasaki and later Chernobyl introduced into both our public and academic consciences a very palpable possibility of the "end of the world". Besides countless other popular and academic accounts, German-Jewish Philosopher Günther Anders strikes the chord of this time with titles like "Mensch ohne Welt" (1984)[3] [Man without world] and "Hiroshima ist überall" (1982)[4] [Hiroshima is everywhere]. Furthermore, with Nazi Germany and Capitalist America as its background, Theodor Adorno's "Minima Moralia – reflections on a damaged life" (in German 1951)[5] provides a tragically ironic twist to the preoccupation of ethics with "the good life". This moral devastation revealed by World War Two was mirrored by the physical destruction of cities all across Europe. The theme of "Wohnungsnot" (housing plight) was not exclusive to Germany in the aftermath of industrial warfare. Nuclear catastrophe, fascism, commercial capitalism, and post-war destruction epitomised an emerging notion of the home under threat. These grand threats of the 20th century, far from having disappeared (Fukushima providing a recent echo), are now accompanied by even more intricate threats of pollution/climate change, migration and urban alienation.

From the chilling recognition that a single event, whether political or nuclear, could devastate much of the physical and/or moral foundation of human life on the planet, has dawned a sense that life itself has fallen ill at the root. Far beyond the possibility that the home, whether in the form of housing, the nation, or even the planet, could be destroyed, there emerges a sense of the home as corrupted, infested, stained internally beyond the possibility of a simple cure. In one word, the understanding of threat shifts from "extermination" to "extinction". The home is not only susceptible to murder but is in danger of "dying-out".

---

3   G. Anders, *Mensch ohne Welt: Schriften zur Kunst und Literatur* (München: CH Beck, 1993).
4   G. Anders, *Hiroshima ist überall* (München: CH Beck, 1995).
5   T.W. Adorno, *Minima moralia: Reflections on a damaged life* (London and New York: Verso, 2005).

Alongside the grand threats of extermination and extinction, alienation in the built environments of urban production and living bear a far more mundane sense of the loss of home. Following the work of French anthropologist Marc Augé, this sense of alienation is crystallised in the built environment by so called "non-places", hypermodern transit zones like airports, highways, and supermarkets.[6] As opposed to places which are marked by their history, the relations they engender, and the identity they evoke, non-places launch themselves through a peculiar transience: in non-places, there is "no room [...] for history unless it has been transformed into an element of spectacle."[7] The 24-hour news cycle displayed on screens becomes the emblematic non-history to a sense of time dominated by "the urgency of the present moment [...] measured in time units."[8] The non-relations of "solitary contractuality", encapsulated in the check-out counter, passport control, etc., oust the "organically social."[9] Finally, the temporary non-identity of the ID card affords a relative anonymity which "can even be felt as a liberation, by people who, for a time, have only to keep in line, go where they are told, check their appearances."[10] Against this (hyper)modern world of transience and the alienation of everyday urban life arises a notion of "the home" as a special, dedicated place. Threatened by the proliferation of non-places, the home becomes the anti-modern *per se*. As this "specific position", the productions of home have entered the rows of "curiosities presented as such: pineapples from the Ivory Coast; Venice – city of the Doges; the Tangier Kasbah":[11] the traditional countryside house; an advertisement of the Serengeti savannah, your uniquely individual coffee prepared just for you, etc. A vast range of "experiences", products, places, personalities, and organisations are now surrounded by an air of

---

6   M. Augé, *Non-Places: An Introduction to Supermodernity* (London and New York: Verso, 2008).
7   M. Augé, *Non-Places: An Introduction to Supermodernity*, cit., p. 103.
8   M. Augé, *Non-Places: An Introduction to Supermodernity*, cit., p. 104.
9   M. Augé, *Non-Places: An Introduction to Supermodernity*, cit., p. 94.
10   M. Augé, *Non-Places: An Introduction to Supermodernity*, cit., p. 101.
11   M. Augé, *Non-Places: An Introduction to Supermodernity*, cit., p. 110.

"belonging" which promises to compensate, protect, or recover the threatened home.

In this context, commercial enterprise is ruthlessly seizing on the notions of "the home" and "belonging". While the explicit invocation of "the home" might be less surprising on advertisements from Swedish furniture giant IKEA, key players in seemingly unrelated industries have recently launched campaigns that (re)figure much of commercial enterprise in explicit reference to the notions of "the home" and "belonging". From Google's "be more at home" (2017),[12] making the home a matter of technological enhancement, to Starbucks' "wherever I go, you bring me home" (2018),[13] retail and technology epitomize the key role the notion of "home" has come to occupy in subtle ways even in seemingly unrelated sectors like banking and finance. At its most ostensible, this "economy of belonging" has culminated in the rise of Airbnb as a key player far beyond the sectors of hospitality and tourism in just a decade since its founding. The business' declared mission of "returning us to a place where everyone can feel they belong" (2014)[14] expressly pits the home against the conditions of industrialised urban society. With explicit reference to the "lost home" of former village life, this notion of belonging, incorporated in Airbnb, has become a major force in regional development, personal finance, and real estate development in the context of austerity after the 2008/9 North Atlantic financial crisis. Two points in this case will indicate the very real impact of this particular notion of "belonging" and "the home": on the one hand, the economic hardship of unemployment post-financial-crisis in communities and individuals in rural southern Europe specifically has been economically cushioned by Airbnb through an integration into the tourism market of formerly "untapped assets" of privately owned homes. On the other hand, with austerity and precarity expanding across many sectors, the increase of rent and housing

---

12   https://youtu.be/EdMFmPEnhlU (last accessed 30.06.19)
13   https://mobile.twitter.com/starbucks/status/9725833289955035648 (last accessed 30.06.19)
14   https://blog.atairbnb.com/belong-anywhere/ (last accessed 23.06.2019)

prices in urban hubs has been compensated by a sort of "market subsidy", whereby the very life of the "host" authenticates the belonging to be enjoyed in their home for Airbnb guests. Subletting through Airbnb now considerably factors into not only the feasibility of renting and buying at ever higher prices, but the very understanding of real estate, urban development, and ultimately the "authentic home". It would thus be a grave mistake to treat the notions of "home" and "belonging" as mere rhetorical or theoretical concerns. In short, Airbnb's "belong anywhere" installs itself as the perfect answer to "being everywhere and nowhere", to the transience of modern urban life. This is the promise of home in one of its ubiquitous formations.

2. Heidegger and the uncanniness of being in the world

2.1 Dasein and Space

Contrary to the picture of transient modernity just painted, wherein a constant being-everywhere-and-nowhere ("homelessness") produces belonging as something to be reached in certain dedicated places ("home") outside industrial urban life, the German Philosopher Martin Heidegger provides a conceptual vocabulary which allows belonging and homelessness to emerge as deeply entwined.

The notion of "Dasein", this foundational hinge of Heidegger's early work (*Being and Time*) that has come to be popularly equated with the philosophical legacy of the "German Existentialist", is based on the understanding that what being-human is (*essentia*) can only be understood from/in its *being/existence* (*existentia*).[15] With *Dasein* the *Was-sein* (being-what) is first of all and always based on its *Zu-sein* (to-be). "The 'essence' ['*Wesen*'] of this being lies in its to be."[16] This existence, the "to be", is however, not just a mere existence in the sense of being-

---

15   M. Heidegger, *Sein und Zeit* (Frankfurt am Main: Vittorio Klostermann, 2006 [19. Aufl.]), p. 42.

16   M. Heidegger, *Being and time* (Albany: Suny Press, 2010), pp. 42-41.

at-hand ("*Vorhandenheit*"). Heidegger's "existentialism" holds "*Existenz als Seinsbestimmung*",[17] that is, not any quality or trait, but existence itself as that which assigns humans their unique being. Humans are those concerned with their existence, their own being-there (*Dasein*), and thus with *being* (*Sein*) in general. On the one hand then, Heidegger's notion of *Dasein* reveals being-human as being "*bestimmt*" (determined/appointed) in its being/character by its very existence. On the other hand – and these two implications are strictly coextensive and can only be separated in analysis – *Da-sein*, literally "there-being", implies a primordial notion of space as existential rather than geometric and external. This resistance to an understanding of space as external should however not be prematurely read as a notion of space as subjective, internal experience. "[S]pace [...] is neither an external object, nor an internal experience.".[18] There is not first a human, and then the space she enters. Heidegger rejects this notion of space by making the "there" ("*da*") inseparably part of "being" ("*sein*"). This subversion is not properly captured in translating *Dasein* as the hyphenated "being-there", which still suggests too much of a distinction between the operations of subjectivity and space. *Dasein*, opposed to the materialist understanding of a subject entering an external space, has no existence prior to, outside of, or apart from its "world". Yet, this world is not the experience of an idealist subject totally internal to itself either. Heidegger's "*in-Sein*" (being-in) breaks the materialist/idealist binary of "being in" as either the subject-in-the-world (external-materialist) or the-world-in-the-subject (internal-idealist).

Thus, in Heidegger's vocabulary, being-human and space are not two separate things, where the former "takes place" inside the latter. Through the notion of Dasein, what common sense separates as subject and space, container and content, are existentially never separable and always arise mutually. *Dasein* as

---

17   M. Heidegger, *Sein und Zeit*, cit., p. 42.
18   M. Heidegger, *Basic writings: from Being and time (1927) to The task of thinking (1964)* (San Francisco: Harper, 1977), p. 358.

"being-in-the-world"[19] always comes with its world. Belonging can, in this vocabulary, never just be the reaching of a dedicated "home". Humans are not first subjects and subsequently "there" in space. On this basis, the attempt to fix homelessness and a crisis of belonging by putting the same subjects in different places reveals itself as out of tune with the existential condition of being-human. Instead, it appears that the question of belonging and homelessness cannot be adequately posed in terms of a division of subjects and places. Around the conceptual hinge of *Dasein*, Heidegger thus provides a grammar that rubs up against common understandings of belonging and home as to be found in special dedicated places external to our being-subject. Dasein provides the possibility of asking the question of belonging differently from the common terms of "where is home?". Being-human as *Dasein* (being-there) allows for the notion of "the home" to open up beyond any specific place "out there", while neither falling into an experience "in here".

2.2 *Dwelling/Building*

Heidegger's own notion of being-in, as opposed to the geometrical, challenges our common understanding of building as the precondition for dwelling/living, and thus opens up to a sense of belonging that is not indebted to a spatial notion of the home.

> "Das In-Sein meint so wenig ein räumliches »Ineinander« Vorhandener, als »in« ursprünglich gar nicht eine räumliche Beziehung der genannten Art bedeutet; »in« stammt von innan-, wohnen, habitare, sich aufhalten."[20]
> "Nor does this term being-in designate a spatial 'in one another' of two things objectively present, any more than the word 'in' primordially means a spatial relation of this kind. 'In' stems from innan-, to live, habitare, to dwell."[21]

Being-in is not primarily a question of spatial/geometrical relations, but a matter of the quality of being-there (*Dasein*). This

---

19   M. Heidegger, *Being and time*, cit., p. 53.
20   M. Heidegger, *Sein und Zeit*, cit., p. 54.
21   M. Heidegger, *Being and time*, cit., p. 54.

quality indicates itself through the etymological root of "in", "*innan*", as "*wohnen*" ("dwelling"). On this basis, Heidegger delivers an understanding of "*Wohnen*" (dwelling) and "*Bauen*" (building), paradoxically inverted from the point of view of common sense:

> "Wir wohnen nicht, weil wir gebaut haben, sondern wir bauen und haben gebaut, insofern wir wohnen, d h. als die *Wohnenden* sind."[22]
> "We do not dwell because we have built, but we build and have built because we dwell, that is, because we are *dwellers.*"[23]

To fully appreciate Heidegger's reversal, it is crucial to understand the German word translated as "dwelling", "*wohnen*", in its common, mundane sense: to live, to reside (for instance: "Ich *wohne* in Berlin." "I live in Berlin."). The English "dwelling" is thus already imbued with too much meaning beyond this basic, everyday sense of "living". In its common usage, "*wohnen*" is always in need of a reference: "Ich wohne *in Berlin*"; "Er wohnt *in der Sandstraße*.". Contained in this referential need (the "in …") is the implication of "*wohnen*" as conditioned by a "*bauen*" (building): only where a village/city, a street, a house has been built can "*wohnen*" (living/dwelling) take place. Heidegger violates this common sense of "*wohnen*" by letting it stand alone, without adding an "*in …*". In order to capture this provocation better in translation, dwelling could be replaced by "residing": "… we build and have built because we *reside*, that is, because we are *residents*". Similarly to the German "*wohnen*" and "*Wohnender*", in English one always "resides" *somewhere* and is "resident" of *someplace* (country, town, building etc.). This common sense of "*wohnen*" and "residing" as always referred to a place is the foundation to an understanding of "the home" as an external place, and of "belonging" as the result of being in that place. This configuration animates a whole range of concerns/ project for preserving existing homes, and building new ones, as

---

22 M. Heidegger, *Vorträge und Aufsätze* (Frankfurt am Main: Vittorio Klostermann, 2000), p. 143.

23 F. Nietzsche, *On the Genealogy of Morals and Ecce Homo* (New York: Vintage, 1989), p. 350.

the reasonable approach to homelessness, thus conceived as the lack of accommodation.

When Heidegger says that it is only *insofar ("insofern")* as "we are dwellers/residents" that we build and have built, he upturns this entire operation of common sense. Building is not the condition for residing. *Wohnen* (dwelling/residing) in Heidegger's sense is not merely a specialised "being in" as "*wohnen in*", but as "*wohnen*" the very foundation of all (geometrical) "being in". Yet again, the English translation too easily allows for a reading of this passage as a simple reversal: the two uses of "*because*" in the first and second subclause suggest that the common sense notion of building-conditioning-dwelling is now simply reversed: dwelling as the *cause* for building. The more subtle translation would have "… we build and have built *insofar as* we dwell/reside, that is, *as* dwellers/residents". This nuance is far more than linguistic, pertaining to the core of the emergence of Heidegger's notion of "the home". Heidegger traces the etymology of the German words "*bauen*" (building) and "*wohnen*" (dwelling), revealing they both imply "das Bleiben, das Sich-Aufhalten" ("to remain, to stay in a place"),[24] a connotation which remains silently in the background of the common sense of *bauen*/building as the condition for *wohnen*/dwelling. The impulse Heidegger takes from etymology is that building (*bauen*) and dwelling/residing (*wohnen*) are neither sequential nor even separate activities. Building is not merely the human activity of constructing houses, and dwelling/residing is not merely occupying the buildings, or towns, or nations called "home(-)".

In this context, "the home" and "belonging" emerge no longer as obtained by building. If building and dwelling do not form a sequential dependency where the former authorises the latter, the obsession with the home and belonging as something "out there" to be obtained and secured through planning and construction begins to dissipate. *Bauen-wohnen* (building-dwelling) mutually

---

24   M. Heidegger, *Vorträge und Aufsätze*, cit., p. 143 (M. Heidegger, *Basic writings*, cit., p. 350).

arise from our being-residents, not just from occupying space but as our way of inhabiting as being-in-the-world. This challenges the unquestionable notion of the human subject as an *occupation* of space. *Dasein* is an *inhabiting*. Statements such as this tend to produce the sensation of a cliff-hanger. We expect something more which we do not get: "inhabiting what?". This sensation of suspense should, however, not be mistaken for an omission. It results from the condition that ...

> "... das Wohnen wird vollends nie als der *Grundzug* des Menschseins gedacht."[25]
> "... dwelling is never thought of as the *basic character* of human being."[26]

Heidegger poses the challenge of thinking *wohnen*/dwelling not as merely one activity amongst others, but as the "*Grundzug*" of being human. Here translated as "basic character", *Grundzug*, literally "ground-pull", evokes the image of a motion of pulling at the heart of being-human. Dwelling is not just something we occasionally get to do as humans, but that which pulls us into being-human to begin with.

> "Das Wohnen aber ist der Grundzug des Seins, demgemäss die Sterblichen sind."[27]
> "Dwelling, however, is the basic character of Being in keeping with which mortals exist."[28]

Following on from the starting point of *Dasein*, which opened up "the home" beyond the either/or of outer place and inner experience, a different notion of being-in has now revealed itself through an existential understanding of *wohnen* (dwelling/residing) as the ground-pull of *Dasein*. Further, the separation and sequentialization of *bauen-wohnen* (building-dwelling) has been traced back to their common origin both etymologically

---

25   M. Heidegger, *Vorträge und Aufsätze*, cit. p. 142, emphasis added.
26   M. Heidegger, *Basic writings*, cit., p. 350, emphasis added.
27   M. Heidegger, *Vorträge und Aufsätze*, cit., p. 155.
28   M. Heidegger, *Basic writings*, cit., p. 362.

and existentially. Dwelling and building, as two expressions
of the shared "basic character" of being-human, here denoted
as "inhabiting", are not just activities humans are occasionally
engaged in. As the *Grundzug*, this inhabiting pulls human
existence... into what?

2.3 *The plight of dwelling and uncanny existence*

Following Heidegger on the path of belonging, the existential
building/dwelling has revealed itself as the ground-pull of
human existence. In order to continue along this way, it is now
necessary to turn to Heidegger's explicit engagement with the
notion of homelessness.

Against the common, circumstantial notion of homelessness
as a certain condition of the urban built environment, in
Heidegger's work "homelessness" receives an existential twist,
situating it at the root of being human as *Dasein*. At the time of
Heidegger's later writings, the destruction of WWII had wreaked
havoc on many urban centres, inducing a "plight of housing"
("*Wohnungsnot*"),[29] haunting/besetting everyday life in post-
war Germany and much of Western-Central Europe. Almost 70
years after the end of WW2, the notion of "*Wohnungsnot*" has
persisted, no longer, however, as an acute result of destruction,
but associated with systematic effects of urban density, ruthless
rent and housing markets, rising homeless populations, as well
as refugee and immigrant streams pushing towards the wealthy
countries in Northern and Western Europe.

Below the surface of homelessness as "*Wohnungsnot*",
Heidegger introduces "*Unheimlichkeit*", a richly ambiguous
notion of existential homelessness. The German word implies
uncanniness, as which it is commonly translated, but contains
the literal connotation of not-being-at-home.

> "Unheimlichkeit meint aber dabei zugleich das Nicht-zuhause-sein."[30]

---

29   M. Heidegger, *Basic writings*, cit., p. 363.
30   M. Heidegger, *Sein und Zeit*, cit., p. 188.

"But uncanniness means at the same time not-being-at-home."[31]

In his early work Heidegger introduces *Unheimlichkeit* in his chapters on anxiety ("Angst"). Not-being-at home is not just a circumstance that can be the cause for anxiety, but homelessness as *Unheimlichkeit* is the ur-experience of anxiety from which all other anxieties issue forth. Paradoxically, *Dasein* as being-there that already comes with its world is characterised by a primordial homelessness. This, then, answers the question where the *Grundzug* of *Wohnen* as inhabiting pulls us: into homelessness, that is, home as withdrawal (*Entzug*). Homelessness in the Heideggerian sense of a withdrawal (*Entzug*) is not opposed to the ground pull (*Grundzug*) of inhabiting. The existential notion of belonging is expressed in this very movement: to be pulled by that which withdraws. Precisely by withdrawing, home(lessness) draws us with, that is, pulls us into our uncanny existence. This withdrawal is not a temporary one that could be remedied. It is part of the very existential structure of *Dasein*. Heidegger's homelessness is thus far more radical than even the most "systematic" analyses of urban modernity's crises of housing and living.

"However hard and bitter, however hampering and threatening the lack of houses remains, the *proper plight of dwelling* ['*Wohnungsnot*'] does not lie merely in a lack of houses."[32]

Homelessness is not just a circumstantial situation we suffer, but the existential dynamic at the core of our being. Ontologically/existentially understood as uncanniness, homelessness is "a threat which concerns *Dasein* itself and which comes from itself".[33] This seemingly "pessimistic" notion of homelessness as a persistent existential withdrawal, rather than a recoverable, circumstantial loss, however, opens up to an "optimism" towards

---

31   M. Heidegger, *Being and time*, cit., p. 182.
32   M. Heidegger, *Basic writings*, cit., p. 363 emphasis in original; German added.
33   M. Heidegger, *Being and time*, cit., p. 189 (M. Heidegger, *Sein und Zeit*, cit., p. 183).

this threat that is at odds with the "promise of home" that has become so ubiquitous, attuning our political, personal, social, and mundane world.

> "Sobald der Mensch jedoch die Heimatlosigkeit bedenkt, ist sie bereits kein Elend mehr. Sie ist, recht bedacht und gut behalten, der einzige *Zuspruch*, der die Sterblichen in das Wohnen *ruft*."[34]
> "Yet as soon as man gives thought to his homelessness, it is a misery no longer. Rightly considered and kept well in mind, it is the sole *summons* that *calls* mortals into their dwelling."[35]

Perplexingly, homelessness in Heidegger becomes a "*Zuspruch*", a summons, an encouragement. It is homelessness that primordially "calls" us into our existence. "Uncanniness is the fundamental kind of being-in-the-world, although it is covered over in everydayness."[36] The covering-over of our existential homelessness lies in our mundane procurements. In our everyday doing we are distracted from the uncanniness of our existence, and this covering-up is absolutely vital and necessary. Homelessness as the existential movement of withdrawing is like a vacuum that pulls us and our everyday homeliness into existence. Homelessness is thus not primarily the circumstance in which home is lost but the primordial pull that is foundational to any and all of our belonging. "Tranquilized, familiar being-in-the-world is a mode of the uncanniness of *Dasein*, not the other way around."[37] Revealing homelessness as primordial uncanniness, Heidegger introduces an understanding of belonging where the danger lies not so much in "losing home" but paradoxically in being "too much at home", that is, forgetting our primordial homelessness. The vital "covering-over" of existential uncanniness by homely existence bears the danger of falling into an excessive fleeing.

---

34 M. Heidegger, *Vorträge und Aufsätze*, cit., p. 156, emphasis added.
35 M. Heidegger, *Basic writings*, cit., p. 363, emphasis added.
36 M. Heidegger, *Being and time*, cit., p. 277 (M. Heidegger, *Sein und Zeit*, cit., p. 266).
37 M. Heidegger, *Being and time*, cit., p. 189 (M. Heidegger, *Sein und Zeit*, cit., p. 183).

"Die verfallende Flucht *in* das Zuhause der Öffentlichkeit ist Flucht *vor* dem Unzuhause, das heißt der Unheimlichkeit, die im Dasein als [...] In-der-Welt-sein liegt."[38]

"Entangled flight *into* the being at home of publicness is flight *from* not-being-at-home, that is, from the uncanniness which lie in *Dasein* as thrown, as being-in-the-world."[39]

As opposed to our common understanding of "falling" *into* homelessness *from* being-at-home – whether historically, biographically, circumstantially, or even "existentially" – the order is reversed here: falling from uncanniness into the home of publicness. The "obsession" with the home in all domains of being-modern now reveals itself as a fleeing from existential uncanniness. This "fleeing from homelessness", while perhaps epitomised in being-modern, pertains not to the circumstances of urban environments and hypermodern transit zones, but can only express itself as such on the basis of the existential structure of being-in-the-world.

"Die alltägliche Art, in der das Dasein die Unheimlichkeit versteht, ist die verfallende, das Un-zuhause »abblendende« Abkehr."[40]

"The everyday way in which *Dasein* understands uncanniness is the entangled turning away which 'dims down' not-being-at-home."[41]

Everyday being-in-the-world is always a turning away from uncanniness. This "dimming down" is the sole possibility of sustaining existence. Yet, in making existential *Unheimlichkeit* into circumstantial homelessness there opens up the excessive falling: the obsession with the home. From this tendency of getting lost in homeliness, it now becomes clear why uncanniness in Heidegger is a "*Zuspruch*", a summons and encouragement. It is the very breaking-through of the covered-up homelessness that is the persistent guard against falling into mundane, dimmed-

---

38   M. Heidegger, *Vorträge und Aufsätze*, cit., p. 189, original emphasis.

39   M. Heidegger, *Being and time*, cit., p. 189 (M. Heidegger, *Sein und Zeit*, cit., p. 183), original emphasis.

40   M. Heidegger, *Sein und Zeit*, cit., p. 189.

41   M. Heidegger, *Being and time*, cit., p. 189 (M. Heidegger, *Sein und Zeit*, cit., p. 183).

down homeliness. "Anxiety, on the other hand, fetches *Dasein* back out of its entangled absorption in the 'world'."[42]

In Heidegger's vocabulary, "the home" is not a place that might be threatened or lost, but a movement of withdrawing that summons *Dasein* in its uncanny being. Being-human emerges as a movement rather than a state. Proximate belonging in our familiar everyday world is always covering-over the ground-pull of homelessness – both the necessary hold in existence and containing the danger of excessive, forgetful falling into the "promise of home" of our mundane reference ("*Verwiesenheit*").

3. *Nietzsche – man as a promise*

3.1 *Promise as existence*

In the language of Martin Heidegger homelessness indicated itself as a *Zuspruch* that summons us into our being, and encourages us not to get lost in everyday homeliness. It remains to get to an understanding of how "mortals [can] answer this summons".[43] In the German lies indicated a linguistic chain from *Zuspruch* to "*entsprechen*" (answer). As the third link in this chain, Friedrich Nietzsche's notion of "*Versprechen*" (promise) will bring this inquiry full circle back to its starting point: the promise of home.

> "Ein Tier heranzüchten, das *versprechen* darf – ist das nicht gerade jene paradoxe Aufgabe selbst, welche sich die Natur in Hinsicht auf den Menschen gestellt hat."[44]
>
> "To breed an animal with the right to make *promises* - is not this the paradoxical task that nature has set itself in the case of man?"[45]

---

42   M. Heidegger, *Being and time*, cit., p. 189 (M. Heidegger, *Sein und Zeit*, cit., p. 182).

43   M. Heidegger, *Basic writings*, cit., p. 363.

44   F. Nietzsche, *Zur Genealogie der Moral. Eine Streitschrift* (München: Goldmann Verlag, 1992), p. 45 emphasis added.

45   F. Nietzsche, *On the Genealogy of Morals and Ecce Homo*, cit., p. 57 emphasis added.

The German *versprechen*, usually translated "promise", finds regular mention in Nietzsche and is indicated as having particular import to being-human. In everyday language, *versprechen* is practically equivalent to "promise". However, etymologically the two notions are far less commensurable. Derived from the Latin *pro-mittere* (to throw ahead; to send forward) the notion of "promise" encapsulates our common sense of a promise as the announcement of a future action: now I say what I will do later. In this sense, a promise is an arrangement for the future involving notions of accountability, reliability, fulfilment, etc. From this emerges an understanding of promise which raises an uncertainty regarding the follow-through ("will she really do what she promised?") and thus calls forth contractual securities and punishment.

Versprechen, on the other hand, does not etymologically indicate the sending-forward of an action. The root *sprechen* (speaking) is modified by the untranslatable and deeply ambiguous prefix "ver-". In words like "*verlaufen*" (to get lost) and "*verfehlen*" (to miss), "ver-" suggests an *active* failure: "*verlaufen*" (*laufen* = walking) is not just a *passive* getting lost, "*verfehlen*" (*fehlen* = to miss from) is missing a target not just the absence of something. There is thus a sense of "getting it wrong" or "failing in an attempt" indicated by the "ver-". In the words "*verlieben*" (falling in love) and "*verstehen*" (understanding), there is however a counterintuitive sense that "getting it wrong" is sometimes the only way to "get it right": to love we have to fall, to understand we have to lose our stance. For something truly new to emerge (whether understanding or love), a certain kind of "getting it wrong" appears to be key. *Ver-sprechen*, then, reveals itself as a kind of speaking (*sprechen*) that indicates a slip or blunder (*Versprecher*) which bears the possibility of enunciating oneself. *Versprechen* is a misspeaking which allows us to come into a different existence. It is in this sense that I propose *versprechen* as the way to answer (*entsprechen*) the summons (*Zuspruch*) of uncanniny, existential homelessness.

The difference between "promise" and "*versprechen*" - sending forth of an action vs. (mis-)speaking oneself - here encapsulates the two sides of Heidegger's inquiry into homelessness: the fleeing into mundane covering-over of homelessness through a contractual "promise of home", and the anxious self-announcement drawn-with by uncanniness.

In tension with the common notion of promise as concerned with action and thus bound up with "morality", Nietzsche's ambiguous *versprechen* pertains to the ontological level of being human.

> "als ob der Mensch kein Ziel, sondern nur ein Weg, ein Zwischenfall, eine Brücke, ein großes Versprechen sei..."[46]
> "as if man were not a goal but only a way, an episode, a bridge, a great promise."[47]

Versprechen, then, is not merely a different "activity" than promising. As humans, *versprechen* is not just something we *do* but what we *are*. Being-human now reveals itself as assuming the way, that is, the "task" (*Aufgabe*) that nature has set itself with regards to man. The reference to man as a "great promise" in tandem with the "not a goal but a way" must perhaps be read as Nietzsche's mocking gesture towards all transcendental notions of promise: the paradox of "man as a promise" is that this promise, as *versprechen*, is strictly immanent. Being-human indicates itself neither as a state, an essence to be preserved, nor as a transcendental ideal, but as a way to be assumed.

3.2 *Maintaining Composure*

> "Ich liebe den welcher goldne Worte seine Thaten vorrauswirft und immer noch mehr hält, als er verspricht."[48]
> "I love him who casts golden words before his deeds, and always does even more than he promises."[49]

The English translation of "*hält*" as "does" misses the subtle

---

46   F. Nietzsche, *Zur Genealogie der Moral. Eine Streitschrift*, cit., p. 116.
47   F. Nietzsche, *On the Genealogy of Morals and Ecce Homo*, cit., p. 85.
48   F. Nietzsche, *Also sprach Zarathustra: ein Buch für alle und keinen* (München: Goldmann Verlag, 2010), p. 14.
49   F. Nietzsche, *The Portable Nietzsche* (London: Penguin, 1977), p. 127-8.

gesture towards a different sense of promise here. Literally "to keep", "*halten*", is not just "doing". To say that one *does* more than one promised falls back into a contractual understanding of promise where one merely overdelivers on an arrangement. In *keeping* more than one promises, however, is contained a violation of this logic of promise as action-sent-forth (pro-mittere). If promise is to be taken at the ontological level, *keeping* of the promise can never just a matter of follow-through. The German *halten*, like "to keep", has in its own right only a tentative relation to action. The associations it evokes are rather of "*Haltung*" (posture), "*aushalten*" (endure), "*festhalten*" (hold onto) and "*behalten*" (keep).

Haltung as "posture" evokes only a superficial bodily composition. In the context of *versprechen* as attaining a new composition by misspeaking, *Haltung* is much more than "standing-upright": it is maintaining composure in facing up to uncanniness. *Aushalten*, then, is not merely an enduring of our circumstantial misery in the hope of eventual relief, but, literally, a "holding-out" *in* being underway. On this background, *festhalten* is released from the gesture of a rigid "holding-onto" a present state, and opens up to a "holding-fast": a paradoxical steadfastness that is not based on firm grounds but takes hold in the very pull (*Zug*) of uncanny being-human. Finally, *behalten*, commonly understood as keeping a possession, now literally implies a "be-holding", a recognition and appreciation of homelessness which already indicated itself in Heidegger's *Zuspruch* of uncanniness:

> "homelessness [r]ightly considered and *kept* well in mind (*recht bedacht und gut behalten*), it is the sole summons that calls mortals into their dwelling."[50]

If being-promise (*versprechen*) is how we answer (*entsprechen*) the summons (*Zuspruch*) of uncanny homelessness, then keeping (*halten*) the promise indicates the task of being-human as

---

50   M. Heidegger, *Basic writings*, cit., p. 363, German added.

maintaining composure on shaky grounds, holding out in being underway, holding fast on the pull, and beholding uncanniness. This "underway-ness" finds expression in Nietzsche's notion of man as the "sick animal":

> "Denn der Mensch ist kränker, unsicherer, wechselnder, unfestgestellter als irgendein Tier sonst, daran ist kein Zweifel - er ist *das* kranke Tier."[51]
> "For man is more sick, uncertain, changeable, indeterminate than any other animal, there is no doubt of that – he is *the* sick animal."[52]

Here translated as "changeable", "*unfestgestellt*" implies both "undefined" and, more literally, un-fast-put/made. In its ambiguity, *unfestgestellt* is thus both a gesture of refusing all essential definitions of man and simultaneously announces a need to "make-fast" which cannot be supplied by any ascertainment. Man, this "sick animal", has not "fallen sick" and is thus in need of a cure to restore a primordial health. Being-sick is rather what it means to be human to begin with, and demands not to be fixed or restored but, first and foremost, to be properly *assumed* as the underlying pull of man as a way.

Conclusion

We have come to an entirely different sense of being at home and belonging. On the basis of existential homelessness, our everyday procurements have revealed themselves as the necessary covering-up of uncanniness, bearing the danger of falling into an excessive fleeing into mundane homeliness. The obsession with the home that constitutes the underlying tune in so many domains of being-modern - from international travel to urban planning, from commerce and consumerism to political rhetoric and "personal" sentiments – now becomes visible as an inability to bear the uncanniness of being-in-the-world. The transience of modern life appears to be too painfully close to the

---

51   F. Nietzsche, *Zur Genealogie der Moral. Eine Streitschrift*, cit., p. 177.
52   F. Nietzsche, *On the Genealogy of Morals and Ecce Homo*, cit., p. 121.

"pull" of dwelling and the withdrawal of the home, and hence calls for the most obsessive preoccupation with the home. While seemingly so anxiety-inducing, mundane modern existence reveals itself as increasingly less capable of holding-out in anxiety, facing uncanniness. A ubiquitous posturing of "belonging anywhere" constitutes the intense lure of everyday homeliness. What is being lost here, if anything, is the capacity to be-with homelessness, not "the home". This being-with homelessness, whether at the level of housing shortage or at the "existential" level, is never a mere "gesture" of solidarity and sympathy, but the very foundation of our being-with ourselves and one another. On this basis, then, building is never just the obtainment of living space, but in itself a dwelling which is always a being-with (-others). It is in this sense that we need to "bear in mind that all building is a dwelling.".[53] Building is never the *pre*condition for dwelling and being at home in the world. Only when building is released from this subservience to our desperate attempts to cure homelessness, can it be re-discovered as the very activity in which we come together in uncanny homelessness. The oppositional pairing of the non-homes (hostile environments) we find ourselves in – from supermarkets and airports, refugees and urban density, to alienation and restlessness - and the home we strive and long for outside of these, gives rise to the notion of a "lost home" which animates a fleeing from our existential homelessness (*Unheimlichkeit*).

At the same time this appraisal of uncanniness never praises, legitimises, or even excuses the troubling realities of everyday existence. The home can never be addressed at the existential level. The home always withdraws. This existential wound draws with it our mundane existence as its covering-up. Both the threat-to/loss-of home and our strategies to recover/secure it are complicit in our necessary forgetting of existential homelessness in everyday existence. The point can therefore never be to cease operations or to simply dismiss political, social, developmental, and personal projects of making-home. However, in bearing

---

53   M. Heidegger, *Basic writings*, cit., p. 350.

with our existential homelessness, we can regain a sense for alternative ways of procuring this existential withdrawal in our everyday lives. The challenge of dwelling – and this is so difficult for our present world of transience – is, as Heidegger puts it: to remain "perpetually under way".[54]

---

54   M. Heidegger, *Basic writings*, cit., p. 262.

PART III
FURUSATO ACROSS SPACE

KAWAGUCHI YUKIHIRO 川口幸大[1]

QIAOXIANG AND *FURUSATO*

A Comparative Study of Homes of Overseas Chinese and Japanese Emigrants

Introduction

Qiaoxiang (僑鄉) is a common noun in Chinese vocabulary, composed of two characters: *qiao* (僑), meaning "sojourner," and *xiang* (鄉), meaning "home." Thus, *qiaoxiang* refers to home of Chinese people living overseas. While Chinese has a common noun to indicate the home of emigrants, Japanese vocabulary does not have a corresponding word to mean the home of Japanese emigrants. Furthermore, Japanese seems not to be the exception, for only Chinese has a word to mean the home of its own particular ethnic group or nation. Specifically, *qiaoxiang* is a neologism constructed for political reasons.

As several previous studies in this volume has shown, no home begins as a home, but is imagined or generated mainly for political or economic reasons. In China, the home of emigrants is frequently referred to as *qiaoxiang* to connect them to their birthplace and motherland and to reinforce their ties to China. By contrast, for Japanese emigrants, though their hardships and successes after migration are frequently discussed, their birthplaces are rarely mentioned. The Japanese language has no corresponding word meaning the home of Japanese migrants, and instead must use the phrase *Nikkeijin no furusato* 日系人 の故鄉 (the hometown of people of Japanese descent) or *imin boson* 移民母村 (the mother village of Japanese migrants).

In this article, I aim to examine how the homes of emigrants are represented and what role they play in the relationship

---

1   Tohoku University

between emigrants and their natal communities in China and Japan through a comparative study of the overseas Chinese (*Huaqiao* 華僑) and Japanese emigrants (*Nikkeijin* 日系人 and *Manmō kaitakudan* 満蒙開拓団).

1. *The Representation of the Homes of Overseas Chinese*

The invention of qiaoxiang *and its transition*

In the pioneering studies on emigrant communities in China, *Country Life in China*[2] and *Emigrant Communities in South China*,[3] the word *qiaoxiang* is not found. *Qiaoxiang* began to be used gradually around 1946 in official documents, and, was seen frequently after 1956.[4] The Chinese government and the natal communities of emigrants expected the term to evoke the emigrants' nostalgia, nationalism, and a sense of duty or obligation to their home, and to urge them to commit to the development of "the New China". Especially after 1978, when the Chinese Communist Party (CCP) initiated reform and the Open Door Policy, the family and natal communities of overseas Chinese longed for remittance and investment from them and were eager to restore bonds with them. The neologism *qiaoxiang* played a crucial role as an intermediator between the overseas Chinese and their homes.

From the beginning of the reforms and the policies that allowed new connections between parts of China and the rest

---

2   Daniel Harrison II Kulp, *Country life in South China: the Sociology of Familism* (New York: Bureau of Publications Teachers College Columbia University, 1925).

3   Ta Chen, *Emigrant Communities in South China: A Study of Overseas Migration and Its Influence on Standards of Living and Social Change* (Shanghai: Kelly and Walsh, 1939).

4   Xiao Canpeng 趙灿鵬, "Muguang xiang wai: Zhongguo xiandai huaqiao yanjiu de yi ge qingxiang ji "qingxiang"chengwei de kaocha" [Looking abroad: A General trend in the overseas Chinese studies in modern China, with special reference to "*qiao xiang*"] 〈"目光向外"—中国現代華僑研究的一個傾向暨"僑郷"称謂的考察〉, *Huaqiao Huaren lishi yanjiu* 『華僑華人歴史研究』 (2008-1), pp. 42-45.

of the world in the 1980s and 1990s, overseas Chinese became essential actors in the development of their homes. From 1978 to 1987, the first decade following the Reform, Jiangmen 江門, one of the largest cities in the western part of Guangdong province and a typical hometown of overseas Chinese, received 146 times the investment and 670 times the remittance for education and welfare from overseas Chinese compared to the previous twenty years.[5] Kaiping 開平 prefecture is one of the most representative *qiaoxiang* and the main field site of this study. In 1984, the education budget of Kaiping was 618 million yuan (~111 million USD), but the prefecture received 860 (~154 million USD) in remittances from overseas Chinese in education fees, more than their own budget.[6] The Kaiping prefecture gazetteer contains several color pictures of the opening ceremonies of the hospitals and schools constructed by remittances from the emigrants during the 1980s and 1990s.[7] These documents show that overseas Chinese played pivotal roles in the growing prosperity of their homes, especially in the early days of the Reform. At the same time, through such contributions, overseas Chinese could reconstruct their relationships with their homes. The cliché "rich overseas Chinese support their poor *qiaoxiang*" was used by local and national governments repeatedly during the 1980s and 1990s.[8]

However, we also have to notice that not all overseas Chinese prospered and made significant contributions their home. It is likely the government and home communities emphasized a few rare cases, and the image of rich emigrants supporting poor homes

---

5   Jiangmenshi difangzhi bianzuan weiyuanhui 江門市地方志編纂委員会, *Jiangmen shizhi* [Jiangmen city gazetteer] 《江門市志》 (Guangzhou: Guangdong renmin chubanshe, 1998), p. 1215.

6   Kaipingxian difangzhi bangongshi 開平市地方志办公室, *Kaiping xianzhi* [Kaiping county gazetteer] 《開平県志》 (Beijing: Zhonghua shuju, 2002), p. 1535, 1537.

7   Kaipingxian difangzhi bangongshi, *Kaiping xianzhi*, cit., frontispieces.

8   Kawaguchi Yukihiro and Inazawa Tsutomu 川口幸大・稲澤務 (ed. by), *Kyōkyō: Kakyō no furusato wo meguru hyōshō to jitsuzō* [Oiaoxiang: The representation and actuality of the home of overseas Chinese] 『僑郷—華僑のふるさとをめぐる表象と実像』 (Ōtsu: Kōrosha 行路社, 2016).

was largely fabricated. Nonetheless, it is certain that from the late 1970s to the 1990s, the word *qiaoxiang* was directed at the overseas Chinese to arouse their nostalgia, nationalism, and sense of duty.

Qiaoxiang *as a cultural resource and tourist site*

As China entered the 21st century, the meaning of *qiaoxiang* and its target drastically changed. First, due to generational change, older emigrants who felt nostalgia for their homes decreased year by year, so the relationships between emigrants and their relatives were not as close as they had been in the 1980s and 1990s. In addition, the southeastern coastal area where *qiaoxiang* are located became wealthy, thanks in no small part to the contributions from overseas Chinese. As a result, the relationship between overseas Chinese and *qiaoxiang* has not been as substantive as in the previous decades.

Instead, *qiaoxiang* are gaining attention as a cultural resource and a tourist site. "Kaiping Diaolou and Villages" (開平碉楼与村落) was registered on the UNESCO World Heritage List in 2007, and since then many tourists visit the Kaiping *qiaoxiang*. Here, at the museum, the history and lifestyle of a home of overseas Chinese is objectified and exhibited as "*qiaoxiang* culture" (僑郷文化). Now *qiaoxiang* is no longer directed at overseas Chinese, but primarily at tourists.

Kaiping Diaolou and Villages, the World Heritage Site

According to the official website of UNESCO, Kaiping Diaolou and Villages is presented as follows:

> Kaiping Diaolou and Villages feature the Diaolou, multi-storeyed defensive village houses in Kaiping, which display a complex and flamboyant fusion of Chinese and Western structural and decorative forms. They reflect the significant role of émigré Kaiping people in the development of several countries in South Asia, Australasia and North America, during the late 19th and early 20th centuries.[9]

---

9   https://whc.unesco.org/en/list/1112

Diaolou were built mainly through the remittances from overseas Chinese or the wealth of returnees, and had many functions, not only as dwellings, but also as fortresses and watchtowers against the bandits who were a particular problem during the early 20th century. The architectural style of *diaolou* is a unique fusion of China and the West, as UNESCO pointed out, an ostentatious display of the success of overseas Chinese in distant lands.

As a result of its registration on the World Heritage List, the *diaolou* in Kaiping are frequented by tourists, especially during the national holiday week in May and during summer vacation. The ticket fee for five particular sites is 160 Chinese yuan, approximately 20€. Compared to the 60-yuan entrance fee of the Forbidden City in Beijing, the price for *dialou* sites is relatively expensive.

The most popular site among the five is Zili Village (自力村), where many *diaolou* tower whimsically in a rural village paddy field. Tourists walk around the village, looking at the distinct scenery. Zili Village, like other spots in this course, is well managed as a tourist site. Tour guides who speak Mandarin, Cantonese, or English are available. Every main *diaolou* displays an explanation not only in Chinese, but in English, Japanese, and Korean as well.

Tourists learn that, as fortresses, *diaolou* had many features for defense. Every window is made from iron and can be tightly closed. Multiple slits for shooting are provided on the outer walls and balcony. Inside the building, a thick safe is provided behind a secret door. According to the explanation, the residents hid themselves there when the Japanese army came inside the tower.

At each floor of a *diaolou*, the former residents' living space is exhibited, with their furniture and housewares. The most distinguishing feature of these items is the cultural fusion of traditional China and the West. Men in some photos wear a suit or tuxedo and women wear wedding dresses. In other photos, they have on *hanfu* 漢服 or *qipao* 旗袍 in the Chinese style. Although tables and chairs are Chinese-style red wood, the floor is made of Italian marble stone. Western-style bath tubs are installed in the bathroom, and a wooden box for shipping whiskey sits on a chest. All these things show that the people's daily lives were surrounded by a variety of imported Western items that were quite rare in rural China in those days. Among them, probably what most impressed visitors were "*Jinshan xiang*" 金山箱 or "Gold mountain trunks." *Jinshan* means California during the gold rush of the late 19th century, where many immigrants, including Chinese, flooded to make a fortune at a single stroke. Successful men returned to their homes with a trunk full of treasure, which was the symbol of their triumph. At the souvenir shop, assorted sweets in a box shaped like a gold mountain trunk are sold.

Like other tourist spots, it takes about an hour to see Zili Village. The location clearly shows tourists the "*qiaoxiang* culture": the East-West fusion lifestyle of the emigrant community and the characteristic functions of *diaolou*.

Kaiping diaolou

Qiaoxiang *culture in the museum*

Qiaoxiang culture is also exhibited in the Jiangmen Museum of Overseas Chinese. As the name indicates, this museum is uniquely focused on overseas Chinese. Many signs are hung on the outer wall of the museum, saying "Base of Patriotic Education" (愛国主義教育基地), "Base of Educational Practice on Overseas Chinese Culture" (華僑文化教育実践基地), "China International Culture Communication Base for Overseas Chinese" (中国華僑国際文化交流基地),[10] and so on. These signs show clearly that this museum is a facility for education and exchange on the theme of overseas Chinese culture.

At the entrance of the Museum, Chinese characters read 「根在五邑」 ("Rooted in Wuyi," referring to the region). This phrase clearly shows that this is the home of the overseas Chinese. The visitors are received by two cartoon characters called Huage (華哥, Brother China) and Qiaomei (僑妹, Sister sojourner), who are third-generation Chinese living in San Francisco and here to visit their grandfather's home. They guide visitors to the exhibition.

The theme of the exhibition is quite simple and clear: that the overseas Chinese's experience mainly consists of hardship, success, and contributions to the home. The first part of the exhibition begins with "traditional" life in this area, including the reproduction of an old house and photos of the local market. Gazetteers of the Republican period (the beginning of the 20th century) show that a food shortage or feud among sub-ethnic groups caused the migration.

In the next section, articles about the process of migration are exhibited, including a Qing-era passport and a timetable for ships leaving for South East Asia or North America. The cabin from which migrants boarded is reproduced and visitors learn how tough the trips to these places were.

The next exhibition shows the hard work emigrants performed in mines, plantations, and laundries, or for the construction of Transcontinental Railroad. Later, emigrants established footholds for living in foreign society through the running of restaurants and other businesses, building shrines, and organizing associations of fellow provinces or prefectures. Some went on to great success. Photos of prominent emigrants with Presidents

---

10   English translation is as found in the source text.

George H. W. Bush or George W. Bush are proudly displayed. Visitors also learn that successful migrants also made various contributions to their homes, such as building schools, ancestral halls, railways, and *diaolou*. They also eagerly supported the revolutionary activity of Sun Yat-sen 孫逸仙, and his famous saying, "oversea Chinese are the mother of revolution" (華僑為革命之母) is displayed beside a statue of him.

In sum, what the Museum represented so thoroughly is that overseas Chinese were not only indispensable actors for the development of their natal communities, but also for the political movement of leaders and construction in their motherland, China. In addition to this Museum, Wuyi University in Jiangmen has a Research Center for Qiaoxiang Culture of Guangdong (広東僑郷文化研究中心). In stark contrast to this, no university in Japan has a research institution specializing in the homes of emigrants. Most stories of Japanese emigrants are not focused on their impact on their homes, but their lives after migration.

2. *The representation of a Japanese Emigrant's Home*

From the late 19th century to the middle of 20th century, large numbers of people from Japan emigrated to North and South America, Hawaii, Manchuria, and elsewhere. In addition, as among Chinese emigrants, there were particular areas from which a great number of people emigrated. How, then, is the home of these Japanese migrants represented in Japan?

The Memorial Museum for Agricultural Emigration to Manchuria

About 270,000 people migrated to so-called "Manchukuo", founded in 1932 as a de facto puppet nation of Japan. Called *Manmō kaitakuda,* (Manchuria/Mongolia pioneer groups), the migrants were encouraged by national policy for military strategy. The largest proportion of the migrants, almost fourteen percent, were from Nagano 長野県 prefecture, and one-fourth of these from the Shimoina 下伊那 and Ida 飯田 area, where twenty-five percent of the population left for Manchuria.

The Memorial Museum for Agricultural Emigration to Manchuria (満蒙開拓平和記念館) was opened in Achimura 阿智村, Shimoinagun 下伊那郡 in 2013 as a general incorporated association. According to staff, the Museum is supported mainly by admission fees and donation. The theme behind the exhibition is remarkably clear: it is an anti-war message that encourages peace through displaying the harm and suffering of the emigrants. Visitors learn that Japanese emigrants had settled the land that Chinese people originally had owned and lived partly by force. Later, the emigrants became victims that had to flee China, with a significant number losing their lives, after the defeat of Japan.

The next part of exhibition, "Repatriation", shows that emigrants faced great difficulties upon returning to Japan, and many had to relocate multiple times to settle in other places around the country. The final part, "Nostalgia", concerns the people left behind in China (中国残留孤児, *Chūgoku zanryū koji*) and the efforts to support their return to Japan. In contrast to Chinese emigrants, home for them was not a place to come back to proudly and in triumph, but a place where hardship and disappointment awaited them. Surely, many people left this area for Manchuria, but the exhibition does not display any benefits they received. From presentation of the Museum, it is clear that this is only the place from which migrants left and not their home.

Kobe Center for Overseas Migration and Cultural Interaction

Kobe and Yokohama were the main ports from which Japanese migrants left Japan for overseas, and they now have similar facilities. The Kobe Center for Overseas Migration and Cultural Interaction opened in 2009 at the site of the former national institution for migration, where medical checks and basic education for migrants had been offered. At the entrance, the title signifies the theme of the exhibition, with "From Kobe to the World" displayed in four languages: English, Japanese (神戸から世界へ), Spanish (*Desde Kobe al Mundo*), and

Portuguese (*De Kobe para o Mundo*). Necessary articles that migrants brought with them abroad included an oil drum for baths and a large wooden box for storage, but nothing like a gold mountain trunk. A few local farm tools, such as hoes, winnowing baskets, planters and similar items, which they used to cultivate the wilderness, are also exhibited. Visitors learn that Japanese migrants struggled hard to settle in a new area and become successful. However, how the migrants might have influenced and changed their homes remains unclear.

Japanese Overseas Migration Museum

The Japanese Overseas Migration Museum opened on the second floor of the JICA Yokohama office in 2002. JICA is the abbreviation for the Japanese International Cooperation Agency, the independent administrative institution that originally conducted the business of migration. So, to some extent, it seems necessary that the Japanese Overseas Migration Museum is there. The exhibition mainly consists of four parts: the history of migration, life at the migration site, the life history of *Nikkeijin* (Japanese migrants), and *Nikkeijin* in the world. Each exhibit is elaborately displayed, especially the reproduction of a grocery store and a dwelling that migrants had built and used and the video archives of their life stories. As a whole, the exhibition shows their stories of hardship and success in the same way as the Museum in Kobe. In short, the contents are focused on just before the migration and their life after, not on their home.

The Museum of Japanese Migration to Hawaii

Suo-ōshima 周防大島, Yamaguchi prefecture 山口県 is the rare case in Japan where the history of migration is closely related to local revitalization. One-third of the first government-contract labor migrants to Hawaii in 1885 were from Suo-ōshima, partly because Inoue Kaoru 井上馨, the Minister for Foreign Affairs at that time, was from Yamaguchi. It is estimated that migrants to Hawaii and the US numbered in ten thousand in total and after World War II, fifteen thousand people returned to Suo-ōshima. Based on this history of exchange, Suo-ōshima established a sister-city affiliation with Kauai in 1963, and then eagerly promoted various events and tourism developments featuring Hawaii. Now, two Hawaiian-styled resort hotels are in business in the area. On the beach side of the hotels, palm trees are planted to create Hawaiian scenery and a "Saturday Hula" event takes place in summer that sees town officials and shop staff don aloha shirts. Tiki, the guardian angel, is displayed in the shopping center and at the entrance of The Museum of Japanese Migration to Hawaii.

The Museum opened in 1999 in a large renovated house donated by Fukumoto Chōemon 福元長右衛門, one of the most successful migrants from Suo-ōshima. In contrast to the three previously discussed museums in Japan, the exhibitions here include the influence from migrants. The exhibit "Favor from Hawaii migrants" (ハワイ移民の恩恵, *Hawai imin no onkei*) shows that migrants send remittances to their families and communities, and offers thanks for their financial support, which provided for the rebuilding and maintenance of schools and temples. "Articles from abroad" (海外からの品々, *Kaigai kara no shinajina*) displays Western-styled clothes, shoes, and irons which returnees brought back in big trunks, like Kaiping's Gold mountain trunks. Other exhibitions mostly consist of migrant's stories of hardship and success, like any other migrant museum.

Suo-ōshima's museum is unique in that the exchange between the local community and Hawaii, which was enabled by migration, is emphasized, and the migration itself is represented positively. However, compared to Kaiping, it seems rather moderate, and the museum attracts far fewer tourists. Suo-ōshima strongly promoted its relationship with Hawaii, but placed less emphasis of itself at the home of the migrants, as in Kaiping's *qiaoxiang*. Local people and the government probably have no expectations that Suo-ōshima will be registered on the World Heritage List as a home of migrants.

Hawaiian scenery in Suo-ōshima

3. *Politics of the Home*

There is great difference in the representation of migrants' homes between China and Japan. In contemporary China, the homes of migrants, objectified as *qiaoxiang*, are made to be tourist attractions, the theme of exhibitions in museums, and a research topic in university. On the other hand, the four similar museums in Japan rarely mention migrants' homes. In contrast to the case of overseas Chinese and *qiaoxiang*, the change of the home by the migrants' support and contribution is hardly addressed except in Suo-ōshima's case. Moreover, there is no particular town or village in Japan that represents the home of migrants and is treated as a tourist site as thoroughly as China's Kaiping *qiaoxiang*. Interest in migrants from Japan seems to be found mostly abroad, not at home. In other words, to Japanese people, real homes can only the places where people were born or grew up, and from where they moved domestically, but never internationally.

According to Narita Ryūichi 成田龍一, home re-experiences the process of imagination and invention of the nation.[11] In particular eras or social contexts, it is treated as a crucial matter.[12] The *qiaoxiang* boom in today's China is surely meant to complement a part of Chinese nationalism or the "Chinese Dream." From this point of view, the fact that in Japan few people give mind to the homes of migrants is by no means exceptional. It is rather China that is unusual, where *qiaoxiang* draw such great attention. For China, people living overseas are a crucial part of the national agenda.

Conclusion

From the beginning, human beings have always been moving. Arising in Africa, homo-sapiens migrated for thousands of years and spread over nearly the entire world. Humans' persistent migration means that there were always other places that they had been previously. In addition, "home" is a word commonly used in every society. However, a place where someone lives does not necessarily become a home. Whether or not the place where people had stayed previously or even their birthplace becomes a home depends on the person's situation or the political economy of that society.

Qiaoxiang is a specific word only seen in China that indicates the home of Han Chinese migrants. This word is a product of the particular politico-economic situation in a particular era of China. In the Japanese language, there is no similar word that means the home of Japanese migrants. It means that the home of

---

11   Narita Ryūichi 成田龍一, "'Kokyō' toiu monogatari: toshi kūkan no rekishigaku' [The story of 'home': a historical study of urban space] 『「故郷」という物語——都市空間の歴史学』 (Tokyo: Yoshikawa kōbundō 吉川弘文堂, 1998).

12   Uchida Ryūzō 内田隆三, "'Kokyō' toiu riarity' ["Home" as reality] 「「故郷」というリアリティ」, in Narita Ryūichi (ed. by), *Kokyō no sōshitsu to saisei* [Loss and restoration of home]『故郷の喪失と再生』 (Tokyo: Seikyūsha 青弓社, 2000), pp. 133-174.

Japanese migrants has never been objectified like those of their Chinese counterparts.

At the same time, the intent implied in *qiaoxiang* and its object has changed drastically in the past few decades. Originally, *qiaoxiang* was a word created and used by the community members of the overseas migrants and governments expecting remittances and investment from them. Conversely, for other people, *qiaoxiang* is only a kind of unfamiliar topic concerning overseas migrants and the rural areas in southeast coast. However, in the 21st century, some *qiaoxiang*, particularly Kaiping, became tourist sites by recognizing their historical value. Now, their main market is not the overseas Chinese whose homes had been that place, but general tourists. Chinese nationalism intends to make "home" not only relevant to locals, but to appeal to Chinese inside and outside of China.

Sonia Favi[1]

ESCAPING HOME, FINDING HOME

The search for Identity in Recreational Travel in the Late Edo Period

Furusato became an established trope in the policies of Japanese domestic tourism only in the 1980s, but I argue that the notion of "home", in a meaning close to that of *furusato*, shaped the premodern culture of recreational travel in fundamental ways. Home was both an ordinary place, escaped from through the extraordinary (real or virtual) practice of travel, and a metaphorical space that shaped the traveler's sense of the local and the national. Moreover, recreational travel was marketed through nostalgia-centered dynamics that were similar in some ways to those at play in the contemporary promotion of tourist destinations as *furusato*, above all in the case of the representations of *meisho* (名所, famous places) in *meisho zue* (名所図会, illustrated guides/maps to *meisho*).

Furusato (ふるさと) is a multi-layered concept. The term literally translates as "old village", but if one refers to the related entry in the Kōjien dictionary, the first definition given for it is far more generic: "*furukunatte arehateta tochi*" (古くなって荒れはてた土地, a land that has become old and has fallen into ruin). This is followed by two correlated definitions: "*mukashi, miyako nado no atta tochi*" (昔、都などのあった土地, a land where in the past places such as the capital were located) and "*koseki*" (古蹟, historic spot). Lastly, come the definitions: "*jibun ga umareta tochi*" (自分が生まれた土地, the land where one was born), "*katsute, sunda koto no aru tochi*" (かつて、住んだことのある

---

1   Marie Skłodowska-Curie Actions Individual Fellow, The University of Manchester

土地, the land where one used to live), and "*najimibukai tochi*" (なじみ深い土地, a land one is very familiar with).

When one looks at current uses of the term, the last three meanings appear to be the ones most commonly associated with the term. Jennifer Robertson,[2] who analyses how the notion of *furusato* was treated in the media in the last two decades of the twentieth century, underlines this, suggesting, as an apt translation, the terms "home" or "native place". One should not forget, however, that the notion embodies also the first set of meanings: that *furusato* is not just *a* home, but a very specific idea of *collective* home that encompasses both a temporal and a spatial dimension. It is something that exists in the past, a past that is generic (*mukashi, katsute, furu*), but also close enough to be reconstructable.[3] *Furusato* is also a place: *sato* 里, the "village",

---

2   Jennifer Robertson, *Native and Newcomer: Making and Remaking a Japanese City* (Berkeley: University of California Press, 1991). It is in reference to Robertson that the present article chooses to adopt the *hiragana* script for *furusato*, even though the term sometimes appears also in *kanji*, as 故郷 or 古里. As underlined by Robertson, the common use of *hiragana* for *furusato* fosters the ambiguity of its meaning and at the same time assures that the Japanese reading of the word is used, as opposed to the Chinese reading *kokyō* – which imbues the term with a sense of cultural authenticity. See also, in this regard, Jennifer Robertson, 'Hegemonic Nostalgia, Tourism and Nation-Making in Japan', *Senri Ethnological Studies* 38 (1995), pp. 89-103.

3   More often than not, this past is identified with an "invented" Edo period. Guichard-Anguis and Moon speak in this regard of a *tabi* (旅, an old term for "travel") culture of contemporary Japanese tourism, where travel becomes a sort of secular pilgrimage where the destination is the Tokugawa past. Sylvie Guichard-Anguis and Okpyo Moon, *Japanese Tourism and Travel Culture* (London and New York: Routledge, 2009), p. 20. Peter Nosco suggests as a possible reason for this the fact that the roots of contemporary nationalism are found in nationalistic ideas inspired by Edo period *Kokugaku* (国学, National Studies), which, much as the cult of *furusato*, was rooted into the nostalgic idealization of a remote past. Peter Nosco, *Remembering Paradise: Nativism and Nostalgia in Eighteenth-Century Japan* (Cambridge, MA: Harvard University Asia Center, 1990), p. IX. According to Carol Gluck, Edo nostalgia is also due to the immediate proximity of Edo to the Meiji period (1868-1912), which makes it work as a direct mirror to "modernity". Carol Gluck, 'The Invention of Edo', in Stephen Vlastos (ed. by), *Mirror of Modernity: Invented Traditions of Modern Japan* (Berkeley: University of California Press, 1998), pp. 262-284.

a synecdoche for the "local" and the "rural".[4] The identification with the countryside is not absolute: some urban settings are very commonly associated with the notion – the most obvious one being Kyoto, framed as *furusato* in light of its role as the old capital and of its quality of *koseki*.[5] On the other hand, the association is common, and is related to a more general, popular connection of agriculture and "Japaneseness".[6]

Furusato is a timeless but old landscape that, as any landscape, works as an "instrument of cultural power",[7] which can be infused with meaning and turned into an icon to construct cultural and even national narratives. It is, as Robertson puts it, "living historical past", a simulation of life in another time that, in spite of being a simulation, has at its center the idea of authenticity.[8] It is an "invented tradition", marking the boundaries of an imagined community: not "the product of either careful preservation or pure invention. Rather, it is a matter of reconciling past with present through the mediation of value-laden symbols, thereby rationalizing a favored agenda".[9] It is, in other words, the result of a strategic use of the past for present purposes.

The association of *furusato* with the trope of the agricultural

---

4   For some examples of this association in the media, see Jennifer Robertson, *Native and Newcomer*, cit., pp. 19-25.

5   See in this regard Christoph Brumann, 'Outside the Glass Case: The Social Life of Urban Heritage in Kyoto', *American Ethnologist* 36-2 (2009), pp. 276-299.

6   Much has been written on this topic. See in particular Amino Yoshihiko 網野善彦, *Nihonron no shiza: rettō no shakai to kokka* [An Overview of the Theories on Japan: The Society and State of the Archipelago] 『日本論の視座: 列島の社会と国家』 (Tokyo: Shōgakkan 小学館, 1993) and Emiko Ohnuki-Tierney, *Rice as Self. Japanese Identities Through Time* (Princeton, N.J.: Princeton University Press, 1993).

7   William John Thomas Mitchell, *Landscape and Power* (Chicago: University of Chicago Press, 2002), p. 1.

8   Jennifer Robertson, 'Hegemonic Nostalgia', cit., p. 90.

9   Scott Schnell, 'The Rural Imaginary', cit., p. 202. As Brumann underlines, moreover, the rural context is a more fertile terrain than the urban one for the creation of this sort of fixed, desubstantiated heritage, not only because the urban environment tends to be more diverse and rich in intellectual and creative resources, but also because there are usually less historical sources available about the countryside, which allows an easier projection of nostalgic desires on it. Christoph Brumann, 'Outside the Glass Case', cit., pp. 291-292.

village is the result of a political and practical project (what Robertson defines as *furusato-zukuri* ふるさとづくり, native-place-making)[10] that invokes it as the dominant narrative (among many possible history-making narratives) through which popular memories of the "Japanese" past are shaped and socially reproduced. Many agents collaborate in its construction, a leading example being the industry of domestic tourism, which commercializes nostalgia and the interest for cultural heritage.[11] The narrative and its success have much to do with

---

10   Jennifer Robertson, *Native and Newcomer*, cit., p. 4.
11   Many case studies shed light on how this commercialization happened. Eyal Ben-Ari, focusing on a rite of passage in the village of Yamanaka-chō, shows for example how "modern" visual media, and in particular photography, have been used to document and promote old ritual performances as "authentic" traditions and how, in this process, rituals came to be decontextualized and deprived of their original meanings: how they turned into a "rite of presentation" of how Japanese society should be – which coincides with how it supposedly *used to be*, in the context of the harmonious, hierarchic community of *furusato*. Eyal Ben-Ari, 'Posing, Posturing and Photographic Presences: A Rite of Passage in a Japanese Commuter Village', *Man, New Series* 26-1 (1991), pp. 87-104. Barbara Green, in her study of tourism connected to Mizuki Shigeru 水木しげる, frames the search of *furusato* as a form of secular, emotional pilgrimage, underlining the historical connections between pilgrimage, travel to national monuments, and recreative travel (tourism). Barbara Greene, 'Furusato and Emotional Pilgrimage: Ge Ge Ge no Kitarō and Sakaiminato', *Japanese Journal of Religious Studies* 43-2 (2016), pp. 333-356. Ian Reader focuses on religious pilgrimage proper, showing how in the context of the nostalgia boom of the 1980s, and of the consequent traditionalist revival, advertisements were consciously used to revive the practice as the legacy of a lost past, at the same time separating pilgrimage from its religious implications (while tradition and culture tended to acquire religious connotations of their own). Ian Reader, 'Back to the Future: Images of Nostalgia and Renewal in a Japanese Religious Context', *Japanese Journal of Religious Studies* 14-4 (1987), pp. 287-303, and Ian Reader, 'Positively Promoting Pilgrimage: Media Representations of Pilgrimage in Japan', *Nova Religio: The Journal of Alternative and Emergent Religions* 10-3 (2007), pp. 13-31. Irit Averbuch focuses on a 1996 revitalization of the Buddhist ritual *Nunohashi daikanjō-hōe* (布橋大灌頂法会, Great Consecration Ceremony of the Cloth-Covered Bridge) of Tateyama, showing how it was deprived of its original religious essence, and turned into a cultural event – a display of a lost "Japanese" identity. She also underlines how, on the other hand, the original religious essence of the ritual was claimed back by the local population, showing how *furusato-zukuri* can also become the place for counter-narratives. Irit Averbuch, 'Discourses of

a sense of dissatisfaction towards the present: with the anxieties generated by urbanization and industrialization and, as Susan J. Napier underlines,[12] with the trend of *kokusaika* (国際化, internationalization) and the fear of the loss of local identity in the face of globalization. At the same time, the urge that shapes *furusato*, the search for identity in an imagined past and outside of the realm of the ordinary, is not strictly rooted in that social context. What I aim to show in this article is how the ways in which the narrative has been marketed are mirrored in some of the dynamics of the pre-modern industry of domestic travel.

By the end of the eighteenth century, the culture of travel in Japan had created a complex landscape. It is hard to make an overall estimate of the number of people who took to the road. Surely, travel was expensive,[13] and Tokugawa authorities maintained strict measures of control over it, including the issue of *ōrai tegata* (往来手形, identification documents) and the establishment of *sekisho* (関所, checkpoints). On the other hand, the current state-of-the-art widely agrees that it became a fairly common practice by the end of the Edo period.[14]

---

the Reappearing: The Reenactment of the "Cloth-Bridge Consecration Rite" at Mt. Tateyama', *Japanese Journal of Religious Studies* 38-1 (2011), pp. 1-54. Millie Creighton shows how marketing strategies have romanticized the agricultural heritage of Japan, elevating *furusato* to a model of "cultural authenticity", and underlines how this trend has impacted remote rural communities, transforming them into tourist destinations, but at the same time decontextualizing them and depriving them of their specificity – that is, turning them into everyone's *furusato*. Millie Creighton, 'Consuming Rural Japan: The Marketing of Tradition and Nostalgia in the Japanese Travel Industry', *Ethnology* 36-3 (1997), pp. 239-254.

12   Susan J. Napier, 'Matter out of Place: Carnival, Containment, and Cultural Recovery in Miyazaki's "Spirited Away"', *The Journal of Japanese Studies* 32-2 (2006), pp. 287-310.

13   For data on the costs of travel in Edo Japan, see Konno Nobuo 今野信雄, *Edo no tabi* [Edo travel] 『江戸の旅』 (Tokyo: Iwanami shoten 岩波書店, 1993), pp. 175-177.

14   I refer the reader, in particular, to Konno Nobuo, *Edo no tabi*, cit.; Ashiba Hiroyasu 足羽洋保, *Shin kankōgaku gairon* [A new outline in the study of tourism] 『新観光学概論』 (Tokyo: Minerva Shobō ミネルヴァ書房, 1994); Constantine N. Vaporis, *Breaking Barriers: Travel and the State in Early Modern Japan* (Harvard: Harvard University Press, 1994); Constantine N.

Movement was partly integrated in the structure of the
Tokugawa state, linked to institutional obligations such as the
practice of *sankin kōtai* (参勤交代, alternate attendance), and
to a growing economic integration within the country. The
development of an efficient road system (the *gokaidō* 五街道,
five routes), and the climate of relative peace brought by the
Tokugawa rule also allowed space for other forms of travel,
such as visits to hot springs (usually motivated, at least formally,
by health reasons) and pilgrimages. Both practices predated
the Edo period, but in Tokugawa Japan they underwent a sort
of revolution, in that, in the context of a developing market
economy, they came to be performed by a public that was larger
and more diverse than before, in terms of both social status and
gender.[15] Religious travel, moreover, often went hand in hand
with recreational travel, centered on *monomi yusan* (物見遊
山, sightseeing) – not only because Tokugawa authorities were
more apt to grant travel permits to people who embarked on
pilgrimages,[16] but also because, as Ian Reader underlines, the two
modalities of travel tend to overlap, as they both encompass the
search for something that lies beyond and requires a movement
from the ordinary.[17] The infrastructure that supported travel grew

---

Vaporis, 'The Early Modern Origins of Japanese Tourism', *Senri Ethnological
Studies* 38 (1995), pp. 25-39; Laura Nenzi, *Excursions in identity: travel
and the intersection of place, gender, and status in Edo Japan* (Hawaii:
University of Hawaii Press, 2008); Carolin Funck and Malcolm Cooper,
Japanese Tourism: Spaces, Places and Structures (New York, Oxford:
Berghahn, 2013).

15 Information about the social status and gender of travellers is gathered from
travel permits and from the records of *sekisho*. See in this regard Laura
Nenzi, *Excursions in identity*, cit., pp. 45-68 (and particularly, for data about
status and gender distribution, p. 47).

16 That pilgrimage was considered as an "acceptable" form of travel is clear
from the fact that it was sometimes treated as a necessary "rite of passage",
a sort of coming-of-age ceremony. And even outside of this ritual, religious
travel came to be minutely and very openly organized, through *kō* (講
confraternities) and through the activities of *okitōshi* (御祈禱師 master of
prayers, usually abbreviated as *oshi*). See in this regard Toshikazu Shinno,
'Journeys, Pilgrimages, Excursions: Religious Travels in the Early Modern
Period', *Monumenta Nipponica* 57-4 (2002), pp. 447-471.

17 Ian Reader and Tony Walter (ed. by), *Pilgrimage in Popular Culture*

steadily throughout the period: *shukuba* (宿場, post stations) evolved into distinctive, transit-oriented cities,[18] and religious and secular organizations came to handle a complex network of advertisements, lodgings, and commercial activities providing services and selling *meibutsu* (名物, famous products).

These factors have led some scholars to speak of an early development of mass tourism in Japan.[19] One has to be wary of looking for traces of "modernity" in Edo Japan, as it is easy to fall in the traps of the idea of the "inevitability" of it. At the same time, a convincing argument can be (and has been) made about the fact that the roots of contemporary travel culture in Japan are at least partly found in the distinctive characteristics of the pre-modern industry of domestic travel. I argue that this is true not only in terms of infrastructure and of styles of travel, but also in terms of how travel was approached and how it was marketed to the public.

"The journey itself is home": Bashō wrote this in *Oku no hosomichi* [The Narrow Road to the Interior] 『おくのほそ道』 (1702)[20] in reference to his travels to the northeastern part of Japan. If one reads this statement from a Buddhist perspective,[21] Bashō can be said to equate departure from one's material, everyday home to freedom from fixity and to the discovery one's true home: the awakening of the mind. "Home", at the same time, may also be understood as the home of cultural (poetic) memory, with which Bashō establishes an intertextual dialogue and which he himself expands with his wanderings (by dialoguing with his contemporaries and including commoners and provinces

---

(Basingstoke: Palgrave Macmillan UK, 1993), p. 9.

18   On the transit-oriented nature of Edo urbanism, see Iderlina Mateo-Babiano, 'How is Urbanism Socially Constructed? An examination of Japan's Post Stations', *Journal of Urban Design* 23-3 (2018), pp. 395-413.

19   Funck and Cooper, among others, argue this idea. See Carolin Funck and Malcolm Cooper, *Japanese Tourism*, cit., p. 10.

20   Sam Hamill, *Narrow Road to the Interior and Other Writings* (Boston & London: Shambhala Publications, 2000), p. 3.

21   See Patricia Huntington, 'Place as a Refuge: Exploring the Poetical Legacy of Matsuo Bashō', *Frontiers of Philosophy in China* 12-4 (2017), pp. 572-590.

as objects and sites of poetic production). As Thomas Heyd highlights,[22] "home" is at the heart of Bashō's poetic journey, as it is at the heart of any journey, and in another sense is also rooted in the interdependent notions of "place" and "space" (as defined by Foucault): place as a well-known location, from which one departs, and space as an unknown location, an "other". The (poet-)traveler fulfills an important role in the cultural life of his community, as he provides a perspective on space, which in turn gives place, the here and now, a horizon that defines it. Travel becomes in this sense a reinvention, a rediscovery of "home" in relation to an "other", be it the cultural memory of a poetic past or an unknown space.

Bashō was an educated traveler, moving across Japan in an age when travel was only just becoming common. By the end of the eighteenth century, the backgrounds of people who embarked in travel had become more varied and the reasons that motivated them more complex. Still, some of his insights resonate with the way travelers approached their journeys in the second half of the Edo period. As Nenzi illustrates,[23] travelers from the cultured strata of the population kept placing emphasis on the sacred and literary-charged dimensions of the landscape. The majority of commoners, who didn't have access to higher levels of education, tended on the other hand to appropriate space through entertainment and commercial transactions, in a way that prompted destinations, *meisho* in particular, to evolve from sacred and lyrically charged spaces into "travel packages", the product of complex marketing strategies where cultural precedents were promoted hand in hand with commercial facilities and attractions. As Robert Goree suggests,[24] the separation between these two dimensions of recreational travel might not have always been so

---

22   Thomas Heyd, 'Bashō and the Aesthetics of Wandering: Recuperating Space, Recognizing Place, and Following the Ways of the Universe', *Philosophy East and West* 53-3 (2003), pp. 291-307.

23   Laura Nenzi, 'Cultured Travelers and Consumer Tourists in Edo-Period Sagami', *Monumenta Nipponica* 59-3 (2004), pp. 285-319.

24   Robert Goree, 'Meisho zue and the Mapping of Prosperity in Late Tokugawa Japan', *Cross-Currents: East Asian History and Culture Review* 6-2 (2017), pp. 404-439.

neat: less educated travellers might have enjoyed the "cultured" aura of famous places, provided that it was "packaged" in a way that was palatable for them, while educated travelers might have enjoyed the more mundane aspects of their visit, in combination with its cultural dimension.

The cultural allure of *meisho* and the promise of entertainment were probably coupled with another, subtler reason for enjoying travel. As seen above, a journey tends to be a liminal experience, in that it involves a removal from the ordinary patterns of everyday life. This, in the Edo period, included a separation from the official way in which space was organized, with its emphasis on fixed status boundaries, and on limited social and geographical mobility. Nenzi,[25] who analyses travel in Edo Japan from the perspective of gender, offers some telling examples of how female travelers challenged legal codes and societal expectations (pretending, for example to be someone else, wandering nuns, or even men in order to obtain passage through *sekisho*). In some cases, above all in the final years of the Edo period and in contexts where a partial immunity was granted to travelers thanks to the involvement of religion, authorities seem to have closed their eyes to behaviors that were openly defiant:

> There were about fifty young women from Osaka, each carrying a ladle [to collect alms]. The blackening had fallen off and their teeth were white. They were all clad in the same outfits with white leggings on their shins. They wore male pongee clothes and pulled up their cuffs with velvet sashes used by men. They also wore silk crepe loincloths and tied their hair in a knot, like men. They hooded their heads with bleached cotton towels and wrote *Okagemairi* [pilgrimage to Ise] on their hats. Each carried a banner that proclaimed "Runaway Pilgrim".[26]

Of course, the change in identity was not material but illusory, and it was only temporary. However, one could argue for the long-lasting psychological effects of such a recreation, which had an almost carnivalesque twist to it. In this sense, while the practice of travel probably did not cause general social disruption, at a

---

25   Laura Nenzi, *Excursions in identity*, cit., pp. 72-91.
26   Laura Nenzi, *Excursions in identity*, cit., p. 87.

psychological and metaphorical level it did offer commoners a way to flee "home", a home made of gendered family and status obligations. It, indeed, "freed" one from fixity, even if not quite in the religious sense intended by Bashō.

This applied also to those who did not *personally* embark on a journey, as the liberating effects of travel were reflected and enhanced by literature: commercial maps, published travel journals, travel narratives (including *kanazōshi* 仮名草子 and *ukiyozōshi* 浮世草子), and "guides" such as *meisho zue*. These works became a way to relive travel, or to indirectly and vicariously experience it, when the actual experience was impractical (for material or legal reasons). This indirect experience was not necessarily less impactful than the real one and had wide resonance as travel literature. Thanks to the growth of the publishing industry and to the diffusion of literacy, this literature found a growing readership in the Edo period. Mary E. Berry speaks in this regard of the birth of a "Library of Public information", a sort of metaphorical space for all those early modern sources that fit together because of their "common purpose to examine and order the verifiable facts of contemporary experience, for an open audience of consumers".[27] This audience came to share common interests and a common social lexicon: to develop, in other words, something akin to a common social knowledge. Travel literature is a mirror of this knowledge and of the "popular" understanding of place and space. It is also an important way to understand how travel was marketed, as, in many cases, it was the product of very deliberate editorial strategies.

Meisho zue are a particularly interesting example of these strategies. The genre consists of large format (27.2 cm x 18.8 cm) multi-volume guides to *meisho* (rarely focused on a single site, and more often on a series of sites within the area of a city or related to some other kind of topography). I use, loosely, the term "guides", but, as Robert Goree underlines,[28] the genre is not easy

---

27   Mary E. Berry, *Japan in print. Information and Nation in the Early Modern Period* (Berkeley: University of California Press, 2006), p. 15.
28   Robert Goree, '*Meisho zue* and the Mapping of Prosperity', cit., pp. 408-411.

to classify, as the books include both *zu* (図, pictures, that may as well be classified maps) and *mondan* (文談, commentaries), with descriptions, historical or legendary narrations, and poetry, all rendered in simple, accessible language. The genre was launched in 1780 by the Kyoto-born poet and editor Akisato Ritō 秋里籬嶋 with a guide to Kyoto titled *Miyako meisho zue* 『都名所図会』 and flourished well into the Meiji period, eventually producing nearly one hundred titles. [29]

Meisho zue weren't necessarily used on site: given their format, they were probably meant to be consulted before travelling, or, as Goree suggests, may have not been designed to work as reference for travel at all, but rather as a form of escapist entertainment, a way to virtually engage with the *meisho* without the dangers and expenses of an actual journey.[30] This was, as mentioned above, a not at all rare modality of travel for commoners and one that puts the books in the category of "meta-traveling" tools, that is, "artifacts that use travel as their subject matter", are "consumed in places and times other than those of the journey and capitalize on the symbolic dimensions of traveling and topography".[31] In other words, works through which travel was experienced as an *intellectual* more than as a physical practice in the context of a shared cultural horizon. This meant that, for a large section of readers, *meisho zue* not only mediated the experience of *meisho* but "created" them, and the meaning associated with them, in a way that was impacted by the strategies of their editors.

The idea of preserving the past as a component of the present, as "living historical past", was at the core of these editorial policies. *Meisho zue* introduced to readers well-established *meisho*, those that had typically acquired their status by virtue of their sacredness, their aura as *utamakura* (歌枕, places of lyrical

---

29   For an overview on the history and readership of *meisho zue*, see Robert Goree, *Fantasies of the real: Meisho zue in Early Modern Japan* (Dissertation Presented to the Faculty of the Graduate School of Yale University in Candidacy for the Degree of Doctor of Philosophy, 2010).

30   Robert Goree, *Fantasies of the real*, cit., p. 18.

31   Jilly Traganou, *The Tōkaidō Road. Traveling and representation in Edo and Meiji Japan* (New York and London: Routledge, 2004), p. 25.

interests), or their connections to historical events. At the same time, they created new associations for them, connecting them to the present, much as Bashō did in his poetic dialogue with *utamakura*. These associations could be commercial, as *meisho* were presented in their new guise of travel packages,[32] or they could be cultured: in *Tōkaidō meisho zue*, for example, the editor (Akisato) deliberately chose to give precedence in *mondan*, to contemporary poems, creating an intertextual dialogue between their cultural aura and the intellectual landscape of present Japan.[33] *Meisho zue* also created new *meisho*: usually commercial sites on the rise that, being included for the sake of faithful representation, came to acquire the same dignity as "official" *meisho*,[34] creating a landscape where the boundaries between the nostalgic enjoyment of cultural heritage and commercialization were blurred.

For the cultured, elite travelers who visited *utamakura* and basked in their lyrical resonances, nostalgia was a way to affirm their status – to indulge in a sense of a cultural superiority that emerged in their emotional and cultural connection with the poets of old. The appeal of nostalgia to commoners may in this sense have been connected with the role that travel played for them in the re-definition of their identity. The search for a golden past helped them disconnect from their status. And while the possibility to access travel varied according to material circumstances, once a space was marketed to them in accessible format, they were equal in front of it. They could play at elevating their cultural status, at traveling to a different time as well as to different places, removing themselves from the time and place socially defined by Tokugawa authorities.

Meisho zue thrived in a travel culture where the commercialization of nostalgia and cultural heritage and the

---

32   See in this regard Laura Nenzi, *Excursions in Identity*, cit., p. 141.

33   Nishino Yuki 西野由紀, 'Miyako kara Fuji ga mieta jidai. "Tōkaidō meisho zue" no mokuromi' [The Era when Mount Fuji Could Be Seen from Kyoto. The Strategy Behind "Tōkaidō meisho zue"] 「都から富士が見えた時代。東海道名所図会の目論見」, *Nihon Bungaku* 60-2 (2011), pp 21-33.

34   See in this regard Robert Goree, *Fantasies of the real*, cit., pp. 68-69.

(re-)invention of tradition were well established.[35] By the time they were produced, these marketing dynamics had become part of structured editorial strategies, which in some ways recall the deliberate narrative policies of *furusato-zukuri*. In reference to *Tōkaidō meisho zue*, for example, both Nishino Yuki[36] and Takada Mamoru[37] speak of an editorial strategy meant to showcase the "cultural advantage of Kyoto over Edo" (江戸に対する京の、文化的優位性),[38] which is revealed for example in the prominence given to Kyoto poets and in the way Mount Fuji, one of the central symbols of Edo, is always represented in strict association with the imperial capital. Goree, more generally, speaks of *meisho zue* as ways through which editors engaged in a "larger project of cultural geography that normalizes a vision of prosperity":[39] that is, works that built a very deliberate narrative that projected an idea of richness and peace over Japan, which probably served the scopes of both the editors (as it enhanced the pleasure of daydreaming about travel, and therefore the appeal of the books) and of the Tokugawa *bakufu* that approved their publication (as it underscored the efficacy of the Tokugawa rule, and at the same time provided the public with a "controlled" form of escapism).

In this sense, *meisho zue* constructed "proto-national" collective narratives, where the past was showcased to reach expressly strategic effects in the present. Their impact is better understood when one considers that *meisho zue* came to represent much of the Japanese archipelago (with the exclusion of Ezo) and reached a vast readership, as they were mostly produced

---

35 Nenzi reports for example that, as early as 1680, the Hachimangū shrine in Kamakura, famous for its association with the assassination of Minamoto no Sanetomo, offered the possibility to attend a *kagura* performance that was presented as a tradition of the shrine, but was, in fact, a commercial production, enacted by innkeepers dressed as Shinto Priests. Laura Nenzi, *Excursions in Identity*, cit., p. 141.

36 Nishino Yuki, 'Miyako kara Fuji ga mieta jidai', cit..

37 Takada Mamoru高田衛, 'Kumitateshiki "kinsei" to iu kūkan no hanashi. "Tōkaidō meisho zue" shigo.' [Fabricated Modernity: The Space of Tōkaidō-meisho-zukai] 「組み立て式「近世」という空間の話 : 『東海道名所図会』私語」, *Nihon Bungaku* 53-10 (2004), pp. 22-32.

38 Takada Mamoru, 'Kumitateshiki "kinsei" to iu kūkan no hanashi', cit., p. 24.

39 Robert Goree, '*Meisho zue* and the Mapping of Prosperity', cit., p. 408.

in peripheral areas but were available in lending libraries and frequently on sale in the major cities of Edo, Kyoto, Osaka and Nagoya.[40] It can rightly be said that they account widely for what might have been the "popular" perception of space at the time: a space that they turned into "place", making it familiar for a vast audience.[41] At the same time, through that space, place – that is "home" – was re-defined: as Matthew W. Shores observes,[42] travel and the popular culture that surrounded it enhanced the commoners' sense of regional identity through the consciousness of difference, laying the foundation for a geographical identity that was part regional and part national.

In this sense, the mapping of *meisho* is akin to the mapping of *furusato* in the multi-layered meanings associated with the term: it is a mapping of a collective past that affects the present. As catering to the desire of travelers by turning them into an object of consumption is a feature of mass tourism, these similarities also add weight to the idea that some of the roots of contemporary travel culture can be found in the Edo period.

Of course, *furusato*, as built in popular interpretations and through the policies of tourism since the 1970s, is very different in nature from the *meisho* of the Tokugawa period. One, moreover, should not forget that *furusato-zukuri* happened though a concerted effort that had very much to do with national image and were undertaken in the context of a modern nation-state, while the policies promoting Tokugawa travel were the

---

40   Robert Goree, *Fantasies of the real*, cit., p. 3.
41   They were, on the other hand, only one of the ways in which "space" was appropriated and turned into "place". Another instance of this were, for example, *Fujizuka* (富士塚, artificial replicas of Mount Fuji), used both as a pilgrimage site in place of the real Fuji and as a recreation site, and which by the end of the Edo period numbered 60 in Edo alone and about 200 in the surrounding areas. Byron H. Earhart, *Mount Fuji: Icon of Japan* (Columbia: University of South Carolina Press, 2011), p. 75. The idea that shaped Fujizuka was, once again, that the essence, the cultural heritage of famous places, could be captured, allowing travelers that couldn't reach the place itself to "live" its atmosphere in a vicarious way.
42   Matthew W. Shores, 'Travel and "Tabibanashi" in the Early Modern Period: Forming Japanese Geographic Identity', *Asian Theatre Journal* 25-1 (2008), pp. 101-121.

result of the scattered efforts of different editors and locations. Still, the early-modern works created a map of landmarks that, coming to be part of the "library of public information", added to a "proto-national" understanding of a previously unknown space, which became place or "home".

Davide Bitti[1]

FROM IBARAKI TO EDO/TOKYO

How the Earthquake Catfish Found a New Home in the Capital

Japan, an archipelago positioned between several tectonic plates, has always been plagued by violent earthquakes. This, naturally, has influenced the life of its inhabitants, becoming part of the religion and the folklore of Japan and giving birth to a variety of myths and beliefs. In this article, I will focus on one of these: the legend of the "Earthquake catfish", also known as *Jishin namazu* (地震鯰), and its three main elements: the *Jishin namazu* itself, the god *Kashima daimyōjin* (鹿島大明神) and the stone called *Kanameishi* (要石), all still well-known in Japan today and part of the folklore of the *Kashima jingū* (鹿島神宮, Kashima Shrine) in the northern Kantō prefecture of Ibaraki. In connection with the theme of *furusato*, the *namazu* provides an interesting example of the mutability of legends and their geographic associations, their homes.

According to the legend, the god of the Kashima Shrine, the *Kashima daimyōjin,* uses the *Kanameishi* to keep the *Jishin namazu* still and to prevent it from creating earthquakes with its movements. Therefore, the role of the god of the shrine is to protect the land from earthquakes. However, over time this function of a local deity, venerated in a local shrine in Ibaraki, was extended to that of the protector of the entire country from the natural disasters brought by the *namazu*. This transformation expanded the scale of the local myth and established the conditions for the legend to spread across Japan.

In truth, the *Kanameishi* was already part of the folklore in various parts of Japan. For example, in a map dated 1624, the

---

Dainihonkoku jishin no zu (「大日本国地震之図」), a huge
dragon encircles the Japanese archipelago and is depicted with a
Kanameishi laid on its head. That is because, before the *namazu,*
dragons were associated with the origins of earthquakes.
However, some question exists as to whether the *Kanameishi* still
found at the Kashima shrine today is the same stone represented
in the legend of the *Jishin namazu.* The stone appears also in the
Kashimagūsha rei denki (『鹿島宮社例伝記』), records of the
Kashima shrine from the Kamakura period (鎌倉時代, *Kamakura
jidai*, 1185–1333). In those records, the *Kanameishi* of the shrine
is connected directly with the *Konrinzai* (金輪際), the pillar
whose base rests at the very bottom of the earth in the Buddhist
cosmology. Thus, the *namazu*'s movements, when it worked
itself free of the stone, shook the pillar and caused earthquakes.
Kanameishi can also be found in other shrines like the *Katori
shrine* (香取神社) in Chiba prefecture (千葉県), but it is important
to note that records of the *Kanameishi* of *Kashima*, that used by
the *Kashima daimyōjin*, can be found in documents dating back
much further than those connected with other shrines. Also, the
namazu as a supernatural creature unconnected with earthquakes
is associated with other shrines like the *Tsukubusuma jinja* (都
久夫須麻神社) on Chikubushima (竹生島), a small island in the
Lake Biwa (琵琶湖) that many believed was protected by a huge
namazu. A number of shrines in Kyūshū, like the *Toyotamahime
jinja* (豊玉姫神社) or the *Otohime jinja* (乙姫神社), have their
own connections to the *namazu* in its role as the messenger of the

gods. This article, however, places its focus on only the legend connected with the *Kashima daimyōjin* that, while well known in various parts in Japan in earlier times, became part of the culture of Edo only after the events introduced in the next paragraph.

After the Ansei Edo earthquake in the middle of the 19th century, the legend of the *namazu* spread more widely than it ever had before as the main theme of the *namazu-e* (鯰絵, catfish images) woodprints that flooded Edo in the wake of the disaster. The earthquake struck on November 11th, 1855, destroying a significant part of the city and claiming many lives, especially among the red light district workers and other inhabitants of the *Shin'yoshiwara* (新吉原) area. Shortly after the earthquake, and seemingly at odds with the tragic effects of the disaster on the city and its people, a considerable variety of woodprints depicting the legend of the *Jishin namazu*, commenting on the post-quake situation, and often directing ironic humor towards it began to appear throughout the city.

This paper examines various *namazu-e* in order to explore how the *namazu* legend, tied to the Kashima shrine in Ibaraki, became the symbol of a natural disaster that happened in Edo. The links between the Edo prints produced after the earthquake, tied in image and word to the city in which they were produced, and the *Jishin namazu* legend, tightly bound to the Kashima shrine, will provide a window onto the processes by which the *furusato* (故郷, hometown) of the *namazu* shifted from Ibaraki to Edo, even as it continued to maintain solid roots at the original shrine.

But first, it is important to understand how the people of Edo came to know about the legend at all and why it only circulated actively in the capital after this particular earthquake. In Edo, the legend of the *Jishin namazu* enjoyed enduring popularity thanks to the *kabuki jūhachiban* (歌舞伎十八番) play *Shibaraku* (『暫く』), in which the *Jishin namazu* appears as a character named *Namazubōzu* (鯰坊主) or *Kashima nyūdō shinsai* (鹿島入道震斎) and is an integral part of the story. Even before its enshrining in *kabuki* popular culture, however, the earthquake catfish was already integrated into the fabric of the capital. Among the floats

paraded around the city in the *Kanda matsuri* (神田祭, Kanda shrine festival) there is one depicting the *Jishin namazu* with the *Kanameishi* on its back, pinning it down. Images of this float are preserved in the *Kanda myōjin sairei emaki* (『神田明神祭礼絵巻』 Picture Scroll of the festival of the glorious Kanda deity). The strength and longevity of the links between the *Kanda* shrine and *namazu* are attested to by the fact that one can still buy *Jishin namazu* amulets at the shrine today.

People in Edo, therefore, were already familiar with the *Jishin namazu*, but why did the *namazu-e* start to spread only after the earthquake of November 1855? In answering this question, the date of the earthquake is key. On the premodern Japanese calendar, the earthquake actually happened not in November but in the tenth month, which was also known as *Kannazuki* (神無月), the month without gods. It was believed that in the tenth month, the gods from all over the country gathered at the *Izumo taisha* (出雲大社, Izumo shrine) to talk about the happenings of the whole year. So, except for the god of *Izumo*, who hosted the congress, all the other gods, including the Kashima deity, were believed to have left their shrines "empty" for the duration of the month. This, then, was the factor that brought the *namazu-e* to Edo. The people of the city, accustomed to the legend of the *Jishin namazu* and the role of the *Kashima myōjin* in keeping it motionless, saw in the absence of the god from the shrine a cause for the earthquake. With the god in conference with the other deities at the *Izumo* shrine, the *namazu* was left without impediment, allowed to move freely under the Japanese soil and to create the devastating earthquake. This was the starting point for the *namazu-e* and the element that created the conditions for the *furusato* of the *namazu* to move from *Ibaraki* to *Edo*.

As the first *namazu-e* under consideration here, we will begin with the example that is most obviously related to the core legend, the print called "*Kashima kanameishi shinzu*" (『鹿嶋要石真図』 "The real image of the *Kanameishi* of Kashima"). This work depicts the Kashima *daimyōjin* restraining the *namazu*, standing upon the creature's head and pinning it to the ground with his sword. In the background, the *Kanameishi* is shown protected by a fence at the Kashima shrine and from it emits a white line that connects it with the deity in the foreground.

The positioning of the god and its use of the sword is not unusual as the *Kashima daimyōjin*, also known as *Takemikazuchi no ono kami* (建御雷之男神), is known as a god of swords. The *namazu* pushed to the ground by the god remains still, and several working tools and coins are scattered all around it. It is clear that the *Kashima daimyōjin* came back to resume his role restraining the fish in a hurry, his speedy return attested to by the kinetic lines that go from behind the *Kanameishi* to the feet of the god, blocking the *namazu*. The coins and various tools surrounding the couplet of god and fish represent a recurring theme in *namazu-e*, making reference to how, while it inflicted harm on many people, the earthquake also bestowed financial benefit to others, particularly those in the building trades, by prompting the reconstruction of large swathes of *Edo*.

The next *namazu-e* is even more symbolic, and is called "*Ara ureshi taianhi ni yurinaosu*" (『あら嬉し大安日にゆり直す』 "What a joy, the lucky days will be back"). Here, the three central elements of the legend are the focus of the scene.

This time, the *Kashima daimyōjin* is effectively pinning the large *namazu* with the *Kanameishi*. More interesting than this standard arrangement, however, are the three small catfish in the right corner of the print bowed in obeisance to the god. This trio is interpreted as representations of the aftershocks of the main quake, a typical way to depict them graphically in *namazu-e*. The small *namazu*, happy at the return of the God, are apologizing for their behavior and claiming that they did not actually want to harm people. For them, the actual problem at the time was that boiled catfish started to lose popularity in *Edo* as a dish in favor of *dojō* (ドジョウ), a fish that had apparently become very popular. Therefore, the catfish moved in response to this trend without thinking about the consequences. But now that the god was back, they pledged to stay calm forever. This *namazu-e* is an example of a type that tries to handle the earthquake in a humorous way. As in other similar works, small details like the changing tastes of the people of *Edo* open a window on the habits and costumes of the era.

The next piece presented for discussion is *"Edo namazu to shinshū namazu"* (『江戸鯰と信州鯰』 "The catfish of Edo and the catfish of Shinshū"), a work that shows even more clearly the transition in the *furusato* of the legend from Ibaraki to Edo. In the print, two huge *namazu*, one with the *kanji* (漢字) for Edo and the other with that for Shinshū printed on their foreheads, are being attacked physically and verbally by a crowd of people. The Edo *namazu* represents the Ansei earthquake while that labelled Shinshū is associated with the *Zenkōji jishin* (善光寺地震, Zenkōji earthquake) of 1847. The people around the two fish are mostly composed of workers who lost their jobs due to the disasters and are now trying to kill the *namazu* with their working tools. A closer look, however, reveals that not everyone has the same murderous intentions. The man on the left side, a craftsman, screams at the crowd to stop this behavior or he will be in trouble, since without the quake, he will lose his coming work in the reconstruction. This is an example of the ways that *namazu-e* often criticized the people who were seen as taking advantage of the earthquake's destruction and reaping profits from the misery it caused. Nevertheless, the most important element

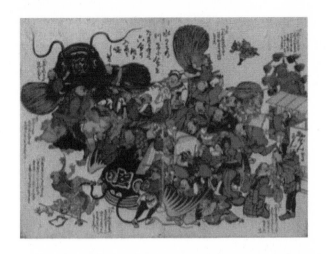

in the print is in the upper right corner. The character is running desperately towards the scuffle screaming, "This is terrible! I have to put a stop to it quickly." (「これはたいへん、早くいってお さえてやらねばなるめえ」, "*Kore ha taihen, hayaku itte osaete yaraneba narumee*"). This is the *Kashima daimyōjin* rushing back from Izumo to stop the earthquake catfish. Here, then, is a very clear representation of the earthquake that destroyed Edo – and the one that destroyed Shinshū earlier – in the form of a catfish and the God himself rushing to stop it. The fact that the two catfish display the names of the cities in which the disasters occurred on their foreheads shows a shift in the *furusato* of the *namazu*, as in this specific picture the fish represent earthquakes that struck two regions remote from Ibaraki. At the same time, the *Kashima daimyōjin* hurrying to stop them indicates that the management of the earthquake catfish is still very much a duty of the god of Ibaraki.

A very similar print is "*Shin'yoshiwara dainamazu yurahi*" (『しんよし原大なまづゆらひ』 "The origin of the *namazu* of Shin'yoshiwara"), which portrays a situation almost identical to that of the previous example but for the absence of the *Kashima daimyōjin*. The scene here is set in the pleasure district of *Shin'yoshiwara* (新吉原), which suffered severe damage from the Ansei earthquake. As in "*Edo namazu to shinshū namazu*", most of the people depicted in the print are attacking the fish using their

working tools, yelling words of hate and violence while trying to kill the *namazu* and his small double on the right (a representation of the aftershocks, similar to those seen in *"Ara ureshi taianhi ni yurinaosu"*). Nevertheless, as in the previous print, there are some people who actually want the *namazu* to live. Three figures in the upper right corner of the image hold the typical tools for fighting fires and run in the direction of the brawl yelling at the crowd to stop attacking the fish.

The next print to be treated is titled *Shibaraku no sotone* (『し ばらくのそとね』 "A brief nap outside"). As discussed above, the legend of the *namazu* was already well known in Edo thanks to the *kabuki* theatre and the play *Shibaraku*. As can be seen in the title the print, the inspiration for its title and theme comes directly from the *kabuki* play. In particular, the work is a parody of *Shibaraku no tsurane* (『暫の連ね』 "the Shibaraku/brief soliloquey"), trading out the word *"tsurane"* (a particular kind of monologue in a kabuki play) for *"sotone"* (outdoor sleep). In the original play, the protagonist begins this monologue by entering onstage and yelling *"Shibaraku"* (暫く). Here again all the three main elements of the legend are represented in the print, this time decked out in elements of *kabuki*, as though the work were depicting an actual play. Notably, the *namazu* is extremely humanized in this representation, with a human face, arms and clothing, but attached to a large fish tail. The title of the *namazu-e* is not only a reference to drama but also a play on words, as it could be understood as "sleeping outdoors for the time being," a reference to the fact that the extensive damage and destruction that the earthquake caused all around *Edo* meant that many would have to sleep outside. The print also states in text that no one in the city escaped injury, and conditions in various areas of the city like *Shin'yoshiwara* are explained in detail. Here, the use of both the legend and the *kabuki* play become useful tools to explain to the print's audience the post-earthquake situation of *Edo* using symbols with which they were already familiar.

In these ways did *namazu-e* depict the legend of the earthquake catfish. Sometimes all the elements of the original legend were present at the same time, and sometimes only the catfish appeared prominently in the scene. Regardless, it is clear that this legend, originally so strongly associated with the *Kashima* shrine in Ibaraki, became part of the folklore of Edo. While the legend of the *Jishin namazu* was already known in Edo and in other regions of Japan thanks, for example, to the *Shibaraku no tsurane* play, and the *namazu* itself was already considered a creature related to divinities and earthquakes in other shrines, with the *Namazu*-e we can see those symbols, clearly related directly to the *Kashima jingū*, moving toward an Edo context. As examined above, the Kashima god runs from his shrine to try to save the infuriated Edo people in the print *Edo namazu to shinshū namazu*. Similarly, in *Ara ureshi taianhi ni yurinaosu* several small *namazu* ask forgiveness from the god and explain to him that they caused the earthquake because of changing culinary trends in Edo. Those symbols, once only related to the Ibaraki shrine and its specific myth, became the means of narrating the post-earthquake situation in the capital. They were mobilized to relate the events of the Ansei earthquake to people both within and outside of Edo in an idiom that adopted distinctive elements of the people, costumes, and culture of the city. These symbols then became related to earthquakes, not only in the capital, but on a wider, national scale.

This shift that arose in the Ansei earthquake prints continues in the present day. In recent years, the *Jishin namazu* has become a symbol not only associated with earthquakes and their destruction, but also with disaster prevention. Walking in Tokyo, it is not unusual to see road signs for earthquake prevention depicting a cartoonish *namazu*, and catfish are used across the country as mascots for such things as the anti-seismic systems for buildings and firefighters, as in Aichi prefecture. There are even videogames, *anime*, *manga*, and mascot characters depicting the *Jishin namazu* in present times.

But what is there about this legend that makes it so adaptable? As discussed, the *namazu* was already well known in the Edo period, in the Ansei era in particular, and the catfish was recognized as a symbol of earthquakes among the masses thanks to Edo shrines like the *Kandamyōjin* that still today use it as a charm against natural calamities. The authors of the *namazu-e*, working in the immediate aftermath of the earthquake and portraying the catfish as a personification of the disaster, were able to convey their messages, their satirical commentary, and their stories in a concrete and direct way using it as a graphical metaphor that they could be confident would be understood at a glance. As a result, we have *namazu-e* depicting a famous nightlife area of Edo and its workers, who are trying to kill the great catfish of Kashima, all to create a satirical work making reference to the actual situation following the disaster that no one in the capital was likely to misinterpret. Similarly, later generations took *namazu* as the incarnation of earthquakes generally, giving this variety of disaster a shape and a face, allowing it to be fought and protested against, and creating an object towards which people can express the complicated range of feelings that earthquakes and related disasters elicit. These factors together provided a foundation that enabled the namazu first to find a new home in Edo, then to plant roots across the country that continue to the present.

Bibliography:

Cornelis Ouwehand, *Namazue minzokutekina sōzōryoku no sekai* [Namazue, A world of ethnic immagination] 『鯰絵・民族的な想像力の世界』(Tokyo: Iwanami Bunko 岩波文庫, 2013; 1st edition by Serika Shobō セリカ書房, 1979).

Kuroda Hideo黒田日出男, *Ryū no sumu nihon* [Japan, where dragons live] 『龍の棲む日本』(Tokyo: Iwanami shoten, 2003).

Wakamizu Suguru 若水俊, *Ansei yoshiwara hanjō-ki dai jishin to yūkaku* [Records of Yoshiwara in the Ansei period, the great earthquake and the red-light district] 『安政吉原繁盛記 大地震と遊郭』(Tokyo: Kadokawa gakugei shuppan 角川学芸出版, 2010).

Kawanabe Hiroya 川那部浩哉, Maehata Masayoshi 前畑政善, Miyamoto Shinji 宮本真二 (ed. by), *Namazu - imeeji to sono sugao* [Namazu - Its image and its real face] 『鯰―イメージとその素顔』(Tokyo: Yasaka Shobo 八坂書房, 2008).

Akishinonomiya Fumihito秋篠宮文仁, Ogata Yoshio 緒方喜雄, Mori Seiichi 森誠一 (ed. by), *Namazu no hakuran-shi (Ikimono bunka-shi sensho)* [Namazu exposition magazine (creature's selected cultural magazine)]『ナマズの博覧誌』(生き物文化誌選書) (Tokyo: Seibundō-shinkōsha 誠文堂新光社, 2016).

Kawaraban・Namazue ni miru edo・Meiji no saigai jōhō - Ishimoto korekushon kara [Edo and the informations about the Meiji Earthquake as seen through Kawaraban and Namazu-e – From the Ishimoto Collection]「かわら版・鯰絵にみる江戸・明治の災害情報－石本コレクションから」University of Tokyo Library System - www-old.lib.u-tokyo.ac.jp/ -

PART IV
FURUSATO IN LITERATURE

KUROIWA TAKU 黒岩卓[1]

FURUSATO IN THE FIRST JAPANESE TRANSLATION OF THE *SONG OF ROLAND* BY BAN TAKEO

Introduction

The *Song of Roland*, probably composed in the 11th century in its original form, is known as the first masterpiece of French Literature.[2] Appreciation of this epic as a "national" work dates from the first half of the 19th century, when French philologists discovered it and considered it a worthy literary monument that could reinvigorate the patriotic spirit of the French people, especially after their

---

1   This work was supported by JSPS KAKENHI Grant Number JP 17K02583. In the introduction and the first chapter of this paper, we adopt some passages from one of our previous papers: Taku Kuroiwa, 'Présence de la Chanson de Roland dans le Japon moderne: les premières présentation et traductions (MAEDA, BAN, SATŌ)' [Presence of the Song of Roland in modern Japan: the first presentations and translations], in *Le Recueil Ouvert*, online, Grenoble Alpes University (2017).

2   The outline of the epic is as follows: "Charlemagne has conquered almost the whole of Spain, but the city of Saragossa remains standing against him. After deliberation, he decides to conduct peace negotiations, and Ganelon, the father-in-law of Roland, is named the ambassador. Charlemagne begins to return to France by leaving the rear-guard behind, to which Roland was nominated as commander. Because of the betrayal by Ganelon, who has become an accomplice of the Saracens, this rear-guard is attacked by considerably large enemy troops. Two thousand Christians, including Roland and his friend Olivier, fight bravely but die in the end. Before his death, Roland blows the horn to make Charlemagne and his troops return to the battlefield, and they annihilate the Saracens. After the battle, Ganelon is tried and given the punishment of being cut into pieces" (translation of a resume by Harano Noboru 原野昇, 'Rōran no uta' [The Song of Roland] 「ローランの歌」, in *Furansu chūsei bungaku wo manabu hito no tameni* [Introduction to the study of French Medieval Literature] 『フランス中世文学を学ぶ人のために』 (Kyoto: Sekaishisōsha 世界思想社, 2005), p. 24).

defeat in the Franco-Prussian War of 1871. In this sense, modern French philology has charged the *Song of Roland* with nationalistic functions since its discovery.[3] However, it should be noted that the death of the heroes in the battle against the Muslims was also considered martyrdom for Christianity in this epic;[4] thus, as we can see in the 176th *laisse* (stanza), the hero of the epic, Roland, goes to the kingdom of heaven after death. This amalgam of secular and religious inspirations has certainly contributed to ensuring the longevity of the work into the modern period.[5]

As we can readily suppose, this religious background could not be fully apprehended by Japanese audiences in the first half of the 20th century, which was when this French epic was introduced in Japan. At the beginning of the century, Maeda Chōta 前田長 太 had explained the love of God and Church among Occidental knights in the Middle Ages as an Occidental variation of the Japanese notion of *chūkun-aikoku* (忠君愛國, fidelity to the lord and love for the country).[6] This kind of transposition, which minimizes the importance of the vertical relationship with the Single God and equates Him with temporal sovereigns, is always present, even in analyses of Japanese translations of the *Song*

---

3   Regarding the status of this epic in France in the modern period, see Marie-Madeleine Castellani, 'Roland, héros de la Patrie française dans les préfaces aux traductions de la *Chanson de Roland* (1870-1919)' [Roland, the hero of the French Patria in the prefaces for the translations of the Song of Roland (1870–1919)], in Caroline Cazanave and France Marchal-Ninosque (ed. by), *Mourir pour des idées* (Besançon: Presses Universitaires de Franche-Compté, 2008), pp. 189-205; Tania van Hemelryck, 'La *Chanson de Roland* aux XIXe, XXe et XXIe siècles. De la glorification nationale à l'instrumentalisation idéologique' [The Song of Roland in 19th, 20th, and 21st centuries. From national glorification to ideological instrumentalization], *Interférences littéraires*, nouvelle série, n. 3 (novembre 2009), pp. 27-35; Isabel N. Di Vanna, 'Politicizing national literature: the scholarly debate around *La chanson de Roland* in the nineteenth century', *Historical Research* 84 (2011), pp. 109-134.

4   For discussion about the origin of inspirations for the *Song of Roland*, see Julian Eugene White, '*La Chanson de Roland*. Secular or religious inspiration?', *Romania* 84, 335 (1963), pp. 398-408.

5   See Di Vanna, cit., pp. 25-26.

6   Maeda Chōta 前田長太 (ed. and trans. by), *Seiyō bushidō* [*The way of Western samurai*] 『西洋武士道』 (Tokyo: Hakubunkan 博文館, 1909), p. 55.

of Roland.[7] Indeed, we invariably find modifications facilitating the acceptance of the epic by members of Japanese society, and this is also the case for the first translation by Ban Takeo 坂丈緒, which makes several notable uses of the word *furusato* (故郷).[8] What, then, are the effects and the meaning of this word as used by Ban when representing the French Middle Ages in Japanese for Japanese readers?

To answer this question, we will begin with a brief introduction to the translation and the translator. Next, we will analyze the occurrences of the word *furusato* and describe how this word is used in the first Japanese translation of the *Song of Roland*. Finally, we will review the meanings of the word that can be derived by its usage in Ban's other writings, as well as in Japanese society of the time.

I. *Ban Takeo and his cultural heritage*[9]

The first Japanese translation of the *Song of Roland*, completed by Ban Takeo, appeared in January 1941. However, according to the standards of French literature studies, the volume –

---

7   We previously investigated the manner of translating calls for God in the first three Japanese translations of the epic. See Kuroiwa Taku 黒岩卓, '*Rōran no uta* sanshu no nihongoyaku ni tsuite no oboegaki' [Notes about three Japanese translations of the *Song of Roland*] 「『ローランの歌』三種の日本語訳についての覚書」, in *Tasha wo meguru shikō to hyōgen* [*Thinking and representation around the Other*] 『他者をめぐる思考と表現』 (Sendai: Tohoku University, Institute of Arts and Letters, Department of French Language and Literature/GPJS International Workshops division, 2017), pp. 1-12.

8   Ban Takeo 坂丈緒 (trans. by), *Rōran no uta. Kaikyō sensō* [*The Song of Roland: Islamic War*] 『ロオランの歌 回教戦争』 (Tokyo: Ars, 1941). There is a Japanese adaptation of this epic by Nobori Shōmu 昇曙夢 published in 1928, but, apparently, it is not based on an old French text (see Kuroiwa, 'Présence de la *Chanson de Roland* dans le Japon moderne', cit., note 2).

9   Regarding this first translation of the *Song of Roland*, we have two pioneering contributions by Harano Noboru 原野昇: see Harano Noboru, 'Historique de l'étude des chansons de geste françaises au Japon' [Chronicle of the study of French *chansons de geste* in Japan], in *Mélanges de langue et de littérature du Moyen Âge offerts à Teruo Sato* (Tokyo: la Comité de Publication des Mélanges Sato II, 1993), pp. 11-17; Harano Noboru, '*Roran no uta* ni miru

though not necessarily the translation in and of itself – appears somehow strange. First, let us look at the title, *Roran no uta. Kaikyō sensō* [*The Song of Roland: Islamic War*] 『ロオランの歌 回教戦争』. This arresting title was a consequence of the nature of the collection in which the work was integrated. As the first volume of *Sekai sensō bungaku zenshū* [Collection of the World's War Literature] 世界戦争文學全集, edited by *Sensō bungakukai* [Association of War Literature] 戦争文学會, this volume aimed to devaluate Occidental civilization in general and demonstrate the superiority of Asiatic civilizations, including those founded upon Islam. This propagandist tendency is strongly present in the abundant annexes to the translation, written by commentators other than the translator. These also include publicities of many pro-governmental works, such as *Nachisu sōsho* [The Nazi Collection] ナチス叢書.

Nevertheless, we have to emphasize the accuracy of the translation, which marks a remarkable contrast to the flood of propagandist discourses in this volume. At the very least, we can affirm that the translation is diligently loyal to the modern French translation by the editor of the original text, Joseph Bédier, despite some peculiar word choices (as will be noted below). The translator's philological and historical commentaries on the epic are numerous, and his conscientious efforts to present in Japanese an outline of the French philological study of the *Song of Roland* are undeniable. Thus, the contrast between the scientific quality imbued by the translator and the arbitrariness of the framework of the entire book presents a surprising and incongruent character.

Without entering into a detailed description of his life, it should be specified that the translator, Ban Takeo, had a hybrid

---

ibunka' [Foreign culture in the *Song of Roland*] 「『ロランの歌』に見る異 文化」, in *Chūsei Yōroppa ni miru ibunka sesshoku* [Cultural exchanges in Medieval Europe] 『中世ヨーロッパに見る異文化接触』 (Hiroshima: Keisuisha 渓水社, 2000), pp. 7-53. (This article is republished in Harano Noboru, *Furansu Chūsei no bungaku* [*Literature in Medieval France*] 『フ ランス中世の文学』 (Hiroshima: Hiroshima daigaku shuppankai 広島大学出 版会, 2005), pp. 165-204.)

cultural background and was familiar with Japanese Classics.[10]
Ban reveals how he sometimes had to explore the antique
vocabulary of earlier Japanese literature in his translation of the
Song of Roland, as we can see below:

> 譯文が多少擬古的になり過ぎた嫌ひがあるが，それは
> 一つには古代佛蘭西語で書かれたこの古い物語の調子に引
> 摺られたせゐであり，一つには又，語感の新し過ぎる言葉
> は，如何に翻譯と雖も避けたかつたので，何れの時代にも
> 存在しなかつたやうな，かゝる奇妙な文體が出來上つた次
> 第である。武具，馬具を始め服裝や風俗を示す單語は，出
> 來るだけそれに近い物を示す和名を用ひ，又さう云ふ物の
> 名所の全く日本に存在しない物には，譯者が適當と考へた
> 和名を發明するより外なかつた。これは何れにしても一種
> の符牒に過ぎないから，それ等が實際何んなものであつた
> かは，別項の説明と圖版によつて出來るだけ明かにして置
> いた積りである。[11]

Perhaps I have made the style of the translation too archaistic. On the
one hand, it is because I was influenced by the tone of this old story written
in old French; on the other hand, it is because I did not want to use words
which sound too modern, although the key purpose was translation. That is
why I created this strange style which had not been utilized in any period.
For the words designating the arms, harness, clothing, and other things, I
tried to use, as much as possible, Japanese words which designate similar
items. When I could not find any, I was obliged to invent new Japanese
words which seemed adequate. In any event, all these words are no more
than signs, and I tried to show, as much as possible, what these words
signified at the time via explanations and images that I grouped separately.

---

10 Born in 1904 as the second son of Ban Masaomi 阪正臣, notorious poète of
    waka, Ban Takeo was educated at the Athénée français, a famous private
    school of French and French Culture, where he studied French, Latin, and
    Greek. He would have thus been familiar with both Japanese and European
    cultural traditions, as shown in his earlier writings. He stayed in Paris in the
    1930s on a scholarship from the French government, and there he studied
    French philology with several prestigious *philologues* of the time, including
    Joseph Bédier, editor of the *Song of Roland*. After his stay in France, he
    taught in the Athénée français. Following the Pacific War, during which he
    worked at the Legation of Romania in Japan, he became a librarian at the
    National Diet Library and taught in several institutions in Tokyo, including
    the Athénée français. As regards the translation of the *Song of Roland*, it
    seems that he participated in the *Collection of the World's War Literature* via
    the mediation of Maruyama Kumao 丸山熊雄, one of his friends in Paris.

11 Ban, *The Song of Roland: Islamic War*, cit., p. 3.

According to this quotation, he preferred to use the vocabulary of Japanese classical culture to elaborate his style before trying to create new words. His way of thinking was analogical, and his efforts aimed essentially at establishing a bridge between old French and the Japanese literary style in order to transfer the sense of the original text while also creating an aesthetically coherent Japanese text.[12]

II. *Translation by Ban Takeo: analysis of the 176th* laisse.

The analogical approach noted in the previous section may tolerate minor differences between the original text and its translation if they are intended to ensure the aesthetic quality of the latter, and this is exactly the case for the word *furusato* in Ban's translation of the *Song of Roland*. Let us take, for example, the 176th *laisse*, where Roland dies and his soul goes to Paradise. This *laisse* is exemplary because of its pathos and its place in the overall plot. The following is Ban's Japanese translation followed by an English translation of the original text:

百七十六
　ロオランは松の根方に伏し、その眼は遠く西班牙の方を睨みながら、數々の思ひ出が胸の内に湧き起こるのを覺えた。自から征め伏せた多くの國々や、良き国フランスの故郷と、その身内の人々や、育ての親たり又主君たるシャルル大王のことを思ひ浮べて、嘆息と涙を押へる事も出来なかつた。しかし自身の後生を先ず願はずには居られなかつたので、胸を叩いて、神の許しを請ひ、『恒に偽り給ふ事なき誠に父よ。ラザロ聖者を蘇らせ給ひし如く、又ダニエル聖者を獅子の牙より救ひ給ひし如く、我等が魂を生涯に犯したる罪科故の、諸々の危難より救ひ出し給へ』と祈り、右の手袋を神に捧げまつれば、天使ガブリエルはこれを受け取り給ふ。腕の上に頭を持たせ掛け、両手を合せて事切れれば、

---

12   In one of his writings, he affirms that he dislikes the mixing of European and Japanese texts. See Gaston Baty, *Engeki no shinzui* [*The essentials of the theater*] 『演劇の神髄』, trad. by Ban Takeo (Tokyo: Hakusuisha 白水社, 1942), pp. 13-14. The original title of Baty's work is *Le Masque et l'encensoir*. On the details of his life and his predilection for an analogical understanding of the relationship between old European and Japanese cultures, we plan to publish another paper in the near future.

神は天使ケルビムと、危難の聖ミカエルを、ガブリエルと共に下し遣はされ、名將の魂を天國に連れ戻らせ給うた。[13]

176. Count Roland has laid himself down beneath a pine tree and has turned his face towards Spain: He began to call many things to mind: the many lands he had conquered, sweet France, and the men of his lineage, and Charlemaine, his lord, who nurtured him. He cannot restrain himself from weeping and sighing, but he is not forgetful of himself; he confesses himself and prays God for his mercy: "O true Father, who didst never lie, thou who didst raise St. Lazarus from the dead and save Daniel from the lions, save my soul from all the perils that beset it on account of the sins which I have committed in my life." He held out his right glove to God, and St. Gabriel took it from his hand. His head was resting on his arm and his hands were clasped, and thus he went to his end. God sent down his angel Cherubin and St. Michel du Peril; with them came St. Gabriel, and they carry the soul of the count to Paradise.[14]

In this quotation, we can find the Japanese word *furusato* (or *kokyō*) in the expression *yoki Furansu no furusato* (良き国フランスの故郷, his hometown in good France,[15] translated into English as "sweet France") in the first lines of the *laisse*. The corresponding original text is 'De dulce France,' where we cannot find any expression that would correspond exactly to the Japanese

---

13 Ban, *Rōran no uta. Kaikyō sensō*, cit., p. 123. The original old French text is as follows: "Le quens Rollant se jut desuz un pin, / Envers espaigne en ad turnet sun vis. / De plusurs choses a remembrer li prist, / De tantes teres cum libers cunquist, / De dulce France, des humes de sun lign, / De Charlemagne, sun seignor, kil nurrit ; / Ne poet muer n'en plurt et ne suspirt. / Mais lui meïsme ne volt mettre en ubli, / Cleimet sa culpe, si priet Deu mercit : / « Veire Paterne, ki unkes ne mentis, / Seint Lazaron de mort resurrexis / E Daniel des leons guaresis, / Guaris de mei l'anme de tuz perilz / Pur les pecchez que en ma vie fis ! » / Sun destre guant a Deu en puroffrit. / Seint Gabriel de sa main l'ad pris. / Desur sun braz teneit le chef enclin ; / Juntes ses mains est alet a sa fin. / Deus tramist sun angle Cherubin / Et seint Michel del Peril ; / Ensembl' od els sent Gabriel i vint. / L'anme del cunte portent en pareïs" (*La Chanson de Roland*, éd. Joseph Bédier (Paris: H. Piazza, [1922], 19e édition)), vv. 2375-2396, pp. 180-182. We would like to be precise that Ban's translation is based on the 92nd edition published in 1931.

14 *The Song of Roland*, trans. Jessie Crosland (Cambridge, Ontario: In parentheses Publications, Old French Series, 1999, http://www.yorku.ca/inpar/roland_crosland.pdf).

15 In this paper, we translate the word *furusato* as "hometown", even if this Japanese expression can be applied to a larger (or smaller) geographic sphere.

furusato. Thus, without producing a complete mistranslation, the translator seems to have tried to mark, through this word, the importance of the hometown for the heroes of this epic.

As is evident in his other translations and in the testimony of his friend Maruyama Kumao, Ban was a very meticulous person.[16] Nevertheless, he introduced a Japanese term that has no counterpart in the original text, and this addition must have been deliberate.[17] An analysis of the five occurrences of *furusato* in his translation reveals that this word is, in general, employed to translate possessive pronouns such as *lor* [their] and *son* or *sa* [his] when the danger of death is approaching Roland, his pairs, and his soldiers.[18] Moreover, Ban (or the editor) adds a phonetic guide in *hiragana* to these Chinese characters; especially when the personal sorrow of Roland is described.[19] So, with this word *furusato*—namely, when accompanied by a phonetic transcription in *hiragana*—the translator (or editor) seems to have tried to express a sense of sadness, linked to the fact that a character can no longer return to the place to which he is firmly attached. In other words, the translator gestures towards the personal history of these characters by introducing this word.

It is also notable that this word is never applied to the troops that accompany Charlemagne himself, even if they are in a

16   See Maruyama Kumao 丸山熊雄, *Sen kyūhyaku sanjū nendai no pari to watashi* [Paris in the 1930s and I] 『一九三〇年代のパリと私』 (Tokyo: Kamakurashobō 鎌倉書房, 1986), p. 102. Ban Takeo's work includes translating subtitles for a film, and we can see his attention to detail in his translations and writings.

17   Still, translating this epic has been undertaken using diverse approaches in modern France. See Christopher Lucken, 'Traduire la *Chanson de Roland*' [Translating the Song of Roland], *Médiévales* 75 (automne 2018), pp. 167-196.

18   See the table at the end of this document for all the occurrences of this word.

19   See the 140th and 167th *laisses* of the translation. In the post-war edition of this translation by Ban, which was integrated into a literary collection without the propagandist discourses that we have seen above, the occurrence of the 167th *laisse* is transcribed only in *hiragana*, without using these Chinese characters: see *Sekai bungaku zenshū. Koten-hen. Dai 3 kan. Chūsei jojishi-hen* [Collection of the World Classics. Tome 3. Medieval epic] 『世界文學全集古典篇 第三巻 中世敍事詩篇』 (Tokyo: Kawadeshobō 河出書房, 1952), p. 48.

battlefield located far from France. The reason is simple: these soldiers will return alive to France after the battle, as winners. In other words, those who are destined to return to their hometowns do not need the word *furusato*. Moreover, there is no use of the word *furusato* in relation to the troops of the great admiral of the Saracens, Baligant, even though they have traveled far from their homelands to fight the Christians. Even if these Muslims are destined to die in battle with Charlemagne in the last part of the epic, the word *furusato* is never used for their affairs. To summarize, then, the word *furusato* is reserved for the Christians who will die on the battlefield, rendering their death more impressive via a nod towards their personal histories. To put it another way, Ban would have introduced these words to express what a dying Japanese person, especially a dying Japanese soldier, would feel in this situation: a feeling that is related to his hometown.[20]

III. *The word* furusato *in other writings by Ban Takeo*

It is worth mentioning that Ban never used the word *furusato* in his pervious writings and translations, nor did he use it in his post-war works; at least as far as could be determined.[21] This

---

20   On the other hand, Ban substitutes the call for God in the text with other emotional displays in his translation (See Kuroiwa, 'Rōran no uta sansyu no nihongoyaku ni tsuite no oboegaki', cit., p. 10). Thus, Ban's translation tends to redirect the identity of the Christian heroes only to the secular community by erasing the religious background of the epic and emphasizing the nostalgia for their secular hometowns. However, the whole appreciation of the semantic system of the translation needs further investigation.

21   We investigated all his writings appearing in the NDL Online of the National Diet Library of Japan and those published in the review *Gekisaku* [Playwriting] 『劇作』 , along with his translations of the *Song of Roland* (both 1941 and 1952 versions) and *Mask and Thurible* of Gaston Baty. Also, we could check many numbers (but not all) of *Kaihō Atene* [Bulletin of the Athénée Français] 『會報アテネ』 (we would like to express our profound gratitude to Ms. Kawaguchi Ayako of the Athnée Français, our consultant for this review). After finishing this paper, we discovered his early writings published in the magazine *Take* [Bamboo] 『竹』 . We anticipate integrating the analysis of these writings for another occasion.

suggests that he had little attachment to the notion of *furusato* in and of itself. Born and living in Tokyo, and profoundly enjoying his stay in France (where he likely found the source of his educational background), we dare to hypothesize that he had rarely experienced strong feelings of longing for his hometown. Even considering the provincial connotations of the word *furusato*, he does not seem to feel an affinity, as is shown in the following passage:

> 甚だ痴〔をこ〕がましい事を云ふ様だが、正直な所僕は東京の田舎臭さに閉口する事が多いので、俳句や川柳——と云つても近頃のは全然知らない、昔のを云ふのだが、さう云ふものを生んだ日本人が何うして斯んなにまで鈍感になつて行くのだらうと、心細い思ひがする。〔…〕
> 日本に歸つて最初に讀んで見たのは、三馬の『浮世風呂』だつたが、これは僕に取つて非常に嬉しい發見だつた〔…〕ちよつと足を踏まれたからと云つて、直ぐ無禮者！と怒つて人を切る様な野暮な日舍〔sic〕侍には考へも及ばない、洗錬された都會文化が、少くとも町人社會には在つたのである。〔…〕 22

I am displaying too much pride, but honestly I am often embarrassed by the provincialism of Tokyo, and I wonder with a certain fear how the Japanese people, who once created *haiku* and *senryū* (I mean those of the old times, because I don't know those of nowadays), can become so insensitive. [...]

The first Japanese text that I read after my return to Japan was *Ukiyo-buro* [The Bathhouse of the Floating World] of [Shikitei] Sanba, and it was a hilarious discovery for me. [...] At least in the society of the townspeople, there was a very refined urban culture that a provincial samurai, who would feel insulted and attack with his saber anyone who happened to step on his foot, could never imagine. [...]

"The provincialism of Tokyo" reflects his critical attitude toward the provincial people coming into Tokyo and living in this place where refined culture had flourished during the Edo era. Furthermore, one wonders if Ban could have any personal affinity with the Christian warriors of the *Song of Roland*, as he

---

22   Ban Takeo, 'Asyāru to sanba no aida de' [Between Achard and Sanba] 「ア
     シヤアルと三馬の間で」, in *Gekisaku* 73 (March 1938), pp. 98–100. This
     passage raises the question of whether we can read in it his antipathy to the
     militaristic mentality.

dislikes the "provincial samurai" who are irascible and cannot understand the refinement of urban culture.[23]

If Ban was not so attached to the word *furusato* or its connotations, why did he introduce it in his translation to aestheticize the death of heroes, as examined above? This question is difficult to answer, but, at least, we can point out that the local communities—*furusato*—of Japanese soldiers played an important role in maintaining the morale of soldiers and even obliging them to die in battle to save the honor of their hometown and avoid leaving their parents open to criticism.[24] In this sense, Ban's translation precisely reflects the mentality of Japanese soldiers of the period by highlighting the sentiments regarding their *furusato* in the minds of dying warriors in *seisen* (聖戦, holy war).

Conclusion

The first Japanese translation of the *Song of Roland* features a mixture of several cultural currents. The translator, Ban Takeo, was generally faithful to the Roland studies of the period and the original text edited by Joseph Bédier. Nevertheless, he introduced a word that does not find any equivalent in the original text, *furusato*, to incorporate the personal histories of the dying heroes. Thus, Ban presents the heroes of the epic as analogous to Japanese soldiers fighting the Occidentals for their *furusato*. Finally, the introduction of this word reflected the atmosphere of Japanese society of the period, where local communities played an important role in keeping soldiers engaged in battle.

---

23 It seems that the epics were never his center of interest; he was more interested in medieval theater.

24 See Ichinose Toshiya 一ノ瀬俊也, *Furusato wa naze heishi wo koroshitaka* [Why did hometowns kill the soldiers?] 『故郷はなぜ兵士を殺したか』 (Tokyo: Kadokawa 角川, Kindle version, 2014).

Use of *furusato* (故郷) in Ban Takeo's translation of the *Song of Roland*
(we quote the old French text of the *Song of Roland* from the modern edition by Joseph Bédier, cited in note 13)

Laisse	Old French text	Japanese translation
4	Francs s'en irunt en France, la lur tere.	フランス軍は［…］故郷へ立ちもどることでございませう。
134	Tere Major mult est loinz ça devant.	まだまだ故郷も遠い事故
140	Tere de France, mult estes dulz païs	吾等が故郷フランスは、いみじくも良い國だが、 （with the phonetic transcription）
167	Forment le pleignet a la lei de sa tere :	故郷の仕来り通りに、誄を述べて云ふやう、 （with the phonetic transcription）
176	De dulce France, des humes de sun lign,	良き国フランスの故郷と、その身内の人々や、

MÁRIA ILDIKÓ FARKAS[1]

"HOMELAND" IN THE DISCOURSES OF COLLECTIVE IDENTITY OF THE EARLY 19TH CENTURY IN JAPAN AND CENTRAL EUROPE

Introduction

The concept of "*furusato*" (ふるさと), understandable as a nostalgic feeling for an idyllic, countryside home,[2] is an important part of the Japanese cultural identity even today, and thus the main concern of several scholarly works from different fields of humanities and social sciences debating its meaning, functions, and the reasons for its popularity. As for its definition, "*furusato*" mainly denotes "homeland", with strong emotional attachment and a sense of nostalgia for something that seemed to be lost during modernization: the harmonious existence of people. "*Furusato*" came to be popularly associated with "pre-modern as opposed to modern Japan" and connected with a mindset in which "the city is attributed negative qualities, such as being cold, artificial, and dehumanizing, while on the other hand, *furusato* is warm, natural, and humanizing."[3] Scholarly works also examine and interpret its effects: "The interpellative power and efficacy of *furusato* resides in the image of „traditional culture" conjured up by the word and in its perception as something broadly 'Japanese'. In this connection, *furusato* connotes a desirable lifestyle aesthetic summed up by the term *soboku* (素朴), or artlessness and rustic simplicity, and its quintessential landscape

---

1   Karoli Gaspar University
2   Lindsay R. Morrison, 'Home of the Heart: the Modern Origins of Furusato',
     ICU Comparative Culture 45 (2013), pp. 1-27, p. 2.
3   Lindsay R. Morrison, 'Home of the Heart: the Modern Origins of Furusato',
     cit., p. 2.

features include forested mountains, fields cut by a meandering river, and a cluster of thatched-roof farmhouses."[4]

These are the most common connotations of *furusato* today. The "genesis" of this concept is usually interpreted within the modernization processes of Meiji (明治) Japan in the second half of the 19th century; and both the idea and the word are generally linked to the ethnographers of the early 20th century (notably Yanagita Kunio, 柳田國男 and Orikuchi Shinobu, 折口信夫). However, its roots can be traced in the process of the formation of the collective identity in the early 19th century (especially in the works of Hirata Atsutane, 平田篤胤, 1776-1843). This paper explores how and why the concept of "homeland", and the idea of the significance of rural life and folk culture, was introduced in the discourses defining collective identity in the early 19th century, and how and why these concepts gained importance during modernization period in the late 19th century, with prevalent effects into the present. The main concern of this paper is interpreting this process with the help of a comparative approach and attempting to draw analogies between Japanese development and similar courses in other parts of the world, namely, East Central Europe. [5]

---

4   Jennifer Robertson, 'It Takes a Village: Internationalization and Nostalgia in Postwar Japan', in Stephen Vlastos (ed. by), *Mirror of Modernity: Invented Traditions of Modern Japan* (Berkeley: University of California Press, 1998), pp. 110-132, p. 116.

5   There is certainly a third historic region in Europe besides western and eastern zones: Central (or East Central) Europe, being part of the western development but with special features and a different scheme of modernization, and with a tradition and culture of its own. It is a historic region, too, with "attempts of a clutch of small and medium-sized peoples to assert their identities against more powerful neighbours on their flanks. ... In short, the geographical region of Central Europe, ... has created the possibility for a historical region, whose different sectors have moved towards disintegration or fusion according to the flux of events." (Okey, 105.) This essay cannot include the debates and views concerning East Central Europe, but can cite some of the most important works on the existence of a third region in Europe: Jenő Szűcs, 'The three historical regions of Europe: an outline', in John Keane (ed. by), *Civil Society and the State* (London: Verso, 1988), pp. 291-33; Catherine Horel, *Cette Europe qu'ondit centrale des Habsbourg à l'intégratio européenne, 1815-2004* (Paris: Beauchesne, 2009); Robin Okey, 'Central Europe/Eastern

The geopolitical situation of this region in some aspects and in some periods can be compared to Japan's: lying on the periphery (or next to) a civilizational centre (China for Japan and "the West" for Central Europe) and being at times integrated into and at others separated from this centre. As each existed within the sphere of influence of a cultural power (Chinese culture for Japan, and Western European or, more narrowly, German culture for Central Europe), their own territory and culture seemed the "periphery" of a cultural centre, and thus, could be seen as inferior to it. One of the consequences of this was that "high culture" originated from outside, the language of officials and the educated (as well as that of science) was mainly or partly "foreign" (Chinese/German). Against the "foreign" cultural influence (sometimes felt as a forceful impact), even before modernity, ethnic groups or communities (ethnies) started to evolve their own national identities with cultural movements focusing on their own language, on exploring or even inventing their "ancient" culture, creating a new sense of collective identity defined by linguistic and cultural affinities. In Central Europe cultural movements aiming at specifying collective identities of ethnic groups flourished in late 18th and in the 19th century, and at the same time in Japan a cultural movement (later) called *kokugaku* (国学, national learning) did the same by exploring, studying, and reviving ancient Japanese language, literature, myths, history, and also political ideology; and thus defined the contours of "Japaneseness".[6] Similar motives of argument can be identified in the discourses of identity in both Japan and East Central Europe: "language" as the primary bearer of collective identity, the determinant role of language in culture, "culture" as the main common attribute of the community; and similar

---

Europe: Behind the Definitions', *Past & Present* 137 (November 1992), pp. 102-133; Marcel Cornis-Pope and John Neubauer (ed. by), *History of the Literary Cultures of East-Central Europe. Junctures and disjunctures in the 19th and 20th centuries* (Amsterdam: Benjamins, 2004).

6   For the idea of *kokugaku* as the source of Japanese collective identity, see mainly Susan L. Burns, *Before the Nation: Kokugaku and the Imagining of Community in Early Modern Japan* (Durham: Duke University Press, 2003).

intentions to explore, search and develop native language, genuine culture, and original traditions.[7] "Folk culture" came to be seen as the preserver of the original, genuine culture of the community, and rural life with its customs as the pure and authentic way of life reflecting the collective "character" ("Volksgeist") of the community throughout the late 19th and early 20th centuries.

During the 19th century modernization, which was achieved and realized mainly "from above" in both Japan and Central Europe in political and social reform programs of "catching up with the modern West", "a self-consciously modern nationalism was constructed by deploying existing culturalist notions of community".[8] Even after World War II, although the term "national character" (with its pejorative connotations) disappeared from academic and public discourse, the newly developed scholarly field of cultural anthropology "discovered" the significant roles of cultural identity and cultural traditions of communities, which seemed to strongly affect the characteristics and way of thinking even of modern societies, especially in the cases where modernization was seen and experienced as foreign influence and/or pressure.

"Rural nostalgia" as a response to modernization

"Rural nostalgia" can be perceived as a "universal" phenomenon, occurring in several societies in different periods of times with sometimes distinct reasons and motives. In the late 18th and early 19th centuries in Europe, Romanticism greatly influenced and determined the rise of a nostalgia for "harmony" that was thought to have been lost during the Industrial

---

7   For a more detailed comparative approach, see Mária Ildikó Farkas, 'Cultural identity, nation building, modernization. Defining identity in Japan and East-Central Europe in the 18th and early 19th century', in Melinda Papp (Pappová) (ed. by), *Encounters with Japan. Japanese Studies in the Visegrad Four Countries* (Budapest: Eötvös University Press, 2015), pp. 51-86.

8   Susan L. Burns, *Before the Nation*, cit., p. 225.

Revolution and the social and political situation, including the rationalization of nature and science, that pervaded as a result of accelerated development. The feeling of disrupted harmony because of the weakening of the old traditional bonds birthed a sense of insecurity: feelings of social alienation and loneliness, which created the need for a sense of new security, and the wish for a "sense of belonging".[9] Some parts of the past (with strong social and community connections) became idealized and crystalized in myths of a "golden age", when people were still sincere and selfless. The search for "unspoiled" people in the present led to the "discovery" and idealization of the common people, the simplest country-folk and the folklore associated with them, including arts, legends, and tales from the oral tradition. Country life became idealized as pure and simple, with strong social bonds between people and a harmony with nature.

The peasantry as untouched by modernization is an idea that was widespread both in Europe (Western, Central, and Eastern) and Japan in the 19th century, but with different interpretations and consequences.[10] This difference was connected to the distinct development of these regions, to their experiences with modernization, and to the different formation of collective identities. While the response of societies to industrialization contained and contains some elements of rural nostalgia almost globally (we can find essays on this topic ranging from 19th century British rural nostalgia up to contemporary sentiments in China or South America), there seems to be significant differences in how societies experienced – and how they reacted to – modernization. Where modernization (which was strongly linked to industrialization and urbanization) was seen and experienced as foreign influence and/or pressure – that is, something "coming

---

9   Miroslav Hroch, 'National Romaniticism', in Balázs Tencsényi, Michale Kopecek (ed. by), *Discourse of Collective Identity in Central and Southeast Europe (1770-1945)*. Texts and Commentaries. Vol. 2. National Romanticism – The Formation of National Movements (Budapest-New York: CEU Press, 2007), pp. 4-21, p. 5.

10   Irwin Scheiner, 'The Japanese Village. Imagined, Real, Contested', in Stephen Vlastos (ed. by), *Mirror of Modernity: Invented Traditions of Modern Japan* (Berkeley: University of California Press, 1998), pp. 67-94, p. 68.

from outside" – it could be seen as threatening to the native culture. This experience generated sentiments and efforts to protect and preserve native culture ("nativism") and pressed the intellectuals of these societies to define the cultural heritage and collective identity of their communities. In this effort, the peasantry – as a social layer usually regarded as untouched by modernization – provided the "storehouse" for tradition and self-definition. An even more interesting – or we might say distinctive – feature linking Japan and East Central Europe is the fact that the basis (the defining elements of collective identity) for modern self-definition was laid in the late 18th and early 19th centuries, before modernization could reach these regions in the second part of the 19th century.

Antecedents – early modern identity formation

The end of the 18th and the first half of the 19th century was a period of defining collective identity in Central Europe. Efforts to attach it to the concept of the "nation", but with a modified interpretation of the notion ascendant in the "West": the nation was defined as a people united by linguistic and cultural affinities. Cultural movements focusing on language and culture produced an intellectual revival that laid the foundation for subsequent national movements.[11]

The evolution, concepts, results, and effects of *kokugaku* in Japan can be compared to the movements in East Central Europe.

---

11   Miroslav Hroch, Czech historian and political scientist, described Central European "national awakening" by an abstract schematization of national development through different phases. He defined three chronological stages in the creation of a nation. That is, Phase A is the "period of scholarly interest," Phase B is the "the period of cultural movement and patriotic agitation", and finally Phase C is "the rise of a mass national movement". "The earliest phase was the period when ... the ethnic group, its culture, past, state in nature, customs and so forth, became a subject of academic interest. In this phase, basic linguistic norms were sought and formulated and historical contexts were traced; in short, the potential nation was defined in a scholarly fashion according to the individual features that distinguished it from other groups." Miroslav Hroch, 'National Romanticism', cit., p. 9.

Kokugaku originally referred to the philological investigation of Japanese historical works and classical literature in the Edo period (江戸時代, 1600-1868) as a tradition of textual study focusing on specifically Japanese sources.[12] As an academic discipline, it relied on philology as its methodological tool; however, over the course of the Edo period, the aim of *kokugaku* studies shifted from the scholarly and philological study of ancient texts to the quest for a unique native ethos and spiritual identity. Scholars tried to bring out the "ethos" of Japanese tradition freed from foreign ideas and thoughts, and to define Japanese culture and Japanese collective identity.

In the cultural movements in Central Europe aiming at the study of one's "native" culture, the earliest phase was philological, when scholars attempted to record and codify native languages, explored folk legends (and wrote romantic epics) of ethnic origins, and compiled national histories – sometimes based on legends. Ancient and vernacular languages were researched, studied, and developed, vernacular literature was encouraged, published and spread throughout the land.[13] *Kokugaku* scholars, in a similar pattern, started to study ancient Japanese texts and wrote scholarly essays on ancient Japanese poetry, literature, and language. In Central Europe, university departments, national academies, and museums were founded and regional associations for cultivating national cultures were organized, first by the elite

---

12   Important works on *kokugaku*: See: Harry D. Harootunian, *Things Seen and Unseen: Discourse and Ideology in Tokugawa Nativism* (Chicago: University of Chicago Press, 1988); Peter Nosco, *Remembering Paradise: Nativism and Nostalgia in Eighteenth-Century Japan* (Cambridge, Mass.: Harvard Univesity Press, 1990); Peter Flueckiger, *Imagining Harmony: Poetry, Empathy, and Community in Mid-Tokugawa Confucianism and Nativism* (Stanford: Stanford University Press, 2011); Mark McNally, *Proving the Way: Conflict and Practice in the History of Japanese Nativism* (Cambridge, Mass.: Harvard University Asia Center, 2005); Mark Teeuwen, 'Kokugaku vs. Nativism', *Monumenta Nipponica* 61-2 (2006), pp. 227-242; Susan L. Burns, *Before the Nation*, cit.; Michael Wachutka, *Kokugaku in Meiji-period Japan. The Modern Transformation of National Learning and the Formation of Scholarly Societies* (Leiden, Boston: Global Oriental, 2012).

13   Miroslav Hroch, 'From National Movement to the Fully-formed Nation: The Nation-building Process in Europe', in Gopal Balakrishnan (ed. by), *Mapping the Nation* (New York and London: Verso, 1996), pp. 78-97.

(nobility) then followed by the middle or lower social strata. The Japanese *kokugaku* movement shows remarkable similarities with this, founding schools to study and research "National Studies", that is, the ancient Japanese language, literature, history, customs and traditions; educating people of all classes; and spreading all these ideas and knowledge about Japanese culture in Japanese language.

A shared feature of these movements is the importance of language as an essential and central element of collective (national) identity. The Hungarian Count István Széchenyi in the 1820s expressed the common idea that "The Nation lives in its language";[14] a Polish scholar wrote in 1836 that "language is a precious national possession, and all Slav nations should cultivate it with devotion, for it expresses their thoughts and ideas;"[15] and a Czech scholar argued in 1806 that "(…) language is what defines nations and their homelands."[16]

The Japanese *kokugaku* scholars had similar ideas about the role of the language in cultural identity.[17] As Burns notes, "the ideal of an original, authentic, and enduring 'Japanese' language was a powerful means to explain and thereby constitute cultural identity."[18] As one of the first great *kokugaku* scholars, Kada no Azumamaro (荷田春満, 1669-1736) expressed in his writings: The *Manyōshū* (万葉集, c. 759) is the pure essence of our national temperament…If the old words are not understood, the old meanings will not be clear. If the old meanings are not clear, the old learning will not revive. The way of the former kings is disappearing; the ideas of the wise men of antiquity have almost

---

14   Emil Niederhauser, *The Rise of Nationality in Eastern Europe* (Budapest: Corvina, 1981), p. 45.

15   Joachim Lelewel, 'Legitimacy of the Polish Nation (1836)', in Balázs Tencsényi, Michal Kopecek, (ed. by), *Disourses of Collective Identity*, Vol. 2, cit., pp. 36-37.

16   Josef Jungmann, 'Second Conversation Concerning the Czech Language (1806)', in Balázs Tencsényi, Michal Kopecek, (ed. by), *Disourses of Collective Identity*, Vol. 2., cit., pp. 106-111.

17   For more detailed analysis, see Ildikó Farkas, 'The Japanese Nation Building in European Comparison', *Acta Asiatica Varsoviensa* 26 (2013), pp. 7-27, pp. 14-15.

18   Susan L. Burns, *Before the Nation*, cit., p. 12.

been abandoned."[19] Motoori Norinaga (本居宣長, 1730-1801) made linguistic claims about the "difference" of ancient Japanese into the foundation of a theory of Japanese cultural uniqueness.[20] He made the "ancient language" of Japan (*Yamato kotoba,* 大和 言葉, やまと ことば), which he "found" in the *Kojiki* (『古事 記』, 712), the basis for a new vision of Japanese community. He used *Yamato kotoba* to distinguish China and Japan, showing ancient Japan as a natural community distinct from the states of China. His ideas determined the new *kokugaku* discourse that appeared in the 18th century, highlighting language as the "primary bearer of identity and difference."[21]

In the discourses of cultural identity in East Central Europe the significance of vernacular language was stressed, with the emphasized necessity of its "rehabilitation". This meant partly the efforts to regain its authentic (or at least what was considered its authentic) forms, and partly the efforts to "emancipate" the vernaculars from the dominance of the languages of "high culture" (usually the languages of the foreign cultural centre). The vernaculars of that time and these regions were the languages of mainly the illiterate peasant populations, and they were thought to preserve the linguistic heritage of their communities (sometimes with language usage seen as "ancient") and thus to reflect the distinctive cultural identity of that community.[22] The linguistic definition of the community in early 19th century soon integrated the peasantry; moreover, it put emphasis on their language as the "basis" of cultural identity.[23] A Czech scholar

---

19 Kada Azumamaro, *Sōgakkōkei* 『創学校啓』 (1728), in Wm. Theodore de Bary, Ryusaku Tsunoda, Donald Keene (ed. by), *Sources of Japanese Tradition. II.,* cit., pp. 7-9.

20 See several chapters in Susan L. Burns, *Before the Nation,* cit., pp. 68-101.

21 Susan L. Burns, *Before the Nation,* cit., pp. 220-23.

22 Paschalis M. Kitromilides, 'The Enlightenment in Southeast Europe: Introductory Considerations', in Balázs Tencsényi, Michal Kopecek, (ed. by), *Disourses of Collective Identity in Central and Southeast Europe (1770-1945). Texts and Commentaries,* Vol. 1, Late Enlightenment – Emergence of the Modern National Idea (Budapest-New York: CEU Press, 2006), pp. 45-56, p. 48.

23 Bessenyei György, 'Beszéd az országnak tárgyárul' [Oration on the subject-matter of the country] (1802), in Balázs Tencsényi, Michal Kopecek,

described one powerful example of this process: "The Czech nation in the true sense of the word rose from the dead... It happened by a resurrection of the Czech language, which had... gradually vanished from the public offices, from the intercourse of the upper classes, from the families of nobles and wealthier burgers, from literature and ultimately also from schools, into which German had been introduced, even in the villages... Czech survived mainly in country huts alone, being called the peasant language and in the towns the speech of the lowest rabble."[24] This idea was attached to the concept of "language" as the determinant of the way of thinking and patterns of behaviour.[25]

In East Central Europe, the peasant culture, possessing the vernacular language, came to be seen as ancient and the preserver of the tradition and autochthonous culture of the entire ethnic group, as opposed to the elites (aristocrats and sometimes city-dwellers), who followed foreign patterns and were attached to the foreign cultural centre.[26] "It had historical reality and explanation in the centre-periphery relations of the modern age. On the periphery, ruling classes imitated cultural forms and behaviour patterns developed in the centre. As a result, the gap between the ruling elite and the rural peasant segment of the society – which at best were only partially affected by changing fashions stemming from the centre – became deeper and deeper. Peasant traditions of Eastern Europe showed much greater originality."[27] Folk culture was considered unchanging from ancient times and untouched by foreign cultural influence, reflecting the collective

---

Disourses of Collective Identity, Vol. I., cit., p. 151.

24   Jakub Malý, *Our National Rebirth* (1880), in Balázs Tencsényi, Michal Kopecek, (ed. by), *Disourses of Collective Identity*, Vol. 2, cit., p. 69. For a comparison of Japanese and East Central European texts, see Mária Ildikó Farkas, 'Cultural identity, nation building, modernization', cit., pp. 51-86.

25   Tamas Hofer, 'The "Hungarian Soul" and the "Historic Layers of National Heritage": Conceptualizations of Hungarian Folk Culture, 1880-1944', in Ivo Banac, Katherine Verdery (ed. by), *National Character and National Ideology in Interwar Eastern Europe* (New Haven: Slavica Publishers, Indiana University, 1995), pp. 64-81, p. 70.

26   Tamas Hofer, 'The 'Hungarian Soul', cit., p. 65.

27   Tamas Hofer, 'The 'Hungarian Soul', cit., p. 66.

"character" ("Volksgeist") of the community.[28] "In culture and tradition native features defined the historical identity of a nation and constituted a supreme, autonomous value that did not have to be rationally justified."[29] In East Central Europe in the 19th century, peasant life, folk poetry, rituals and costumes were discovered and researched, folk literature collected and studied, and a coherent picture of the folk culture of the communities were compiled based on these. It became a common conviction among researchers and the public alike that the peasantry preserved the ancient and authentic culture of the community and reflected the collective identity of the group, which, with the rising of the national idea, became the basis for the national identity.[30] Elements of national symbols could be derived from language (phrases, poems), folklore, customs, the characteristic landscape, mentality (regarded typical of that ethnic group), gastronomy, animals, sacred places, myths, legends, history, and heroes. They covered the social, material, regional, and other distinctive aspects of the community and provided the feeling of equally belonging to the group.[31] One of the most important components of national symbolism showed the picture of the "Homeland", which was regarded as not only exceptionally or uniquely beautiful, but also sacred (as some East Central European national hymns show it even today).[32] The concept of "Home" connected to the countryside and rural life was also elaborated: "Home ... represents an oasis of simplicity, of directness, and of transparency in human relations. One may not be free of worries there, but one will definitely be free of envy, and of all striving for sham values. The home as a retreat from the world, and the country as a retreat from the madding

---

28 Tamas Hofer, 'The 'Hungarian Soul', cit., p. 70.
29 Jerzy Jedlicki, *A Suburb of Europe: Nineteenth-century Polish Approaches to Western Civilization* (Budapest: Central European University Press, 1999), p. 22.
30 Tamas Hofer, 'The 'Hungarian Soul', cit., p. 64.
31 Kiss Gy. Csaba, *"Hol vagy, hazám?" Kelet-Közép-Európa himnuszai* ["Where are you, my homeland?" The Hymns of East Central Europe] (Budapest: Nap Kiadó, 2011), p. 33.
32 Kiss Gy. Csaba, *"Hol vagy, hazám?"*, cit., p. 86.

crowd of rapacious civilization…"[33] There were similar motives in the image of the homeland: sacred mountains, rivers, seas, and characteristic landscapes like mountains, hills or plains, and all these elements were attached and related to the "national character" of the ethnic group and the nation.[34] "Homeland" was frequently portrayed as "paradise" on earth, or a divine land, the land of the "Golden Age" when people lived in harmony and peace and had an idyllic relation to nature and to God, and the innocence of the people made conflicts mong them unknown.[35]

These notions and ideas closely connected to national sentiments are presented in the romantic poetry of the 19th century in East Central Europe. Poems praised the beauty of the homeland (some of them even became national anthems):

> Josef Kajetán Tyl: Where is my homeland? (Czech hymn, 1834)[36]
> Where is my homeland?
> Where is my homeland, where is my homeland?
> Waters murmur through the meadows,
> forests rustle all over the rocky hills,
> spring blossoms glitter in the orchards,
> paradise on earth to look at!
> This is a beautiful country,
> the Czech country, my homeland,
> the Czech country, my homeland!

> Antun Mihanović: Our beautiful homeland (Croatian hymn, 1835)[37]
> Our beautiful homeland,
> O so fearless and gracious.
> Our fathers' ancient glory,
> May you be happy forever.
> Dear, you are our only glory,
> Dear, you are our only one,

---

33   Jerzy Jedlicki, *A Suburb of Europe,* cit., p. 110.
34   Kiss Gy. Csaba, *"Hol vagy, hazám?",* cit., p. 103.
35   Kiss Gy. Csaba, *"Hol vagy, hazám?",* cit., p. 113.
36   The English translation of the Czech hymn can be read on Wikipaedia: https://en.wikipedia.org/wiki/Kde_domov_m%C5%AFj (last download 05. 20. 2019.)
37   The English translation of the Croatian hymn can be read on Wikipaedia: https://en.wikipedia.org/wiki/Lijepa_na%C5%A1a_domovino (last download 05.20. 2019.)

Dear, we love your plains,
Dear, we love your mountains.
Drava, Sava, keep on flowing,
Danube, do not lose your vigour,
Deep blue sea, tell the world,
That a Croat loves his people.
Whilst his fields are kissed by sunshine,
Whilst his oaks are whipped by bura's winds,
Whilst his ancestors lie buried,
Whilst his live heart beats.

One of the greatest Hungarian romantic poets and a national hero, Sándor Petőfi, is well-known for his love of his homeland, the Hungarian Great Plain, which he praised in many of his poems.[38]

Petőfi: Az Alföld (The Great Plain)
What do I care about you, wildly romantic
pine forests of the grim Carpathian mountains!
I may admire but do not love you, and my imagination
does not roam over your mountains and valleys.
(...)
Beautiful you are, Great Plain, beautiful at least to me!
Here my cradle was rocked, here was I born,
here should be the shroud cover me,
here should the earth entomb me.[39]

His poem about going home after many years reflects almost all aspects of the concept of *"furusato"*: home as the scene of the happy and pure childhood, innocence, harmony; the sorrow of an adult man at having lost something since leaving home.

Sándor Petőfi: My Birthplace (1848)
Here was I born, these the scenes I treasure,
Vast Lowland plains, stretching at their leisure,
Born in this old town which seems to creep with

---

38   Sándor Petőfi (1823-1849), died as a soldier in a battle during the Hungarian War of Independence (1848-49) against the Habsburg rule. His life represented what his poems were about: romantic love, the love of his homeland, the wish for independence, the fight for liberty, and self-sacrifice for patriotism.
39   John Neubauer, 'Petőfi: Self-Fashioning, Consecration, Dismantling', in Marcel Cornis-Pipe, John Neubauer (ed. by), *History of the Literary Cultures*

Lullabies my nurse sang me to sleep with,
Still I hear her singing, though she has gone,
"Cockchafer cockchafer, fly away home!"
Child when I left, a little thing so high,
I come back as a man with years put by,
Twenty of them have passed, and the grown boy
Has had his fill of sorrow and of joy...
Twenty long years... and how the time has flown!
"Cockchafer cockchafer, fly away home!"
Playmates of my youth, now how do you do?
If only I could meet but one of you!
Sit down beside me here, cheer me again,
Let me forget that I'm become a man,
Twenty five years the sum of all I own...
"Cockchafer cockchafer, fly away home!"
(…)[40]

In Japan, 18th century *kokugaku* focused on ancient forms of Japanese literature, language and religious practice as the sources of "genuine" Japanese culture. However, in the early 19th century, mainly due to the works of Hirata Atsutane, peasantry, folk culture and rural life were increasingly identified with the original Japanese culture ("Ancient Way", *Kodō*, 古道).[41] This idea of the "Ancient Way" centred on daily life "as an authentic and natural reality that demanded to be liberated from the constraints of culture, and its fragmenting consequences; by escaping from culture – second nature, as it were – it was possible to return to a natural and unmediated relationship between the deities, land, and people, to secure once more a union with the tangible real, the quotidian experience of the folk, which had

of East-Central Europe. Junctures and Disjunctures in the 19th and 20th Centuries. Volume IV: Types and Stereotypes (Amsterdam-Philadelphia: John Benjamins Publishing Company, 2010), pp. 40-55, p. 43.

40   Translated by George Szirtes. Hungarians in the Tower of Babel. http://www.magyarulbabelben.net/works/hu/Pet%C5%91fi_S%C3%A1ndor/Sz%C3%BCl%C5%91f%C3%B6ldemen?interfaceLang=en (last download 05.20. 2019.)

41   Harry D. Harootunian *Things Seen and Unseen: Discourse and Ideology in Tokugawa Nativism* (Chicago: University of Chicago Press, 1988), pp. 17, 23.

been realized first in antiquity".[42] Hirata Atsutane's concept was that the "Ancient Way" (which should be searched out, studied, and then re-established in order to restore the original Japanese culture) meant agricultural production and rural life and was preserved and followed by the ordinary folk, the peasantry.[43] As he wrote: "When thinking about agriculture, it is something that must be esteemed. Still more, Japanese, belonging to a realm founded on rice seedlings, must search out the basis of their country."[44] He also believed that language reflected the "spirit of Japan", but he was convinced that it was the language spoken by the folk.[45] He reconstructed (established?) a religious practice of the reverence of ancestors, tutelary and guardian deities based on the households (*ie*, 家) of the villages, which containing the collectivity of households, became the centre of collective worship and also the model (village society) of social order.[46] Special emphasis was put on rice cultivation as the basic life-supporting form of production and rice as staple food granted by the *kami* of Japan for the Japanese people. The village community came to be seen as a corporate body, a self-governing, self-sufficient, cooperative, and communal integral unit.[47] The "*ie*" as the fundamental unit of ancestor worship and the community (and the whole society) was an idea that gained increasing ground and significance during and after the Edo period, remaining in focus even in the 20th century (e.g. Yanagita Kunio, 柳田國男, or Murakami Yasusuke, 村上泰亮 in the 1980s).[48] The concept of a society based on small village farming was "linked to Japan's climate (*fudo*, 風土), natural setting, distinctive forms of social organization, and indigenous

---

42   Harry D. Harootunian, *Things Seen and Unseen,* cit., p. 37.
43   Harry D. Harootunian, *Things Seen and Unseen,* cit., p. 185.
44   Harry D. Harootunian, *Things Seen and Unseen,* cit., p. 159.
45   Harry D. Harootunian, *Things Seen and Unseen,* cit., p. 186.
46   Harry D. Harootunian, *Things Seen and Unseen,* cit., pp. 203-207.
47   Harry D. Harootunian, *Things Seen and Unseen,* cit., pp. 243-244.
48   Harry D. Harootunian, *Things Seen and Unseen,* cit., p. 245; Murakami Yasusuke, 'Ie Society as a Pattern of Civilization', *Journal of Japanese Studies* 10-2 (1984), pp. 302-312.

deities",[49] and thus was a fundamental part of the Japanese early modern collective identity, which consisted of the combination of these elements with the language.

"Hard work and frugality would seem to be virtues common to the peasantry the world around, but perhaps they were present in excess among the Japanese farmers."[50] Even ideologies and religious or ethical movements arose with the aim of reinforcing these values among the peasantry (*Shingaku* 心学, *Hōtoku* 報徳 movements), closely tied to the family system and the duty of filial piety.[51]

"Rural life" as part of modern national identity

When modernization reached the regions of East Central Europe and Japan in the second half of the 19th century, the societies of these regions were confronted with the Western program of rapid modernization and faced the problems of re-defining identity in line with the newly rising importance of the ideas of nations and nationalism. In this struggle, early modern cultural identities played a significant role, and the peasantry played an important role as the purported preserver of the original, genuine culture of the community.

The expansion of Western industrial civilization in the 19th century in the areas of East Central Europe (and also in Japan) resulted in the appearance and spread of similar debates about the possible responses to this challenge in these societies. The range of possible reactions ranged from the extremities of complete rejection (resulting in attempts at cultural isolation, ethnocentrism, and xenophobia) to boundless acceptance and adoption; however, even the latter approach faced the dilemma

---

49   Thomas R. H. Havens, *Farm and Nation in Modern Japan. Agrarian Nationalism, 1879-1940.* (Princeton-London: Princeton University Press, 1974), p. 22.

50   Robert Bellah, *Tokugawa Religion. The Cultural Roots of Modern Japan* (New York: Free Press, 1985), p. 126.

51   Robert Bellah, *Tokugawa Religion,* cit., p. 127.

of how to adopt modernization (closely linked to Westernization) while not losing identity and culture.[52] In these discourses native culture and traditions were often identified with the countryside, agriculture, and patriarchal social relations.[53] Folk culture was supposed to be unchanging from antiquity and untouched by history and different cultural influences, thus it seemed a rich storehouse for the newly defined national culture: vernacular literature; history; mythology; legends; folk tales; poems; songs; ballads; customs; and also symbols, which became increasingly important during the era of nation building.[54]

In the Meiji (明治) period (1868-1912), similar ideas were wrestled with in a Japan facing the consequences of (Western) modernity. The early years of the Meiji period, featuring a rapid and abundant importation of aspects of Western cultures, stimulated many in Japan to reflect and reconsider their own national culture; therefore there was a growing tendency to "rediscover" and/or "preserve" Japanese tradition and values from the 1880s onward. In the efforts to create a modern identity with "genuine" Japanese values and morals (besides *kokugaku* ideas of emperor-centred state *Shintō* (神道) as ideology and Confucianism as morality), elements of folk culture had a special role as the possible basis for a common background for all the Japanese people. Already in the late 19th century, folklore (fairy tales, legends, and stories of mythology) "was collected, rewritten and standardized. Editions suitable for children were published with illustrations and supplemented with introductory texts, songs and poems."[55] One of the most important aims of the compilation of children's literature on the basis of folklore in the 1890s was "to inspire patriotism, pride, a sense of virtue and

---

52   Jerzy Jedlicki, 'Native Culture and Western Civilization (Essay from the History of Polish Social Thought of the Years 1764-1863)', *Acta Poloniae Historica* 28 (1973), pp. 63-85, p. 63.

53   Jerzy Jedlicki, 'Native Culture and Western Civilization', cit., p. 69.

54   Tamas Hofer, 'The 'Hungarian Soul', cit., p. 71.

55   Michael Wachutka, *Kokugaku in Meiji-period Japan. The Modern Transformation of "National Learning" and the Formation of Scholarly Societies* (Leiden-Boston: Global Oriental, 2013), pp. 227-228.

Japaneseness."[56] These collections of folk tales and stories based on legends and mythology preceded the later folklore studies of Yanagita Kunio and Orikuchi Shinobu.[57]

The notions of rural society offered "a comprehensive view of state and society which was intended to be a common basis of loyalty for everyone in the country."[58] Practices that were regarded as originating in the premodern period seemed to be exempt from the corrosions of modernization. Besides the spread of the ideas of leading Meiji bureaucrats, thinkers and scholars about the importance ("the backbone of the nation") of the traditional Japanese work and life ethic (frugality, duty, hard work, and the village economy),[59] a political ideology with these convictions also developed in the early 20th century. *Nōhonshugi* (農本主義, "Agrarianism") represented an ideal Japanese social and political order based on farming and rural society as the foundations of Japanese civilization.[60] Its proponents firmly believed that rice cultivation had shaped the unique qualities of Japanese culture, village communities were the model upon which to build society, and rural life represented the true ethics to be followed.[61] *Shintō* also reinforced the concept of *kyōdōtai* (共同体, corporate body), the "authentic Japanese rural community" closely connected to wet rice cultivation, with its complicated irrigation and labour-intensive agriculture that gave rise to a special cooperative form of social organization.[62] *Nōhonshugi* "was also an important ideological current in the nation's struggle to clarify its self-image during the years from the Meiji restoration to World War II."[63] Early 20th century native ethnology (*minzokugaku*, 民俗学) as formulated by Yanagita Kunio and Orikuchi Shinobu tended to construct the image of an authentic folk culture that was

---

56 Michael Wachutka, *Kokugaku in Meiji-period Japan,* cit., p. 228.
57 Michael Wachutka, *Kokugaku in Meiji-period Japan,* cit., p. 228.
58 Thomas R. H. Havens, *Farm and Nation in Modern Japan,* cit., p. 188.
59 Thomas R. H. Havens, *Farm and Nation in Modern Japan,* cit., p. 9.
60 Thomas R. H. Havens, *Farm and Nation in Modern Japan,* cit., p. 7.
61 Thomas R. H. Havens, *Farm and Nation in Modern Japan,* cit., p. 296.
62 Jennifer Robertson, *Native and Newcomer: Making and Remaking a Japanese City* (Berkeley: University of California Press, 1991), p. 89.
63 Thomas R. H. Havens, *Farm and Nation in Modern Japan,* cit., p. 317.

untouched throughout history by the changing cultural horizon of the elites – and that consequently was seen as the preserver of the "genuine" culture of the ethnic community and the nation.

Several works of the past decades concerning modern Japanese development have taken features of modern Japanese culture regarded as "traditionally Japanese" to be "invented traditions" from an era of building a modern nation and national consciousness as a part of modernization in the 19th century.[64] According to this interpretation, the idea of Japanese farm villages representing "the core values and habits that shape the Japanese national character" is a relatively recent invention. Although one can find resonance in Tokugawa nativist thought, "the valorization of the farm village as the heart and soul of Japan belongs to a modern discourse that developed in reaction to social cleavages and national anxieties attendant on industrialization."[65] It is important to note, however, that 'invented traditions' are never completely invented; rather, they almost always need to resonate with the inherited experiences and memories of ordinary people if they are to be accepted and internalised.[66] We have to add that "traditions do not of course spring up ex nihilo; genealogies, if not origins, can be found",[67] therefore the question of the origins and history of these "invented traditions" cannot be neglected. These were crucial in the process of "the Japanese defining/ maintaining a sense of identity during the acutely Eurocentric late 19th and early 20th centuries."[68] By the term "invented traditions" we may perceive the selecting, choosing, reinforcing, stressing, emphasizing, or institutionalizing of some of the existing or

---

64   Mainly exposed by Stephen Vlastos in his introductory essay: Stephen Vlastos, 'Tradition. Past/Present Culture and Modern Japanese History', in Stephen Vlastos (ed. by), *Mirror of Modernity*, cit., pp. 1-18.

65   Stephen Vlastos, 'Agrarianism without Tradition: The Radical Critique of Prewar Japanese Modernity', in Stephen Vlastos (ed. by), *Mirror of Modernity,* cit., pp. 79-95, p. 80.

66   F. G. Notehelfer, 'Review on Mirror of Modernity', *Journal of Japanese Studies* 25-2 (1999), pp. 432-438, p. 436.

67   Dipesh Chakrabarty, 'Afterword. Revisiting the Tradition/Modernity Binary', in Stephen Vlastos (ed. by), *Mirror of Modernity*, cit., pp. 285-296, p. 288.

68   Ann Waswo, 'Review on Mirror of Modernity', *Monumenta Nipponica* 54-1, pp. 133-135.

earlier traditions, rather than the exclusive invention of new ones from whole cloth.[69]

Conclusion

As this paper has tried to present, the idea of an authentic folk culture preserving the ancient traits of the community had its origins in the early 19th century in both Japan and in East Central Europe. This suggests that this development cannot be considered a unique or isolated feature of Japanese (or East Central European) history, but may be interpreted as an inevitable trend or pattern of development in certain circumstances. The significant role of cultural identity and cultural traditions of communities cannot be denied as they may have determined the characteristics and way of thinking of even modern societies, especially in the cases where "Western" modernization was experienced as foreign influence and/or pressure and a "threat" to native culture.

The present-day rural nostalgia in both Japan and Central Europe may have some features of these identity issues among other elements widely discussed in scholarly works on *furusato* and is undeniably strengthened by business interests (rural tourism), but it may also represent an important source of development for rural regions and societies. Rural tourism based on cultural heritage can provide possibilities and means of developing for not only rural economy, but also for "revitalising" local communities and regional identities.[70]

---

69   For a more detailed interpretation, see Mária Ildikó Farkas, 'Reconstructing Tradition. The Debate on "Invented Tradition" in the Japanese Modernization', *Acta Asiatica Varsoviensia* 29 (2016), pp. 31-46.

70   Bernadett Csurgó, 'Nostalgia for the rural. Cultural heritage based tourism and community building in rural Hungary", in *Proceedings of Heritage. 5th International Conference on Heritage and Sustainable Development* (Barcelos: Green Lines, 2016), pp. 1583-1592.

Zakota Yutaka 座小田豊[1]

REASONING ABOUT *FURUSATO* AS THE ORIGIN OF LIFE (生命) AND SPIRIT (心)

Introduction

Stars and constellations have long served as guides and goals for travelers returning home. The goal or landmark in this case is "*furusato*". This chapter will focus on the guiding lights that will lead us to *furusato*, in a structure based on the two perspectives drawn from Japanese culture and the Western philosophic tradition, respectively. It is hoped that the results will help us better understand the statement by the esteemed Japanese poet Matsuo Bashō (松尾芭蕉, 1644–1694) at the opening of *Oku no Hosomichi* 『奥の細道』 that "the months and days are the travelers of eternity".[2] In my opinion, this must mean indeed that "life is an eternal journey to *furusato*".

A. Furusato *and Japanese Culture*

A-1. *Furusato* as the Origin of Life and Spirit

Generally speaking, *furusato* is the place where one was born and raised. But *furusato* is not limited to just one place. If you move somewhere else away from your birthplace, spend years there, and find yourself feeling affection for that place, it would become another *furusato* for you. *Furusato*, in this way, is closely tied to our memories associated with the places where we spend our time.

---

1   Tohoku University
2   Matsuo Bashō, *The Narrow Road to Oku* (Tokyo: Kodansha, 2007), p. 159.

Furusato is not just a place, but encompasses the whole atmosphere, such as the people nearby, mountains and rivers, paddy fields, and streets. One experiences and absorbs these, and they stay in one's mind as memories. *Furusato* can become a source that guiding people sentiments like these. That is to say, *furusato* can be regarded as the source of people's lives and spirits. Of course, some may be lonely or feel alienated from their homes or families, but it seems to me almost certain that even such alienated people harbor a yearning for home within themselves. Evidence for this can be seen in the tendency for this sense of alienation to manifest itself as a reverse sense of nostalgia.

How is *furusato* seen now? The Great East Japan Earthquake in 2011 is still vivid in Japanese memory. When the tsunami hit the coastal towns across the three prefectures in the Tohoku Region, it deprived people of their loved ones as well as damaging and destroying outright *furusato*. Eight years and three months have already passed since the earthquake and tsunami struck. Still, I am overwhelmed by sorrow every time I think of it. I feel that the affection of people for *furusato* seems stronger than ever, even among those who had their *furusato* taken from them. In fact, it is precisely because people lost their *furusato* that they may be harboring such strong affection for them.

It is often said that we feel stronger ties to *furusato* when we are far away from it. I am totally sympathetic to this view. It is true that distance from *furusato* makes us more aware of this feeling than when we are in our hometown. The distance here includes not only space but also time. And of these two gaps, time is the more essential. I may be the oldest member from Japan at this symposium. My memories of *furusato* that hark back more than 50 years are becoming clearer as time goes by. Approaching this subject now has caused me to begin to wonder why this is so.

Let me introduce to you the words of an Italian philosopher who also refers to the same feeling. When I was a university student more than 40 years ago, his thesis written in German was a guiding beacon for me in my research on Hegel's philosophy.

His name is Norberto Bobbio (1909-2004). He writes in his book *Old Age and Other Essays* the following:

> "When in your memory you return to places of the past, the dead crowd around you, and their numbers increase with every passing year. You have been abandoned by the majority of those whose company you kept. But you cannot erase them from your memory as though they had never existed. When you recall them to your mind, you bring them back to life, at least for a moment, and they are no longer entirely dead—they have not disappeared completely into nothing."[3]

As Bobbio says, our memories of the people of our pasts and the landscapes of our "hometown" create *furusato*, because the memories make it possible for our spirit to penetrate the gap in time and to build a bridge between the past and the present day. And in due course we will all return to that place. So *furusato* could be the ground and destination of our life and our spirit.

Let me give you an example from oldest Japanese Text, the *Kojiki*『古事記』.

A-2. *Furusato* is the best place for each of us (*mahoroba*, まほろば) in the world

大和は	As for Yamato,
国のまほろば	the most secluded of Lands,
畳なづく青垣	retired behind Mount Awogaki
山籠れる	encompassing it with its folds –
大和し	Yamato
うるわし	is delightful.[4]

This song is well-known even to school children in Japan as the final words sung by Yamato Takeru no Mikoto (日本武尊), the second son of Emperor Keiko (景行天皇), the 12th

---

3   Norberto Bobbio, *De senectute e altri scritti autobiografici* (Torino: Einaudi, 1996), English translation in: Noberto Bobbio, *Old Age and Other Essays* (Cambridge: Polity, 2001), p. 13.
4   In: *The Kojiki: Records of Ancient Matters* (Tokyo: Tuttle, 1982), p. 265.

Emperor of Japan, on his deathbed. Prince Takeru is one of the most renowned heroes in the *Kojiki*, the oldest known text in Japan. He was neglected by his father and was sent far away on a military expedition without even the briefest respite from his previous assignment. His expedition ranged as far as Kumamoto in Kyūshū to the west and Azuma in Ibaraki to the east. Finally, on his journey home, he became sick and sang the lyrics of the *Song yearning for my hometown* on his deathbed, in view of the clouds across the Suzukayama mountains. This nostalgia for hometown, sung here by the prince, offers an early example of a sentiment that is shared in the hearts of many people in Japan.

"*Mahoroba*" means that the particular "hometown" for each person is the place which inspires us. "*Mahoroba*" is translated in this song as "the most secluded of Lands". I believe that what this translation implies is that *mahoroba* is a hidden place at the bottom of our heart. Needless to say, in the real Yamato, the circumstances surrounding Prince Takeru were very severe due to feuds in the Imperial Family. Driven out from Yamato, the prince could have subsumed into the word *mahoroba* the true sense of *furusato*. Therefore, *mahoroba* can be taken to mean "the delightful place in everyone's mind". I am now reminded of Leibniz's *Monadology*, which states that in the pleats of our souls lie living mirrors in which the universe is folded.

A-3. *Hozo no o* ("Umbilical Cord") is a Symbol of *Furusato* in Matsuo Bashō

古里や	Alas, *furusato*!
臍の緒に泣く	Crying for the umbilical cord
年の暮れ	At the end of the year

At the end of 1688, the well-known traveling poet Matsuo Bashō had the opportunity to return to his hometown of Igaiyō (伊賀伊陽). Some historians record that Bashō saw his umbilical cord there. It is known that his memory of his father and mother simply overwhelmed him and caused him to weep bitterly. In those days, Japanese people commonly believed that the souls of their ancestors returned to their original homes at the end of the year to become guardians for their descendants. Bashō must have felt strong ties with his *furusato* and his mother and ancestors, through his sentiment for his remaining umbilical cord. This poem simply calls for such emotion in us as readers.

What this *haiku* tells us is that the umbilical cord not only ties us with our mothers but strongly ties us with our hometown as a whole. In this sense, the umbilical cord symbolizes various features that tie us with our hometown, for example, the sound of wind blowing through the air and tree branches, the sound of wind swirling across paddy fields and farmlands, the sound of rivers and seas, the muffled voices of people, the various odors of the town, and the breath and energy of people close by. All of these are essential elements that build the overall sphere of the "hometown". The Japanese people have been calling their hometown in their mind "*mahoroba*" from ancient times.

Of course, "hometown" is not limited to mountains and villages. It could be a farm village or a city functioning as the center of some kind of cultural zone. Augustin Berque, a French geographer, Prof. of the École des Hautes Études en Sciences Sociales, regards the essence of Japanese "hometown" as the concept of *trajectivité*.

A-4. *Furusato* is the Milieu as a whole: *trajectivité*

Berque proposes *trajectivité* as the key concept of the Milieu (*fūdo*, 風土) in Japan. He says that the Milieu comprises a combination of three propositions. The Milieu is both natural and cultural, both subjective and objective, and both collective and individual. In the Japanese Milieu, these six elements are tightly connected with each other. Prof. Berque calls the dimension of this connectedness "*trajectivité*" (*tsūtaisei* 通態性 in Japanese).[5] I consider this *trajectivité* to be a distinctive

---

5   Augustin Berque, *Le Sauvage et L'Artifice—Les Japonais Devant la Nature* (Paris: Gallimard, 1986); Japanese Edition in: Augustin Berque オギュスタン・ベルク, *Fūdo no nihon* [Climate Japan] 『風土の日本』 (Tokyo:

feature of *furusato* in Japan. We see here, as Berque says, the relationship between causality and metaphor working to integrate past, present and future. That is to say, complementarity and reciprocity permeate, and nature and culture, individuals and others—or the community—are closely bonded while evoking sympathy. Berque states that the frequent lack of a subject in Japanese sentences is an example of this concept. He says that there is a certain horizon for understanding each other without emphasizing oneself.

B. *From the standpoint of European philosophical history*

Novalis (Georg Philipp Friedrich von Hardenberg, 1772-1801), a German poet and philosopher of Romanticism, states in an aphorism that "Philosophy is actually homesickness, so to speak, a compulsive desire to be at home anywhere." (*Die Philosophie ist eigentlich Heimweh—Trieb überall zu Hause zu seyn.*).[6] This means that philosophy is an inquisition into *furusato* for the soul.

1. *Furusato* is the beginning and destination of existence (cf. Anaximander and Aristotle)

2. *Furusato* is the spring of Memory (*Anamnesis*) (cf. Plato)

3. To do Philosophy is to be at Home (cf. Fichte, Schelling and Hegel)

Novalis's words prompted me to remember that philosophy is an inquisition into *furusato*. He gained these thoughts through his research into the philosophies of Kant, Fichte and many others. I would like to introduce to you here some digested versions of the thoughts of philosophers. For example, it is said that ancient Greek philosophy began with a question to *arche* (ἀρχή, the origin of all things in the universe). I think that the

Chikuma Gakugei bunko ちくま学芸文庫, 1988).

6   Novalis, *Das allgemeine Brouillon*, Nr. 857, in: *Novalis Schriften*, Bd. 2 (München Carl Hanser 1978), p. 675.

question, "What is *arche*?" is equivalent to the question, "What is *furusato*?"

B-1. *Furusato* is the beginning and destination of existence

1. Ancient Greek philosophers, especially so-called Greek "natural philosophers" were seeking the origin of the universe in the sense of *"arche"* (the beginning of all things). E.g.: According to Anaximander (ca. 610–546 BC) *arche*, "the source of coming-to-be for existing things is that into which destruction, too, happens, 'according to necessity (*kata to chreon*); for they pay penalty and retribution to each other for their injustice according to the assessment of Time'."[7]

For Aristotle, the ultimate aim of philosophy is *"on he on* [being in itself]"* which was regarded as the origin as well as the end of all things in the universe. In his *Physics* (204 b 30f.), Aristotle says "for whatever things come out of when they come into existence, that they return into when they pass out of existence."[8]

B-2. *Furusato* is the spring of Memory (Plato)

Plato's Idea World is the home of all human souls, and these souls fall down to a human body, and are said to become confined to the human body, which is a kind of grave or prison for a human being (*"Soma"* is *"sema"*).[9] That is to say, Plato thought that the Idea World is the home of the soul, the *"noumenon"*, and that this world is *"eikon"* (εἰκών, a shadow or phantom of the Idea), *"phainomenon"*. According to Plato, man can learn mathematics or algebra, which are generally referred to as the truth, by means of *"anamnesis"* (ἀνάμνησις, reminiscence of the Idea World), because the soul is immortal and lives in a perfect Idea World and is repeatedly incarnated into this world, and then forgets the memory of that world. The only way we can learn truth is by remembering the memory of when we were in

---

7   Anaximander, Fragment B 1, in: G.S. Kirk, J.E. Raven (ed. by), *The Presocratic Philosophers* (Cambridge: Cambridge University Press, 1973), p. 117.

8   Aristotle, *Physics* (Cambridge MA: Harvard University Press, 1957), p.235.

9   Cf. Plato, *Cratylus* 400c; *Gorgias* 493A; *Phaedrus* 250c.

the Idea World (*ontos on*, ὄντως ὄν, the world of Truth); this is the reasoning behind *anamnesis*. I also think that this kind of idea of the eternity of the soul has been inherited down to this day as part of European tradition. For example, in Plato's dialog *Meno* (81c-d): "For as all nature is akin, and the soul has learned all things, there is no reason why we should not, by remembering but one single thing—an act which men call learning—discover everything else, if we have courage and faint not in the search; since, it would seem, research and learning are wholly recollection (*anamnesis*)."[10]

B-3-1. Philosophy is to be at Home (cf. German Idealists)

I will introduce here three German Idealists who insist on this thesis.

J.G. Fichte (1762–1814): His concept of the conscience (*Gewissen*), the depth of the pure ego, is the place where righteous and holy people can assemble together. A community embracing friendly people is formulated here.[11]

F.W.J. Shelling (1775–1854): His concept of *Urwissen*: "unconditional knowledge itself, which is quite simply 'the one (*das Eine*),' and the idea of knowledge, where all knowledge is only one and the same, namely the idea of original knowledge."[12]

G.W.F. Hegel (1770–1831): "Man has already entered the homeland of the truth, when he has attained the consciousness of himself as a human being." This "Homeland of Truth (*das einheimische Reich der Wahrheit*)" is identical to *furusato*, which is a symbiotic zone of all things and a place where people live close together. ("*Mit dem Selbstbewusstsein sind wir also nun in das einheimische Reich der Wahrheit eingetereten.*")[13]

---

10   Plato, *Meno* (Cambridge MA: Harvard University Press, 1924), p. 303.
11   Cf. J.G. Fichte, *System der Sittenlehre (1798)*, in: *Fichtes Werke*, Bd. 4 (Berlin: de Gruyter, 1965), p. 255.
12   F.W.J. Schelling, *Vorlesungen über die Methode des akademischen Studiums (1803)*, in: *Schellings Werke*, Bd. 5, 3Hb. (München: Beck, 1927), p. 215.
13   G.W.F. Hegel, *Phänomenologie des Geistes*, in: *Hegels Werke*, Bd. 3 (Frankfurt am Main: Suhrkamp, 1970), p. 138.

I think German idealists have also been investigating *furusato* as the origin of knowledge and the ego.

B-3-2. *Furusato* always emerges as the present

I believe these concepts of the Homeland of Truth, original knowledge, and the community of holy people could be interpreted as the philosophical concept of *furusato*. They transcend the limitations of time and can penetrate time from past to future. This is because truth can be considered to be universal and eternal, valid everywhere and at all times. So the time that passes in *furusato* is not objective and empty, but significant and therefore eternal. It subsumes the past, the present and the future, and therefore presents us with the lasting present (*nunc stans*).

Furusato is the home of the soul. That is why even though *furusato* may be part of our memory, it still exists as a whole of our present. For example, according to Jacob Burckhardt (1818-1897), an Austrian historian, in his book *The Civilization of the Italian Renaissance*,[14] Dante Alighieri never lost the sentiment that he lived in his *furusato*, Florence, wherever he may have been, drifting and being in exile away from his *furusato*. Moreover, he is conjured up with the image of a pioneer who strolled around the world as an "individual" with a sense of universality. I think Kant's concept of a "Citizen of the world (*Weltbürger*)" belongs to this individual in the form of universality. In this way of life, if I may use a reversed expression, *furusato* was always with and in him wherever he may be. My assumption is that this did not mean that he felt he was always living in *furusato*; rather, *furusato* was always living in him.[15]

---

14   J. Burckhardt, *Die Kultur der Renaissance in Italien* (Basel: Schweighauser, 1860); English translation in: J. Burckhardt, *The Civilization of the Renaissance in Italy* (London: Penguin classics, 1990).
15   Cf. Jacob Burckhardt, *Bilder des Ewigen* (Darmstadt: Wissenschaftliche Buchgesellschat,1997), pp. 335ff, particularly p. 339f.

My Reminiscence

Whenever I think of the coastal towns lost in the tsunami in the wake of the Great East Japan Earthquake, it comes to my mind that I had better review and consider people's thoughts on their lost "hometown". This is a starting point for my study on "hometown". The timing of launching this study could be closely related to my age. This is because people like me with a relatively short future are likely to live in the "memory" of the past, while young people live in the future filled with "hope". On the other hand, we harbor "hope" with the support of "memory". That means that even young people's spirit is fundamental supported by "memory" at the bottom as well. Of course, memory can change by degrees, and moreover, we would like to change the facts and often create favorable memories for ourselves.

Finally, I would like to cite Bashō again, but this time my reference goes to the beginning of his most famous work, *Oku no Hosomichi*:

> "The months and days are the travelers of eternity. The years that come and go are also voyagers. Those who float away their lives on ships or who grow old leading horses are forever journeying, and their homes are wherever their travels take them. Many of the men of old died on the road, and I too for years past have been stirred by the sight of a solitary cloud drifting with the wind to ceaseless thoughts of roaming."[16]

We ought to remember the fact that Bashō just started his journey to Michinoku (陸奥) next March after he had an opportunity to see his own umbilical cord, and had cried bitter at his hometown of Igaiyō. Here, Bashō is referring to mortality. Japanese people express this emotion as *"mujō"* 無常. *Mujō* means that everything passes by every moment and nothing stays the same. There are three exclusive elements, however, from my point of view, that continue to exist and endure. They are the truth, the eternal present, and our memory of the past, as they are

---

16   Matsuo Bashō, *The Narrow Road to Oku*, cit., p. 159.

with us belonging to the present moment. The second has been named "*nunc aeternitatis*". This consideration is also shared by Novalis in his statement, "Memory or recollection is the present" (*Erinnerung ist Gegenwart*).[17]

The deceased people and lost towns are preserved (conserved) in between the pleats of our heart as memory and the memory vividly appears in front of us every time our thoughts turn to that memory. If we follow this logic, *furusato* in our heart exists everywhere and yet concurrently never exists anywhere. This is because even though *furusato* occupies our hearts, we don't know where *furusato* is, and cannot identify where it is. It is certain that our *furusato* lies in our heart as an "original village or landscape". The only thing I can say with confidence is that our life is nothing but a journey from *furusato* to *furusato*. And *furusato* is the ultimate Pole Star for this journey of our life.

I wish and pray that the people who have lost their *furusato* to some disaster will be able to keep their *furusato* in their memory as a source of emotional solace.

---

17   Novalis, *Das allgemeine Brouillon*, cit., p. 349.

Yoshida Shigeto 吉田栄人[1]

MODERN YUCATEC MAYAN LITERATURE AND THE CONCEPT OF HOME, *MAYAB*

In 1982, bilingual cultural promoters of the Direction of *Culturas Populares* in the state of Yucatan started a workshop of Mayan literature under the advisory support of the Mexican writer Carlos Montemayor. This literary workshop stimulated an interest among Yucatec Mayan people[2] in writing literary works in their own language, encouraged also by the interculturalism adopted by the Mexican government as national ideology that offered various kinds of support for revitalizing indigenous languages and cultures. This cultural movement has made for a "renaissance" of indigenous literature in Mexico that can be witnessed at present.[3] This paper discusses the ways these emergent modern indigenous writers represent cultural traditions in their literary works, especially focusing on their discourse about the home of the ethnic group or their native place.

Most modern indigenous writers tend to depict their "*usos y costumbres*" (traditional practices and customs) in an idealizing

---

1   Tohoku University

2   It might be necessary to mention that not all of the Mayan people speak Maya, the original language in the Yucatan peninsula. There are many Mayans who identify themselves as Mayan but who don't understand Maya. The literary workshop played a role in promoting the language among them, as well as in teaching to the Maya-speaking people how to write in Maya. This situation determined the writers' role as cultural promoters and opinion leaders in the early stage of modern Mayan literature.

3   Abbey J. Poffenberger, 'The Renaissance of Mexican Indigenous Literature: Resistance, Reaffirmation and Revision', Dissertation (University of Kentucky, 2006); Emilio Del Valle Escalante, 'Chapter 2 The Maya World through its Literature', in Robert Warrior (ed. by), *The World of Indigenous North America* (Abingdon: Routledge, 2014), pp. 27-50; Paja Faudree, 'What is an Indigenous Author? Minority Authorship and the Politics of Voice in Mexico', *Anthropological Quarterly* 88-1 (2015), pp. 5-35.

mode. They try to write about a history of the survival of
Mayan culture under colonialism (both Spanish rule before the
Independence and subordination to the National State after) and
search for its complete and optimal form, which they believe
has been buried by the Spanish conquest and its colonial rule.
In this historical matrix, they present themselves as people
banished from their home, and thus pre-conquest Mayan society
is envisioned as their native place in their literary imagination.
This way of essentializing[4] the remote past is considered an
ideological premise that all the indigenous writers have to share.
But Sol Ceh Moo, the Yucatec author of *X-Teya, u puksi'ik'al
ko'olel* ("Teya, A Woman's Heart"),[5] acclaimed as the first novel
written by an indigenous woman writer in Latin America, rejects
this essentializing mode of talking about Mayan culture. She
believes that the idea of an idealized Maya culture that must be
shared by all Mayan people makes readers forget the negative
aspects of their traditions. So in most of her works, she prefers
to depict the actual lives of the Mayan people, particularly of
the people suffering under traditional moral standards and
oppression by the social establishment of the traditional societies.
Her novella *Sujuy k'iin* ("Holy day"),[6] an ethnographic fantasy
of a traditional Mayan village in a day of feast in honor of the
Catholic Virgin Mary, shows this perspective at work. And also
Sujuy k'iin is the first novel in the history of Mayan literature
that describes an actual Mayan village as home for the Mayan
people. It is interesting to ask why other Mayan writers have not
created similar works. In discussing these points, I want to show
how *Sujuy k'iin* has challenged the idea of home for the Mayan
people and how it stands as a landmark in the history of modern
Mayan literature.

---

4   To essentialize means here an act of believing and declaring something innate
     or given *a priori*, and considering it as an essential attribute for oneself to be
     a member of a certain group, in this case, the Mayans.
5   Marisol Ceh Moo, *X-Teya, u puksi'ik'al ko'olel / Teya, un corazón de mujer*
     (México: CONACULTA, 2008).
6   Sol Ceh Moo, *Sujuy k'iin / Día sin mancha* (Mérida: Instituto de Cultura de
     Yucatán, 2011).

1. *Literary missions of modern indigenous literature*

In Mexico and other Latin American countries, only literary works written in indigenous languages are considered as indigenous literature, in contrast with the Native American literature in the United States, which is usually written in English. The use of indigenous languages is the decisive and unique indicator of indigenous literature in Latin America, although works are always published with Spanish translations provided by the authors. Despite the fact that most of the audience read the translated text, the indigenous text is necessary because Spanish language only publications are considered the literature of *mestizo*, or non-indigenous people. Before the advent of the so-called boom in Latin American literature, there was a literary tradition known as *indigenismo* in which non-indigenous writers wrote about indigenous societies and their cultures. In this literary tradition, whose origin goes back to the literary romanticism in the nineteenth century, indigenous peoples and their cultures were objects for discussion of national identity.

On the contrary, the modern indigenous literature was born in the 1980s under the pluriculturalism and interculturalism initiated as a part of the restoration of rights of indigenous peoples,[7] in which indigenous languages have acquired importance as a marker of ethnicity. Therefore, the use of indigenous language has been and continues to be encouraged as a right of indigenous people.[8]

---

7   In Mexico, the revolutionary government adopted *indigenismo* as an ideological base for building a unified and homogenous nation state in which indigenous peoples must be "educated" to modernize their ways of life. But this government's paternalistic *indigenismo*, in a mode of prohibiting their cultural rights, practically destroyed the indigenous culture. For further discussion, see Luis Villoro, *Los grandes momentos del indigenismo en México* (México: Colegio de México, 1950); Analisa Taylor, *Inidigeneity in the Mexican Cultural Imagination* (Tucson: University of Arizona Press, 2009); Omar Fabián González Salinas, 'La utopía de forjar una sola raza para la nación. Mestizaje, indigenismo e hispanofilia en el México posrevolucionario', *Historia y Memoria* 13 (2016), pp. 201-330.

8   In México, the General Law of Indigenous People's Linguistic Rights was approved and the National Institute of Indigenous Languages was created in 2003.

The language has constituted a social space for recovering the opportunities of learning their "own" culture, lost under policies that forced indigenous minorities to learn the "national way of life", especially the national language of Spanish. Moreover most indigenous writers usually work as cultural promoters in governmental organizations, a profession that leaves their literary efforts as the obligatory space to work in their native language. But we must not forget that in Latin America it is not possible to make a clear distinction between indigenous people and *mestizo* people by means of physical features or cultural practices. In this socio-cultural situation, indigenous languages serve as the last resort to reclaim an indigenous identity, because non-indigenous people do not speak it. Therefore, the use of native language in the indigenous literature in Latin America is not only necessary but also obligatory for the indigenous writers in order to be considered as such. If they write in Spanish, their works will be considered the same as those of the *indigenismo* literature.

As the indigenous writers are native speakers of indigenous languages (thus signaling their membership in an indigenous group), although they are also native in Spanish, they are considered to possess sufficient knowledge, or to be capable of obtaining such knowledge, to write about their own cultures. What they narrate in their literary works is considered an authentic representation of indigenous cultures that they have inherited from their ancestors. For example, Jorge Miguel Cocom Pech, a Campechano laureate writer who has won various international prizes, has written in his novel *El Abuelo Gregorio, un sabio maya*[9] ("The Grandfather Gregorio, a Mayan sage") of his experience of receiving from his grandfather an initiation to become a narrator or transmitter of Mayan knowledge to the next generation. In this biographic reminiscence of his childhood, his grandfather appears as the repository of the cultural knowledge of the Mayan people. This knowledge has been passed down over generations, and Jorge is selected by the power of corn seed

---

9   *J-nool Gregoio'e, juntúul miats'il maya / El abuelo Gregorio, un sabio maya* (Mexico: CONACULTA, 2012). This book was first published under the title *Secretos del abuelo* "The secrets of the grandfather", 2001.

to be the one to transmit it to the next generation. Here corn is used as a symbol to validate the millenary origin of the Mayan culture, because it is the principal staple of the Mayans from the pre-Columbian era and is often considered a sacred food for the Mayan people. In this manner, Mayan culture is presented as something that has its origin in the remote past and is eternally unchanging. However, we cannot forget that it is just Jorge Miguel Cocom Pech who interprets and finds meaning in the secrets passed down by his grandfather in the initiation rituals. It is clear that Mayan culture is interpreted and reinterpreted by those to whom it is transmitted. Its meaning can change over time, because it must be adapted to the particular social and cultural situations of the Mayans who are initiated as sages, repositories of Mayan knowledge.

In writing about their indigenous cultures, indigenous writers usually recount or reconstruct the stories about traditions that they heard from their grandparents. In this writing process, authenticity and value are given to the lost or disappearing traditions so as to be restored. For them it is important that Mayan culture be glorious and divine because it gives them a basis for their ethnic identity and a decolonial tool that enables them to be indigenous in a pluricultural society. Here the indigenous writers resemble the young Japanese writers in the Meiji era who had feelings of alienation in the capital city Tokyo. These Japanese writers idealized their hometowns as a means of relieving their anxieties in a drastically changing life.[10] Both groups of writers share deep feelings of unfulfillment. For all of them, the *furusato*, the place of origin, appears as an idyllic place or time that one looks to in order to escape from alienating situations and restore mental health.

Although both groups have in common a sense of uprootedness and loss, the Mayan writers usually do not depict their village of origin as a *furusato* (native place) to return to. As we have seen, they rather consider that they, and all of the Mayan people, have

---

10   See Stephen Dodd, *Writing Home: Representations of the Native Place in Modern Japanese Literature* (Cambridge: Harvard University Asia Center, 2004).

been banished from their homeland. Living in Mayan villages, they feel themselves alienated because they were conquered, subjugated, exploited, and discriminated against. Therefore, a native place where they can feel at home does not exist in the land where they live and must be looked for in the remote past before the conquest. This literary imagined home of the Mayans is often called *mayab*.

Mayan intellectuals mainly use the term *mayab* as a toponym that refers to the land of Mayan people. Although *mayab* seems to be a Yucatec word, the ordinary Mayans do not know that word as such. To them, it is the name of a bus company, a hotel, or a restaurant. The word *mayab* first appeared in a document known as the *Pérez Codex* compiled by Juan Pío Pérez, a Yucatecan philologist of the nineteenth century. In that document, *mayab* is recorded as a name of the land where the indigenous people lived before the Spanish conquest.[11] It is unclear where Pérez discovered this meaning or if its use was common at that time. Regardless, it became a favorite term for intellectuals to refer to the land of Mayan people, especially when they talk about the remote Mayan age before the conquest or an idealized Mayan world.

The main difference between the Japanese writers of the Meiji era and the Mayan writers may come from the difference in the physical location of their home villages. The villages of origin for most of the Mayan writers are located not far from Merida, the capital city of the state of Yucatan where they live or work. They can travel in a few hours by commuter taxi or bus service between their home villages and the capital city, and, in practical terms, the villages are not separated from the city. For many of them it is possible to live in their home village and go to Merida for work in one or two hours. Thus, for the Mayan writers, their home villages are not recognized as places to be recalled and enshrined in the Mayan identity, although many recall noticing the cultural differences between their home villages and Merida upon their initial visits to the capital. Therefore, Mayan writers tend to dedicate themselves to re-narrating the stories of the

---

11   "*mayab*. nombre que tenía esta península antes de su conquista."

Mayan traditions they heard from their grandfathers in order to look for a *furusato* that they think they have lost.

But which Mayan traditions are to be narrated is of course arbitrary. Writers choose examples to suit their idealistic view of Mayan culture and describe them in an essentializing mode. The *furusato* as a home to go back to is depicted as the internal harmonious world of the writers. A laureated Mayan poet Wildernain Villegas confessed to me in an interview that writing poems in Maya language is for him a kind of trip to his internal world. In modern Mayan literature, there are no narratives about Mayans who return to their home villages to visit their family or friends, nor portrayals of daily life in the village that should remind them of happy days in their childhood. Mayan writers do not envision happy childhoods for Mayans, as these were taken from them. For them, childhood was unhappy because they were deprived of a "true" life as Mayans under colonial rule and the post-independence national regime. The joyful days of the Mayan people are believed to be kept only in the memory of the grandfathers (or Mayan sages, the repository of the Mayan culture, like a grandfather of Jorge Miguel Cocom Pech), to whom the writers have to turn for their telling. Writers tend to narrate the lost idyllic world their grandfathers recount to them, just like the Native American shamans who have mystical encounters with their ancestors in dreams.

2. *Home as an idyllic village*

In the context of modern Mayan literature described above appeared the novella *Sujuy k'iin* by Sol Ceh Moo, which describes the typical traditional life of the Mayan people on the annual feast day of the patron saint of an anonymous Mayan village. Interestingly this novella has all the elements of the idyllic chronotope Mikhail Bakhtin identified in idyllic novels.[12] The time that predominates in the novella is a folkloric

---

12   Michael Holquist (ed. by), *The Dialogic Imagination: Four Essays by M. M.*

one synchronized with the movement of the sun. Rather than chronometrical time, the movement of the sun gives the timeline to the activities and scenes that comprise the novella. The story begins with the sunrise, to which Mila the protagonist and all the other beings in the world wake up, and they sleep after they finish their activities each, laying in rest until the next day's sunrise. Life in the village is presented as cyclic and never-ending in a chronotope "where the fathers and grandfathers lived and where one's children and their children will live."[13]

The book's scenes are concerned mainly with the basic realities of folkloric life such as "love, birth, death, marriage, labor, food and drink, stages of growth"[14] and religion. All of these are narrated in the reminiscences of villagers speaking in the present. The novella begins with a description of domestic fowls searching for food in a pattern that repeats every morning with the sunrise. This scene gives readers a strong impression that life in the village is cyclic, eternal, and resists any change over the generations.

The idyllic nature of the village also comes from its existence as a closed society separated from the outside world.[15] Villagers consider their own village safe and peaceful and the outside world dangerous. They go out only to look for non-traditional work in pursuit of adventure. In the novella, the villagers mainly go to Playa de Carmen, a tourist spot on the Caribbean coast, to earn money. When Tomás, the second son of Mila, tells the family that he wants to go to work there, his parents think:

> There have been many boys who, in search of work, have embarked on the thousand-times-traced route. For some it was a good decision, for others it was a failure. Vices, criminal attitudes and other evils found in them the way to seize their will. Some returned touched by the hands of the misfortune of drugs; to others, their tricks made them guests of prisons.[16]

Bakhtin (Austin: University of Texas Press, 1981).

13   Michael Holquist (ed. by), *The Dialogic Imagination*, cit., p. 225.

14   Michael Holquist (ed. by), *The Dialogic Imagination*, cit., p. 225.

15   Bakhtin says: "This little spatial world is limited and sufficient unto itself, not linked in any intrinsic way with other places, with the rest of the world." (in Michael Holquist, *The Dialogic Imagination*, cit., p. 225).

16   Sol Ceh Moo, *Sujuy k'iin*, cit., p. 159. Translation from the original text by the present author.

Today the traditional village feasts in honor of the patron saint or the Virgin Mary give the outgoing villagers a pretext and a good occasion to go back to their home. This habit of returning home during the village feast has a basis in the yearning of the Mayans for returning to the peaceful village in order to recover from their stressful lives in the city. In this sense, the home villages must remain unchanged and as peaceful as it was when they left it. Thus the stories of the outgoing villagers play an important part in the novella: Doña Juliana (female godparent of Agapito, the son of Mila) and Fabián (a brother of Julio, the fiancé of Socorro, the daughter of Mila) who went to the United States; two young boys, Crisanto Euán and Aristides Tinah, who went to the Caribbean coast to work and returned dead; and Canijito who returned home addicted to drugs.

Apart from these, all of the scenes inside the village take place in a home-centered landscape. The village is configured as a small place where the villagers can travel on foot. The story begins with a description of the house of Mila, the protagonist of the story, the center of which is the *cocina* (kitchen and eating space) where all the family members gather in order to eat and chat. Mila and her family members exit the home in order to work in the field, grind the corn, and participate in a virgin procession downtown. When they return home, they chat in the *cocina*. This *cocina*-centered life of Mila's family will remind the Mayan readers of their own homes where they grew up.

The novella is filled with words and phrases referring to physical senses, such as the aromas and tastes of foods, the sounds of animals and the village feast, the heat of the sun, and beautiful views of the village. These sensory appeals surely help Mayan readers to thaw their frozen memories of childhood. They may feel as if they were in their own home villages. The depiction of the procession as a picturesque scene may signal exoticism to non-Mayan readers, but it makes Mayans recall vividly the scenes of the processions they participated in in their own villages. When Mayan readers read the following passage, they will say that they know the best places to take photos of the procession.

Armed with their cameras and video cameras, tourists have chosen the right places for their best shots. The movement has become more intense. In the sunset, around the church, thousands of lit candles create a mystical atmosphere. The smell of wax fills the environment.[17]

It will be also easy for the Mayan readers to recall their memories of their home village, because the village in *Sujuy k'iin* is given no name. The anonymity of the village in the novella helps the readers to remember the scenes they saw in their own villages. They may want to write the name of their own village on the vivid descriptions presented in *Sujuy k'iin*.

3. *Shadows of the home*

The novella *Sujuy k'iin* closely resembles an ethnographic account written by a native anthropologist. At its heart, it is a description of a typical Mayan village and its customs in Yucatan. Some Mayan writers have expressed criticisms toward Sol Ceh Moo's works. They alleged that she is not qualified as indigenous writer because she does not follow the model of other indigenous writers praising Mayan culture, and they doubt her knowledge about Mayan culture because she never lived with her grandfathers. To answer these criticisms, Sol Ceh Moo needed to publish connected to Mayan traditional culture. But this placed her in a dilemma, as she was critical of the essentialization of Mayan culture. Her use of ethnographic discourse solved this dilemma, because there exist many ethnographic accounts of Mayan life by professional ethnographers. Few would criticize the content of the novella if she based her writing on these academic accounts. In practice, she moves her narrative position in *Sujuy k'iin* between the subjective Mayan (ourselves) and the objective ethnographer in order to justify her childhood experiences.

Most Mayan writers believe that traditions are transmitted over generations from parents to children. If the parents do not

---

17   Sol Ceh Moo, *Sujuy k'iin*, cit., p. 156. Translation from the original text by
      the present author.

have sufficient knowledge, as in the case of the modern Mayan writers, the grandfathers will teach the grandchildren. Sol Ceh Moo relativizes this essentialized vertical transmission of tradition by inserting a sociological observation:

> Girls learn from mothers when they go in search of firewood; when they do no do it, in the evenings they gather under a tree of oranges or plums and exchange their knowledge they have learned.[18]

However, her real purpose in publishing *Sujuy k'iin*, which she tells us is a chapter of an unpublished novel she had written earlier, was not to add another example to the list of ethnographies of Mayan villages but to criticize the writing style of other Mayans. In writing an idyllic Mayan village life with its harmonious culture, she likely intended to caricature other Mayan writers' essentializing view of Mayan culture. Weight is given to this speculation by her subsequent publication of two books, *Tabita y otros cuentos maya* and *El alcohol también rompe otros corazones*, in 2013, two years after the release of *Sujuy k'iin*. In *Sujuy k'iin* she described the traditional Mayan village as a society without any impurity, as the Spanish rendition of the title *Día sin mancha* (Day without Stain) indicates. But the two later books are collections of short stories about people who suffer from the abuse and oppression that can occur in a traditional Mayan society. This suggests that she wrote *Sujuy k'iin* first as a base for her later discussions about the impurities concealed in Mayan societies.

If we take into account the literary history of the Japanese writers of *furusato* novels, the point will get clearer. Stephen Dodd says that "(*Furusato*) is the product of native influences as well as new ways of perception drawn from the West".[19] In the Mayan case, the literary imagination of their *furusato* (native place) offers the Mayan writers a site for negotiation between local knowledge and Western knowledge, but their *furusato* appears as a place where the local is granted a supremacy over

---

18   Sol Ceh Moo, *Sujuy k'iin*, cit., p. 111. Translation from the original text by the present author.
19   Stephen Dodd, *Writing Home*, cit., p. 1.

the West. This type of discourse is based on an essentialization of the local and its mystification. Sol Ceh Moo rejects this literary scheme because essentialization makes inconvenient realities invisible. She depicts traditional cultures as harmonious in *Sujuy k'iin*, but in reality they have a shadow of unhappiness, which she might have called *mancha*, impurity. For example, she makes Socorro, one of Mila's two daughters and a good student, confess her resignation to the traditional norms of the village when a teacher asks her why she does not want to study at high school. She answers:

> I do the same thing other women do in the village. I will get married and have children. My mother was married when she was fifteen years old. What's the problem for me in doing the same things?[20]

And Socorro also says:

> For what do I have an illusion? [...] We the women do not have many alternatives, maybe in other places the customs are different, but here among us, this has always been the case and I do not think it will change, not for now.[21]

In the Mayan villages portrayed as idyllic worlds, there is no chance, no hope for women to go to school. They have to give up their dreams of studying, not because they are poor but because it is a cultural norm for women not got to school and to dedicate themselves to housekeeping. To be idyllic, everything in life must remain unchanging and cyclic. The intention of Sol Ceh Moo in depicting an idyllic chronotope is surely to denounce this unhappy situation of Mayan women, as she expresses her hopes later in *Tabita y otros cuentos mayas* through Evencia's monologue. Evencia talks to her daughter in her womb:

---

20   Sol Ceh Moo, *Sujuy k'iin*, cit., pp. 113-114. Translation from the original text by the present author.
21   Sol Ceh Moo, *Sujuy k'iin*, cit., p. 104. Translation from the original text by the present author.

If Fidelio helps me as he has done up to now, you will study in the school of the village and go to the secondary school, maybe you will study more and realize my dream of working in a big store.[22]

Her message in *Sujuy k'iin* is that a narrative of a harmonious traditional Mayan culture blinds the readers to social contradictions and abuses.

It is clear that the novella *Sujuy k'iin* is not a simple ethnographic account of romantic Mayan villages, although it apparently pretends to be a praise of Mayan culture. It reminds us of the existence of persons who have to endure the negative aspects of the traditional societies and obliges us to reconsider the home depicted as an idyllic world. In this sense, this novella becomes a strong criticism of other indigenous writers who think that it is their mission to write only praise for indigenous cultures. But they could not have noticed the message of So Cel Moo's novella. It became necessary for her to write more explicitly about the impurities (*manchas*) in villages in *Tabita y otros cuentos mayas* and *El alcohol también rompe otros corazones*. In these two collections of short stories she talks about the lives of the forgotten persons suffering from the mercilessness of the traditional Mayan society: Cleofas, a woman who endures sexual abuse from own father and is deported from the village when she takes the matter to court; Evencia, a woman who challenges the discriminating and oppressive norms that declare that women are born guilty; Febronio, a male diviner who is forced by his father in his youth to work in the jungle and is shunned by the villagers after becoming a diviner; among others.

In this context, the idyllic life described in *Sujuy k'iin* takes the form of a caricature of the essentialized Mayan world. We have to understand that Sol Ceh Moo published it in order to criticize an essentializing way of viewing authentic Mayan villages as holy (*sujuy*) for all the Mayan people. Maybe this is the reason why she generally does not use the term *mayab* for

---

22   Sol Ceh Moo, *Tabita y otros cuentos mayas* (Mérida: Maldonado Editores del Mayab, 2013), p. 37. Translation from the original text by the present author.

the land of Mayan people, choosing instead to refer to it as "our land" or "this land". There is just one short story "Don Maxito"[23] in which she uses the term *mayab*, but it appears only in Spanish version. This suggests that *mayab*, the homeland for the Mayan people, is not for the Mayan people at all. In the Mayan version, the corresponding word is "*tu'ux kaja'an máaya máako'ob*", which means "the place where the Mayan people live" (p.174). For her, "our land" is not a paradise but a patriarchal society plagued with impurities.

4. *Home as a place for imagination*

In talking about the *furusato* concept, *Sujuy k'iin* shows the Mayan people that they have their own home village to return to. The novella does not reveal information about either the location of the village or its name. It is an anonymous village located in an unspecified place on the Yucatan Peninsula (the name of Yucatan also never appears in the novella). This anonymity makes it possible for the Mayan readers to believe that the village is also their homes. The idea of Mayan village as a home to go back to, especially during the village feast, is not new. But in the history of modern Mayan literature, *Sujuy k'iin* is the first novel that depicts the modern Mayan village as the home of the Mayan people.

In summary, Sol Ceh Moo placed the home of the Mayan people in the present time, while other Mayan writers look for it in the remote past or in their internal worlds. For the most Mayan writers, home is an ideological construct that must be remembered as a lost or disappearing world, but for Sol Ceh Moo, it is both the place where she was born and brought up and a patriarchal and oppressive society. Sol Ceh Moo most likely published the novella *Sujuy k'iin / Día sin mancha* to say to other Mayan writers that by essentializing Mayan culture

---

23 Sol Ceh Moo, *Kaaltale', ku xijkunsik u jel puksi'ik'alo'ob / El alcohol también rompe otros corazones.* (Mérida: SEDECULTA/CONACULTA, 2013).

and remaining obsessed with looking for a lost Mayan world, Mayan literature will always be local and never universal. In contrast, she has written novels herself whose themes are more universal than local: *X-Teya, u puksi'ik'al ko'olel* ("Teya, a woman's heart"), *T'ambilak men tunk'ulio'ob* ("The call of the tambors"), and *Chen tumeen chu'upen* ("Only by being a woman"). In fact, she has declared her will to one day win the Nobel Prize in Literature, probably at least partly in an effort to encourage other indigenous writers to be universal and compete with writers from all over the world. Certainly she is looking far beyond the Mayan world. For her, the Mayan world represented as a traditional village in *Sujuy k'iin* is a home that enriches her literary imagination, because it is a part of her native place. She will never stop writing in her mother tongue, Yucatec Maya, nor will she refrain from criticizing patriarchal oppression because these are the sources of her literary imagination.

This paper has discussed the literary representation of home by modern Yucatec Mayan writers and its possible effects on Maya-speaking readers. However, it is necessary for us to remember that indigenous literature is also read by non-Mayan peoples because literary works written in indigenous language in Latin America are generally published with Spanish translations. Whatever the purpose of these works are, we the Western readers might impose interpretations of the noble savage and our "lost" traditions on indigenous literature. Idyllic representations of the home invite us to make a journey to our internal and idealistic world. Western readers may also feel nostalgia toward the idyllic life of the remote Mayan past. Sol Ceh Moo has broken with this literary convention of representing the lost native place and introduced a new perspective on the home. She described the realistic life of a traditional Mayan village, however, she did so in an idyllic manner in order to draw attention to the existence of people oppressed by traditional morals, which is concealed behind the standard literary view of an authentic and beautiful home. When we pay attention to the people who are suffering, our attentions are directed toward the same type of suffering in our own society. We – both indigenous peoples and Western readers – share the same problems when we live under patriarchal social systems. The novels of Sol Ceh Moo remind us that we should deconstruct our idyllic views of indigenous literature.

MIMESIS GROUP
www.mimesis-group.com

MIMESIS INTERNATIONAL
www.mimesisinternational.com
info@mimesisinternational.com

MIMESIS EDIZIONI
www.mimesisedizioni.it
mimesis@mimesisedizioni.it

ÉDITIONS MIMÉSIS
www.editionsmimesis.fr
info@editionsmimesis.fr

MIMESIS COMMUNICATION
www.mim-c.net

MIMESIS EU
www.mim-eu.com

Printed by
Geca Industrie Grafiche – San Giuliano Milanese (MI)
March 2020